EVANGELICALS
AT THE CROSSROADS

WILL WE
PASS THE
TRUMP
TEST?

MICHAEL L. BROWN, PhD

Equal Time Books
CONCORD, NORTH CAROLINA

EVANGELICALS AT THE CROSSROADS

Will We Pass the Trump Test?

DR. MICHAEL L. BROWN

Contents

Other Books By the Same Author

Answering Jewish Objections to Jesus, Volumes 1-5

"Jeremiah," in The Expositor's Bible Commentary, Revised Edition

60 Questions Christians Ask about Jewish Beliefs, Practices and History

Revolution in the Church: Challenging the Religious System with a Call for Radical Change (Grand Rapids: Chosen)

The Revival Answer Book: Rightly Discerning the Contemporary Revival Movements

Revolution! The Call to Holy War

Go and Sin No More: A Call to Holiness

From Holy Laughter to Holy Fire: America On the Edge of Revival

Israel's Divine Healer

It's Time to Rock the Boat: A Call to God's People to Rise Up and Preach a Confrontational Gospel

Our Hands Are Stained With Blood: The Tragic Story of the "Church" and the Jewish People

Whatever Happened to the Power of God: Is the Charismatic Church Slain in the Spirit or Down for the Count?

How Saved Are We?

The End of the American Gospel Enterprise

Compassionate Father or Consuming Fire? Who Is the God of the Old Testament?

Preface

For better or worse, we have never had another president quite like Donald Trump. On the one hand, he can be the most unchristian of presidents, with a thoroughly unchristian past. On the other hand, he has taken some of the most Christian stands of any of our presidents, and that without apology. What do we do with Donald Trump?

There are some who seem to feel that a vote for Trump is tantamount to siding with Satan. There are others who seem to feel that a vote for Trump is tantamount to siding with Jesus. Some see Trump – and when I say "some" I mean some evangelical Christians – as an antichrist. Others see him as a savior. How do we sort this out?

There are well-meaning Christians who feel that Trump has destroyed our country and that, to the extent we identify with him, we have destroyed our witness. And there are well-meaning Christians who feel that Trump has saved our country and that, as followers of Jesus, we owe it to him to stand with him. Again, how do we sort this out?

Normally, in political discussions and in books about Trump and the church, the focus is on how we vote. In this book, however, the focus is not so much on how we vote but on how we live and act. In that sense, the presidency of Donald Trump presents a unique challenge and test. Will we pass that test? Will we make righteous decisions in our voting without compromising our Christian witness? Will we be loyal citizens while always putting the cross before the flag?

For those of you who do not believe a Christian can vote for Trump, I hope that the pages that follow will help you understand a different perspective, even if you don't change your vote. For those who cannot see how a Christian *cannot* vote for Trump, I hope that you, too, will gain perspective on those who differ with you, regardless of how you choose to vote. And for all who read this book before the 2020 elections – less than six months away as I write – I hope the pages that follow will help inform your decision. More importantly, I hope the pages that follow will help you live a life worthy of the Lord, without getting caught up in election fever. And for those of you reading these pages who do not profess faith in Jesus (or, any religious faith), I hope you will gain insight into one of the most divisive questions of our day: what do we do with Donald Trump?

In 2018, shortly before the elections, I felt strongly moved to write a book titled *Donald Trump Is Not My Savior: An Evangelical Leader Speaks His Mind About the Man He Supports as President* (published by Destiny Image). But because I had so little time to put the book together, I decided to write new material for the beginning and the end, then reprint about 100 of my most relevant articles on Trump in chronological order. I was blessed to hear from readers who found the format and approach helpful.

This time, however, almost everything you read here is new, with the exception of several articles which have been rewritten, updated, and adapted for inclusion here. But everything else is, so to say, hot off the press, especially since we have chosen to release this through our own publishing arm, EqualTime Books, meaning we could go to print shortly after the writing was finished. (Note that all weblinks cited in the endnotes were reconfirmed and accessed between May 24 and June 3, 2020. That being said, the book was largely completed before the death of George Floyd at the hands of Minneapolis police, which triggered major protests and riots across the country, with the president in the center of much more controversy regarding race relations in America. So, I did not add in new material on this very important topic, but I did cover it day and night on radio, internet, and in writing, and my relevant commentary is available online.)

If you do not follow our larger ministry work, including our daily radio show, the Line of Fire, our op-ed pieces (normally, five per week), our videos, our debates, and our Jewish outreach materials, please connect with us at AskDrBrown.org. And while you're there, sign up for our emails and then join us on our Facebook, YouTube, Twitter, or Instagram pages, all of which are linked on our website. And if you are helped by this book, please tell a friend and then take a moment to post a review on Amazon.com.

Now, for the big question. Will we pass the Trump test? Will you? Will I? That is a question only you and I can answer. What will it be?

My appreciation to the great team at AskDrBrown, including my faithful producer, Matt Corbin, who has labored sacrificially for years for our ministry work, Cindy Panepinto, who has so expertly run our organization, Brandon Paul, who carefully proofread the manuscript and filled out the many internet references, and Mark Pedosiuk, who so beautifully designed the cover and book layout. To every other member of our team – thank you!

My appreciation also to Steve Bremner (stevebremner.com), for formatting the e-book with meticulous care, to Prof. James Beverley, who also read every page of the manuscript, making many valuable suggestions, and who gave me permission to quote extensively from his new book *God's Man in the White House: Donald Trump in Modern Christian Prophecy* (published by Castle Quay Books), and to James Robison, one of my dearest friends in the world and a man who is constantly encouraging me to be redemptive in all that I write or say. To those who regularly labor in prayer for our work and to those who support us financially, I express my heartfelt appreciation as well. And to my precious bride of more than forty-four years, Nancy, for being an unwavering, unshakable bastion of truth and reality, whether I like it or not – thank you. Your honesty has been a mainstay for me over the decades.

May Jesus be glorified in His Church, and may we pass the Trump test with flying colors!

Michael L. Brown, June 3, 2020

ONE

The Enigma of Donald Trump and the Quandary of Evangelicals

It would not surprise me if, in many evangelical homes in America, Donald Trump is discussed more often than Jesus Christ. After all, hardly a day goes by without the President making major headlines, for better or worse. Hardly a day goes by without controversy swirling around him. Hardly a day goes by when he is not being bashed by the media on the left or praised by the media on the right. And it seems that everyone has a strong opinion about Donald Trump. Everyone has something to say, quite passionately at that.

No name stirs up more emotions than the name "Trump." No name stirs up more dissension or triggers more disagreements. And no person alive today is more widely loved or hated than Donald Trump.

This presents a unique dilemma for evangelical Christians, a group historically known for its strong moral stands on family, character, and the sanctity of life. What are we to make of President Trump? How closely should we be associated with him? To what extent is he an answer to prayer? To what extent a blessing? To what extent a curse?

If we fail to stand with him, are we missing a gift from God because we don't like the packaging? If we do stand with him, are we diminishing our Christian witness in the eyes of the nation? What do we do with Donald Trump?

Evangelical journalist Warren Smith puts it like this: "The real story of Trump's presidency will not be written until he is out of office, and we learn whether Trump delivered us from four years of Hillary Clinton, or whether he doomed conservatives to 40 years in the political wilderness."[1] That is saying a lot.

President Trump has surrounded himself with evangelical leaders. He has a strong evangelical Vice President and perhaps the most evangelical cabinet in history. And he welcomes prayer and receives it humbly. At the same time, no president in memory has a less evangelical past and behaves publicly in a less evangelical manner.

One of my evangelical colleagues was asked by an interviewer how he would evaluate Trump's presidency so far. He answered, "On policy, I give him an A-. On demeanor, I give him a D."[2] And a Pew Research article posted on March 12, 2020 stated that,

> White evangelicals largely see Trump as fighting for their beliefs and advancing their interests, and they feel their side generally has been winning recently on political matters important to them. But when it comes to Trump's personal qualities and conduct, many express mixed feelings. Even among this strongly supportive constituency, most do not view Trump as a *very* religious, honest or morally upstanding person (though many white evangelicals say he is *somewhat* religious, *fairly* honest or *fairly* morally upstanding).[3]

I reduced my own assessment to a simple formulation. Much of what Trump *does* is praiseworthy. Much of what Trump *says* is cringeworthy. To this my wife Nancy responded, "But *saying* things is often *doing* things as well." Quite so!

Who Is Right?

Evangelical supporters of Trump say, "So, he's rough around the edges. He offends people. He exaggerates. And sometimes he even lies. What politician doesn't lie? But he's a fighter. He's fearless. He's pushing back against forces that want to destroy our nation. In fact, he's done more for evangelical causes in just a few years than other presidents did in two full terms. I'll vote for Trump any day of the week."

Evangelical detractors of Trump say, "Yes, he's done a lot of good, but at what cost? Forget about his past immorality and godlessness. That's not the issue. The man is dangerous. He has dragged down the office of the president. He has been abusive and divisive. He has brought out the worst in us as a people. And to the extent we make excuses for his behavior, we bring reproach on the gospel."

A supporter replies, "He is the most effective pro-life president since the Roe v. Wade decision. He is a champion of religious liberties. He is pushing back against aggressive LGBT activism. And he is the best friend Israel has ever had. Who cares about some nasty tweets? You're missing the forest for the trees."

A detractor answers, "Yes, those are all good things. Very good things. And I don't minimize them. But words have the power of life and death as well, and his words have degraded us nationally. His words have opened a floodgate of hatred, of ugliness, of division. And it is outrageous for the President of the United States, the most powerful man on the planet, to use his office to disgrace and attack and malign and belittle others. When we stand with him, we degrade ourselves too."

A supporter says, "Then what do we do? Sit out the 2020 election? Cast a meaningless protest vote? Just do nothing and let a radical liberal become president? Not a chance. Trump is the man for me."

A detractor replies, "I would rather stand on principle than compromise my convictions for the sake of political expediency. And in the end, what have we gained if the laws are changed and the courts are changed but hearts are hardened to the gospel? Maybe we *would* do better if a radical liberal was elected. Maybe *then* we would wake up as a church and stop putting our trust in the government and the White House."

A supporter answers, "Oh, that's a great idea, kind of like not treating cancer so we can see God perform a miracle. Not on my watch!"

This, in short, is the enigma of Donald Trump and the quandary of evangelicals. What are we to do?

Weighing the Good Against the Bad

When it comes to his positive accomplishments, they are substantial to say the least. In fact, many of them are huge – as in YUGE. Theologian Wayne Grudem listed nineteen of the most major accomplishments through the end of 2019. These are the first ten:

1. The appointment of two Supreme Court justices, 50 judges to federal circuit courts of appeal, and 133 federal district court judges (plus two other judges to specialized courts). All of them are committed to interpreting the Constitution and the laws according to the original meaning of the words and not according to their personal policy preferences. This is a good result of immeasurable benefit to the future of the country, for it guarantees that laws must be made by elected legislators who are accountable to the people, not by judges who are appointed for life and have no effective accountability to the people as a whole. Many of these judges will serve for decades to come.

2. Significant tax cuts that have resulted in remarkable growth in jobs and wages. The good results are already seen in the paychecks of millions of workers, with the highest percentage growth occurring in low income jobs, the lowest unemployment rate in 50 years, and the lowest black and Hispanic unemployment rates ever recorded.

3. Massive elimination of wasteful government regulations, giving a strong boost to business and job growth.

4. Strengthening our military with passage of the largest defense budget in our history.

5. Standing up to China and firmly opposing their long-time theft of our intellectual property, including much copyrighted and patented information.

6. Moving the U.S. Embassy from Tel Aviv to Jerusalem, and in general being a strong friend of Israel.

7. Supporting laws and actions that protect the unborn child's right to life, including permitting states to defund Planned Parenthood, reinstating and expanding the Reagan

administration's Mexico City Policy which halts funding to groups that promote abortion overseas, strengthening conscience protections for individuals and organizations that have sincerely held religious beliefs about the sanctity of human life, and requiring insurance companies to disclose to customers if their plans cover abortions.

8. Building as much of a truly effective border wall as could be built in the face of intransigent opposition by Democrats.

9. Withdrawing from the misguided Paris Climate Accord, which would have significantly increased energy prices in the U.S.

10. Issuing executive orders that protect religious freedom, such as rescinding the Obamacare HHS mandate that forced groups such as Little Sisters of the Poor to provide access to abortifacients through their health care plans or face massive fines, finalizing new rules that protect the rights of conscience for pro-life medical professionals, and the Department of Justice issuing 20 principles of religious liberty to guide the Administration's litigation strategy and protect religious freedom.[4]

Tens of millions of lives (if not hundreds of millions of lives) have been positively affected (or will be positively affected) by these policies, and evangelicals can point to these with pride. President Trump has done a *lot* of good.

Washington Post columnist Marc Thiessen listed these as Trump's best accomplishments in 2019 (he presented them in reverse order, as here):

10. He continued to deliver for the forgotten Americans.

9. He implemented tighter work requirements for food stamps.

8. He has got NATO allies to cough up more money for our collective security.

7. He stood with the people of Hong Kong.

6. His withdrawal from the Intermediate-Range Nuclear Forces (INF) Treaty is delivering China and North Korea a strategic setback.

5. His "maximum pressure" campaign is crippling Iran.

4. His tariff threats forced Mexico to crack down on illegal immigration.

3. He delivered the biggest blow to Planned Parenthood in three decades.

2. He ordered the operation that killed Islamic State leader Abu Bakr al-Baghdadi.

1. He has continued to appoint conservative judges at a record pace.[5]

But Trump's evangelical critics would argue that the good Trump has done has been outweighed by the bad. Many of them would agree with the assessment of the *Los Angeles Times*, in a scathing piece posted by the newspaper's editorial board October 20, 2019. The editors wrote: "Trump has cheapened his office, instilled distrust in essential institutions of justice and democracy and replaced knowledge and professionalism with ignorance and amateurism." In their view, "In the corrosive and dangerous Trump presidency, the outrages fly so fast and the chaos mounts so thoroughly that it's easy to pass off the entire unsettling phenomenon as one more made-for-TV-and-Twitter unreality show. New outrages drive the previous ones from our minds."

More specifically, they accuse him of causing "thousands of children to be interned in inhumane conditions, often for months, resulting in deaths, injuries and traumatic separations from families, and without access to even rudimentary schooling." They claim that Trump "has insulted and alienated the nation's friends and allies, rendering the democratic world leaderless. . . . He has cozied up to right-wing nationalist dictators and autocrats at a moment when citizens of faltering democracies and the many peoples around the world aspiring to freedom most need an advocate on the international stage."

Yes, the *Times* continued,

He has rejected the honorable American presidential tradition of seeking unity and instead has indulged in the politics of division, willfully alienating a large segment of the American electorate while among his own supporters drumming up hatred for and suspicion of others.

He has transformed the White House, which should promote policies based on reality, into the world capital of ignorance, dishonesty and misinformation by reciting verifiable falsehoods, from the size of his inauguration crowd to the direction of a hurricane to the (disproven) prevalence of election fraud. . . .

He has made the United States unreliable, erratic and foolish in international affairs by disparaging its diplomatic corps, engaging in frequent and jarring changes in foreign affairs and defense advisors and repudiating international allies and partners.

And on and on the list goes: "He has undercut the nation's moral standing . . . . He has sullied the office of the presidency. . . . He has appealed to the basest part of our culture . . . . More than any president in living memory, Trump has cheapened his office . . . ." And then, the closing words, "This partial list represents a mere slice of what makes Donald Trump unacceptable as president of the United States and what makes it of utmost importance that Americans of all political parties and positions reject and replace him." [6]

Coming from more of a psychological perspective, Peter Wehner, who is a Republican, a Christian, and a Never Trumper, wrote this in *The Atlantic* September 9, 2019:

Donald Trump's disordered personality—his unhealthy patterns of thinking, functioning, and behaving—has become the defining characteristic of his presidency. It manifests itself in multiple ways: his extreme narcissism; his addiction to lying about things large and small, including his finances and bullying and silencing those who could expose them; his detachment from reality, including denying things he said even when there is video evidence to the contrary; his affinity for conspiracy theories; his demand for total loyalty while showing none to others; and his self-aggrandizement and petty cheating.

It manifests itself in Trump's impulsiveness and vindictiveness, his craving for adulation, his misogyny, predatory sexual behavior, and sexualization of his daughters; his open admiration for brutal dictators; his remorselessness; and his lack of empathy and sympathy, including attacking a family whose son died while fighting for this country, mocking a reporter with a disability, and ridiculing a former POW.

The title to Wehner's article said it all: "Donald Trump Is Not Well."[7]

Talk about extremely different evaluations of the same person! It's almost as if some think of Trump as a 21st century reincarnation of Christ while others see him as the Antichrist himself.

A viewer using the name Love of Trump posted this on my YouTube channel:

> Rejoice!
>> Donald J Trump has been called forth by Christ!
>> With Cross in one hand and Sword in the other,
>> And the Holy Spirit rushing through his pure soul,
>> He will defeat the enemies of our beloved Israel,
>> And bestow peace and love throughout the world!
>> Amen.

In stark contrast, Big Al wrote,

> My God republicans look at the type of low life you are worshipping? He had an affair with a pornstar right after his wife gave birth to his son, he paid $150,000 to hide it from you. Would you be proud of your son if he did this? He lied to you, to your face about no relationship with Russia, while he had a signed intent to build a damned tower in Moscow. He bribes a foreign leader to get dirt on a challenger that he is too scared to face one. This is your new Jesus?[8]

Oh my! The hyperbole on both sides is telling.

The Convictions Run Deep

In January, 2020, leading evangelical journalist Stephen Strang published a book carrying this very forceful title: *God, Trump, and the 2020 Election: Why He Must Win and What's at Stake for Christians if He Loses.*[9] In stark contrast, evangelical editor Napp Nazzworth felt he had "no choice" but to resign his position at the online *Christian Post* when the website issued a strong editorial in support of Trump in December, 2019.[10]

One evangelical leader says that his fellow-evangelicals must get behind Trump or the consequences will be dire. Another evangelical leader resigns his job rather than be associated with Trump. Who's right? Nazzworth actually noted that he and the rest of *Christian Post* editors published a February, 2016 editorial "Donald Trump Is a Scam."[11] (The full title was, "Donald Trump Is a Scam. Evangelical Voters Should Back Away.") What changed?

The 2016 editorial began with these words:

Editors' Note: The Christian Post has not taken a position on a political candidate before today. We are making an exception because Trump is exceptionally bad and claims to speak for and represent the interests of evangelicals.

We the senior editors of The Christian Post encourage our readers to back away from Donald Trump.[12]

Almost four years later, two senior editors with the *Christian Post* responded to an evangelical attack on Trump and his evangelical supporters with these words:

You may think Trump is a narcissistic, morally challenged, belligerent cad who has no business being president — except for the pesky constitutional fact that over 60 million American voters elected him to it. You may see Trump as a modern day Cyrus, the Persian king who did God's bidding in assisting in the restoration of Jerusalem. You may think Trump is a Samson-like hero called to realign the Supreme Court, to redirect the economy toward the American worker, and/or to tear down the pillars of Deep State corruption in modern Washington. But whatever you think — and however you vote — America will certainly survive and is, in significant ways, thriving under a Trump presidency — even if it lasts another four years.[13]

To ask again, what changed?

Even in the broader, conservative vs. liberal culture, opinions about

Trump are both widely and wildly divided. Historian Victor David Hanson wrote *The Case for Trump* in 2019,[14] drawing effusive praise from conservative giants like Rush Limbaugh, Mark Levin, and Newt Gingrich. How different this is from the title of the 2017 book edited by Dr. Brandy Lee, *The Dangerous Case of Donald Trump: 27 Psychiatrists and Mental Health Experts Assess a President.*[15]

Conservative actor Jon Voight dubbed Trump "the greatest president of this century" (apparently meaning over the last 100 years).[16] And a poll conducted in late 2019 indicated that, "A majority of Republicans (53%) think Trump is a better president than Abraham Lincoln."[17] In stark contrast, Democrat leader Chuck Schumer claimed in early 2020 that, "no person has done more to destroy the honor and values of America than Donald Trump, and that's why I think he's got to go."[18] Similarly, Democrat strategist James Carville opined that Trump was "the greatest threat this country has faced since the fall of communism."[19] Talk about polar extremes!

To be sure, some Americans revered President Obama as the Chosen One while others reviled him as the Antichrist. And I understand that many public figures are deeply polarizing, especially in the world of politics. But have evangelical Christians ever been as deeply divided over the same national leader, at least since the Civil War? Even when we think of differences between black evangelicals and white evangelicals when it came to President Obama, those differences were more understandable, as Obama apparently lied about his views on same-sex "marriage" to gain conservative black votes in 2008.[20] And, to be candid, the honor of having a black president outweighed Obama's views on things like abortion in the eyes of many a black Christian voter.

But the divisions regarding Trump are much more extreme and much more pointed. The massive good he does for certain Christian causes is undeniable. The massive damage he brings to the Christian name is also undeniable. Consequently, evangelical loyalty to Trump is very intense, as is evangelical loathing of Trump. How do we sort this out?

Christian activist Shane Claiborne tweeted in early 2020:

I love Jesus.

And it is precisely my love for Jesus that creates my outrage at Trump.

When I look at the things Jesus said and compare them to the things Trump says... it is impossible to reconcile the two.

I don't know how any Christian can defend Trump.[21]

Even more bluntly, he tweeted:

Trumpevangelicalism is a cult.

Let us rebuke it... in the name of Jesus.[22]

Yet already in 2016, megachurch pastor Robert Jeffress had said that, when it came to Christians who would not vote for Trump, "I think the Bible has a word for people like that—it's fools." He added that "any Christian who would sit at home and not vote for the Republican nominee [if it were Trump] ... that person is being motivated by pride rather than principle."[23]

Here, then, are two Christian leaders, both of whom profess a deep love for Jesus and both of whom claim to take the Bible quite seriously.[24] Yet they hold completely opposite views of Donald Trump, and they do so in Jesus' name. And each of them represents countless thousands (or millions) or others who hold to their view of Trump. To repeat my question: how do we sort this out?

TWO

Since When Was Loyalty to Trump the Dividing Line for Christians?

I really don't understand it. It's baffling and disturbing. Why do Christian supporters of Trump get so touchy with anyone who dares criticize him? Why is loyalty to Trump the new test of evangelical orthodoxy?

Of course, I'm quite aware of the flip side of this, where *disloyalty* of Trump is the test of orthodox Christian faith, as in, "No true Christian could ever support a man like that!" That's a sentiment we'll tackle often in this book (see especially Chapter Four, "Does Character Still Count and Does Morality Still Matter?").

But for the moment, I want to focus on the extreme loyalty of Trump supporters, to the point that those who criticize him – even if they voted for him, as I did – are looked at with disdain. "How dare you express any disloyalty to God's appointed man! How dare you strengthen the opposition! How dare you weaken our side!"

If you say, "I support the President, but I do believe he lies and exaggerates," you are now worse than an unbeliever. You are challenging God's choosing of Trump.

If you say, "Assuming he's the Republican candidate in 2020, I'll certainly vote for him, but I'd rather see another Republican candidate take his place," you are guilty of heresy. The Trump believers will eat you alive.

In January, 2020, I received this Facebook message from an old, evangelical friend who is also a staunch critic of Trump. He wrote, "I'm going to Hell!!!!!"

What prompted those words? His message was linked to an article from the very liberal *Huffington Post* titled, "Jim Bakker To Christians: You Must Love Trump To Prove You're 'Saved.'"[1] What? Did Bakker really say this? According to the article, which was critical and mocking in tone, "Disgraced TV evangelist Jim Bakker says President Donald Trump is a test of faith and that Christians can pass by loving him.

"'You know what? Trump is a test whether you're even saved,' he said in a clip going viral on Twitter. 'Only saved people can love Trump.'"[2]

Now, in context, it seems that Bakker was saying, "Trump is so offensive to so many people that the only way you can love someone like that is by being a Christian. In fact, Trump is a test for your salvation. Only a real Christian could love him!"

In other words, as far as I can tell, he was not saying, "You are not saved if you do no support Trump!" Instead, he was saying, "Loving someone like Trump is a proof of your salvation." Either way, it's easy to see why a leftist publication like the *Huffington Post* jumped all over this. And it's easy to see why my friend took it the way he did. "If Jim Bakker is right," he was saying in jest and in protest, "then I'm going to hell!!!" Unfortunately, some Trump supporters act as if that were true: "If you don't support Trump, you're not saved!"

Where Is the Christian Balance?

As much as I differ with some parts of Never Trumper Ben Howe's book *The Immoral Majority* (see especially Chapter Four and Chapter Seven), I absolutely agree with him when he writes, "It's not that these supporters can't acknowledge that something Trump did or said is sinful. It's that when he errs, they seem to feel obligated to shield him from consequence in service of the greater good they imagine he serves. He is inerrant in the sense that he is free of the burden of accountability."[3]

He adds, "Instead of noting that God often uses people He does not (and we should not) endorse, Trump evangelicals took it upon themselves to canonize Trump, claiming a divine approval for him that he'd never claimed for himself."[4] God is with him, and therefore anyone who dares to express a difference with him publicly is somehow opposing the Lord.

Howe also chronicles the change in attitude among many Trump voters, which, for some, started with cautious support, then became enthusiastic support, and then became almost fanatical support (my words, not his). This is really baffling.

After all, Trump's flaws are neither hidden nor subtle. He wears them openly and even proudly to the point that they are an essential part of his persona. Can you even imagine a public Trump who was not self-centered, hyperbolic, and, at times, downright nasty? (I say "a public Trump" because quite a few have told me how gracious and even humble he is with them in private.) So, it should be very easy for an evangelical Trump supporter to say, "Hey, I don't like those aspects of his personality either, but it's a small price to pay for all the good he's doing."

The problem is that it is *not* easy for many of his supporters to say this. Instead, they get touchy with you if you agree with a criticism of the President and, worse still, they find it necessary to defend his bad behavior. Some go as far as *extolling* his faults and weaknesses. The man can do no wrong in their eyes.

How in the world did this happen to us? Many fine Christians seem to be infected with this almost blind loyalty to Donald Trump and, in all candor, I don't get it. What is so sacred about evangelicals supporting Trump, meaning, supporting him without qualification or caveat? Since when was an elected official above criticism, even by his voters? Why must we swear our undying loyalty to a very flawed man? Since when has it been heretical to be objective and honest about the president?

Despite the subtitle to my previous Trump book ("An Evangelical Leader Speaks His Mind About the Man He Supports as President") I got blasted by many for the book's title: *Donald Trump Is Not My Savior*. But why? Is President Trump *your* Savior? Did he shed his blood for you? Was he the perfect Son who came down from heaven to take our place on the cross? Does he deserve our hearts and souls, our bodies and minds?

Some would say (and, in fact, did say to me, in anger and rebuke), "No one thinks he's our Savior!"

Then why are they upset with me for saying it? How am I aiding and abetting the enemy by making this proclamation? I want everyone on the planet to know that Jesus alone is my Lord and Savior, and that no human being has my heart the way He has mine. How much greater should our loyalty to the Lord be than our loyalty to the President!

Some would protest, "But you're missing the point. You discourage Trump supporters when you talk like this, and you give fodder to the opponents of the President."

Seriously? I discourage Trump supporters when I say he is not my Savior (or, for that matter, America's Savior)? I give fodder to the President's enemies when I proclaim that my ultimate loyalty is to the Lord, not to a person? Really?

From my perspective, as far as giving fodder to the President's enemies, it's the exact opposite. When we acknowledge Trump's weaknesses, this can actually garner more support for him. I tell the opponents of Donald Trump that I, too, see his failures and shortcomings, but I'm voting for him for other reasons, which, in my mind, outweigh the negatives. (We'll revisit this question several times in the book: Does the good outweigh the bad?) I am hardly blind to his flaws, and I do not follow him mindlessly. Yet I voted for him in 2016 and plan to do so in 2020.

From my perspective, talking like this only helps our witness for the Lord. Talking like this tells non-believers that we did not drink the Trump Kool-Aid, that we remain people of conscience, and that we do struggle with certain aspects of our President's character. Of course, they might still judge and malign us for voting for him at all, which is not a surprise given the radically leftist ideology of many of the Trump haters and the offensiveness of some of his behavior.

So be it. But at least we're showing the world that our eyes are open and our brains are functioning, and it's with open eyes and working brains that we are pro-life, pro-family, pro-Israel, and more. That's why Trump got our vote.

But, to repeat: rather than losing Trump voters by being candid about our differences with him, we might actually gain Trump voters. People will see we haven't lost our minds or our souls. They'll see we are thinking people who believe our nation is under existential attack. And perhaps – just perhaps – some will say, "I can see their point, and I'm willing to take a chance voting for him." In contrast, the more we push the "Trump cannot be criticized" narrative, the more we drive potential voters away.

When Loyalty Goes Too Far

Speaking of these extreme pro-Trumpers, Howe writes,

> As a conservative myself, and one who described himself as an evangelical Christian his entire life, it is difficult not to have reached the conclusion that Trump is less of a vessel to these people and more of an idol. It has gotten to the point that one wonders if Jesus Himself would be branded as a purveyor of "fake news" if He were to come down from heaven and condemn an action or utterance by President Trump."[5]

There might be some overstatement here, but not that much. Some Christians today seem more passionate about Trump than about Jesus – at least, that's how it feels, based on how they respond to criticism of the President. They seem far more thin-skinned about Trump than about the Lord, far more defensive, far more ready to fight.

And what happens when Trump takes the Lord's name in vain? Some are outraged (although, frankly, this is probably one of the least of his offenses). But others either excuse his behavior or simply look the other way. Their philosophy seems to be, "Why quibble over such inconsequential matters when we're in an existential battle with the left?"

To be sure, I do believe the soul of America is at stake in many ways, and it's because I felt Trump would do a better job fighting for the things that were most important for America that I support him. But I didn't vote for him in 2016 because I thought he was a Christian (God knows whether he is or not, but Trump didn't get my vote because I thought he was some kind of red hot follower of Jesus). And I see no reason for us to make excuses for him as a "new Christian" or a "baby Christian." Better to pray that he would have a radical, life-changing encounter with the Lord than to make excuses for his Christianity. (Again, only God knows the true state of his soul.)

Doesn't this demonstrate more integrity, more honesty, more consistency?

I would assume that, behind closed doors, especially when talking with non-evangelicals, Trump's speech is laced with profanity and with taking the Lord's name in vain or the like. (Think back to his days campaigning for the Republican nomination. He was certainly "saltier" back then, before learning to restrain his speech publicly.) And personally, I'm not surprised when he "slips" in one of his rallies, using inappropriate language.

That's who the president is, and I see no reason to crown him Saint Donald. And I imagine many, if not most of our presidents, have had foul mouths in private. It's not the end of the world. Yet even saying, "He's not Saint Donald," creates a firestorm among the most ardent Trump loyalists. Some of them have become such skilled apologists for the President that they do a better job of defending him, despite his many flaws, than they do defending Jesus, despite Him being perfect in every way. How did this happen?

I understand that Trump, by his own design, is a tremendously polarizing figure. He attracts just as strongly as he alienates. Those who love him really love him and those who hate him really hate him. So, it's only natural that, the more Trump stands up for causes near and dear to us and the more his opponents attack him, the more we stand up for him. I can understand that. It's called loyalty and appreciation.

But have we lost our bearings in the process? Have we lost our spiritual sensitivity, our insight, our perception? Have we become totally unaware of how we sometimes present ourselves, how we fail to listen, how we so easily lash out – all in defense of a very far from perfect man?

Ben Howe wrote,

> Trump's unapologetic and arguably narcissistic approach to politics undoubtedly helped him secure the nomination against the backdrop of more traditional candidates, who were seen as spineless and pandering. He was viewed as speaking the truth, no matter how uncomfortable, and whenever that truth telling seemed more like cruelty, he dismissed those concerns as weak. Evangelicals in recent years have taken it upon themselves to adopt those same attitudes in defense of anything Trump says or does. This goes way beyond typical

political spin and water carrying. They seem to believe it is their job to protect this president, to shield him. Even from God.[6]

Why is that the case? Is it because the media is so hostile to him? Is it because he fights for our causes? Whatever the reason, we do best to step back and take a deep breath. We can vote for Trump and support his presidency without doing so blindly. And we can stand *with* the president without becoming *like* the president. There's quite a difference between the two.

THREE

Have We Failed the Love Test?

Speaking to His eleven closest followers shortly before His betrayal, Jesus said, "By this everyone will know that you are my disciples, if you love one another." (John 13:35) And what if we do not love one another? What then will "everyone" know? What if we treat one another with disrespect? If we mock one another? If we savage one another? If we cruelly insult one another? What will "everyone" know then?

They will know that, no matter how much we profess to be His disciples, we are not. Our harsh words will outweigh our confession of faith – at least in the eyes of the world. Our cruelty towards each other, our hateful speech, our judgmental attitudes will speak much more loudly to a watching world than our Christian clichés and Bible memes. Not only are we failing to "walk the walk," but we are failing to "talk the talk" – at least insofar as our treatment of one another is concerned.

And in what context, these days, do we put our lack of love on the clearest display? It is in the context of our attitudes towards Donald Trump, where we not only exhibit our deep divisions, but where we put our flesh on full display on social media, as we viciously assault each other with vitriolic words. We are crude. We are nasty. We are easily provoked. We are condescending. And we do it all as professing, unashamed, zealous Christians.

What does this say to the world? How are we better than the world? How are we different? How do we manifest the fruit of the Spirit? The character of Christ? The new life from above?

I could easily imagine an honest seeker reading our social media posts, then reading the words of Jesus – that the world would know we were His disciples by our love for one another – and concluding, "I guess these people are not His disciples." Could you blame that person for coming to this conclusion?

Paul wrote to the Galatians, "You, my brothers and sisters, were called to be free. But do not use your freedom to indulge the flesh; rather, serve one another humbly in love. For the entire law is fulfilled in keeping this one command: 'Love your neighbor as yourself.' If you bite and devour each other, watch out or you will be destroyed by each other." (Galatians 5:13–15)

Yet that is exactly what we are doing. We are biting and devouring each other rather than loving each other. (And be assured that you can have deep differences while still loving each other and treating each other with kindness, love, and respect.) We are indulging the flesh rather than walking in the Spirit, because of which we are in the process of destroying each other. And over what? Our different positions on President Trump. How can this be?

Some years ago, Nancy and I were in Israel, driving with a friend of ours from the States who had been living in the Land for some years. She was a very sweet, gracious, godly woman, with a genuinely Christian spirit. But living in Israel had taken a toll on her, more than she even realized, and as another driver cut her off on the road, she rolled down her window and laid into him, which would be considered quite normal for an Israeli.

Nancy turned to her and said, "What happened to you?", at which point she put her head in heads and began to weep. She had become as aggressive and mean-spirited as the non-believers around her in this tough environment, and she was ashamed.

The same question can be asked of many a believer today: What happened to us? What became of our Christian conduct, of our civility, of our restraint?

The Reactions Are Extreme

In some circles, if you dare speak a critical word about the President because he offends your Christian values, you will be inundated with an avalanche of mean-spirited criticism. Your faith in God will be questioned. Your loyalty to America will be questioned. Your intelligence will be questioned. You will be labeled a traitor and a coward and a secret, liberal Democrat – and this will all happen in an instant. From here on, rather than being viewed as a trusted brother or sister, you will be viewed as suspect, even as an enemy. Your own family may turn against you.

In other circles, if you dare speak a positive word about the President because he is acting on behalf of your Christian concerns, you will be slammed with an equally intense barrage of hateful criticism. Your Christian testimony will be questioned. Your love for the Lord will be questioned. Your character will be questioned. You will be labeled a carnal compromiser, a racist and a misogynist. You will be accused of backing a man as evil as Hitler. And from here on, rather than being viewed as a trusted brother or sister, you will now be viewed as suspect, even as an enemy. Your own family may turn against you.

And I remind you: This is how *other believers* will treat you (on both sides of the Trump debate). How this must grieve the heart of God. How He must hate to see His children so divided and so hostile to each other. And all the while, sinners who need to know about our Savior, are pushed away from Him – all because of our constant squabbles over Trump. "If that is what it means to be a follower of Jesus," the world says, "I want nothing of it."

Just look at Paul's description of the works of the flesh and the fruit of the Spirit, then ask yourself: Does our interaction about Trump resemble the flesh or the Spirit? Which of these two is being manifested more clearly in our lives, fleshly attitudes or Holy Spirit attitudes? Paul wrote:

> The acts of the flesh are obvious: sexual immorality, impurity and debauchery; idolatry and witchcraft; *hatred, discord, jealousy, fits of rage, selfish ambition, dissensions, factions and envy*; drunkenness, orgies, and the like. I warn you, as I did before, that those who live like this

will not inherit the kingdom of God. But the fruit of the Spirit is *love, joy, peace, forbearance, kindness, goodness, faithfulness, gentleness and self-control.* Against such things there is no law. (Galatians 5:19–23, my emphasis)

In our internet discussions about the President, I see far more hatred than love and far more discord than joy. I see far more anger, dissension, and factions than peace, forbearance, kindness, goodness, faithfulness, gentleness, and self-control. In fact, some of you reading these words right now are getting angry with me, feeling that I am "weak" or "spineless," judging me as "compromised" or "cowardly" – all because I will not get nasty and dirty in defense of Trump or in accusation against Trump. Does this not reveal something to you?

With great passion, Paul wrote, "As a prisoner for the Lord, then, I urge you to live a life worthy of the calling you have received. Be completely humble and gentle; be patient, bearing with one another in love. Make every effort to keep the unity of the Spirit through the bond of peace." (Ephesians 4:1–3) Is this how we conduct ourselves? Are we humble – let alone "completely humble" – and gentle towards each other? Are we patient? Bearing with one another in love? Are we making any real effort – let alone "every effort" – to "keep the unity of the Spirit through the bond of peace"? Or do we feel that, when it comes to Trump, division and dissension are somehow justified?

In Romans 13, Paul again emphasized that "the one who loves his neighbor has fulfilled the law," adding, "Love does no harm to a neighbor. Therefore love is the fulfillment of the law." (Romans 13:8, 10, NET) Yet we are harming one another by our words and attitudes. This is anything but love.

John took things even further, writing, "We know that we have passed from death to life, because we love each other. Anyone who does not love remains in death. Anyone who hates a brother or sister is a murderer, and you know that no murderer has eternal life residing in him." (1 John 3:14–15) He continued, "Dear friends, let us love one another, for love comes from God. Everyone who loves has been born of God and knows God. Whoever does not love does not know God, because God is love." (1 John 4:7–8)

And what, exactly, does this love look like? Paul gives us the most concise and yet comprehensive definition of love in all of literature. Writing to the Corinthians he explained that, "Love is patient, love is kind. It does not envy, it does not boast, it is not proud. It does not dishonor others, it is not self-seeking, it is not easily angered, it keeps no record of wrongs. Love does not delight in evil but rejoices with the truth. It always protects, always trusts, always hopes, always perseveres." (1 Corinthians 13:4–7)

God calls us to walk in this kind of love, and by His grace we can. And yet somehow, when it comes to our interaction concerning Donald Trump, we have failed the love test miserably.

The Internet Is Filled with Cruelty, Anger, and Hate

Of course, for many years now, our internet conduct has been anything but civil, especially when we can hide behind an anonymous online identity. Just call yourself "Megaman" or "Blue Eyes" and blast away. You can say whatever you want however you want to say it, since no one – other than God Himself – knows who you are. Be rude. Be crude. You can even be vulgar. The internet will keep you safe.

But it hasn't stopped there. Even with our identities known, we still act in ungodly ways, saying things in a post that we would never say face to face. Just let those fingers fly, or dictate to your heart's content, and post your comments for the world to see. *I'm going to say whatever I want to say and nobody's going to stop me.* That seems to be the motto of the internet age, for saint and sinner alike.

What an absolutely, tragic shame. And how utterly inexcusable for a follower of Jesus. We are held to a higher standard by our Lord.

Over the years, I have been called just about every name under the sun by professing Christians, some of whom will quote Scripture and blast me with the f-word in the same post. People who are supposed to be the living witnesses of Jesus can be so mean to each other, so utterly cruel. And this has become so commonplace online that we are now completely used to it. Yet when you add in the question of our views on Trump, things go to a whole new level or vulgarity and cruelty and judgmentalism. It is the exact opposite of love. Yet, to remind us again, Jesus said, "By this everyone will know that you are my disciples, if you love one another." (John 13:35)

Have we completely forgotten how to be gracious towards each other? How to disagree without being nasty? Do we even try?

Some would reply, "I've had it with your mamby-pamby, play-nice nonsense. It's done no good at all. That's why we needed a fighter like Trump. And it's only when we as Christians start speaking up and fighting that things will change. We've been walked on like doormats for long enough. It's time to show our guts."

To be honest with you, I believe we *should* push back against the world's sinful agenda. I've written about that myself, quite forcefully, not to mention sought to live it out.[1] And I deeply appreciate the president's backbone and courage when he stands for what is right and refuses to bend or break. That's not easy to do, especially with the immense pressure that must come against him every moment of every day.

But what on earth does this have to do with the way we treat each other? What does this have to do with loving one another and pursuing unity? Do we just dismiss all the verses quoted in this chapter as if they were meaningless words from an antiquated religious book? Dare we?

Again, I understand why so many evangelicals have rallied around Trump. At last, we have a leader who will fight for us. But he will also fight for us (and others) in his particular, Trumpian way, and that way is often anything but Christlike.

There Is a Right Way and a Wrong Way to Fight

Writing for *Politico* on September 23, 2019, Michael Kruse, a frequent Trump critic, noted insightfully that,

> Regardless of the outcome—up, down or somewhere in between—when one tussle is done, Trump reflexively starts to scan the horizon in search of a new skirmish.
>
> "If he's not in a fight, he looks for one," former Trump publicist Alan Marcus told me this weekend. "He can't stop."
>
> "He's always in an attack mode," former Trump casino executive Jack O'Donnell said. "He's always got adversaries."
>
> "He does love a confrontation—there's no question about it," added Barbara Res, a former Trump Organization executive. "Trump

thinks he's always going to win—he really does believe that—and he fights very, very, very dirty."

"A street fighter," Louise Sunshine, another former Trump Organization executive, once told me.

Trump, of course, has said all of this himself, and for as long as people have been paying him any attention. For decades, he has been redundantly clear. "I go after people," he has said. "… as viciously and as violently as you can," he has said. "It makes me feel so good," he has said.

As president, he's changed … not at all.

"I like conflict," he confirmed last year.[2]

Now, would any self-respecting evangelical say that this is in keeping with the fruit of the Spirit? That this kind of attitude is exemplary and godly? That it is not worldly and carnal?

In his viral article, "He Fights," comedian and conservative speaker Evan Sayet wrote,

My Leftist friends (as well as many ardent #NeverTrumpers) constantly ask me if I'm not bothered by Donald Trump's lack of decorum. They ask if I don't think his tweets are "beneath the dignity of the office." Here's my answer:

We Right-thinking people have tried dignity. There could not have been a man of more quiet dignity than George W. Bush as he suffered the outrageous lies and politically motivated hatreds that undermined his presidency. We tried statesmanship. Could there be another human being on this earth who so desperately prized "collegiality" as John McCain? We tried propriety — has there ever been a nicer human being than Mitt Romney? And the results were always the same.

This is because — while we were playing by the rules of dignity, collegiality and propriety — the Left has been, for the past 60 years, engaged in a knife fight where the only rules are those of Saul Alinsky and the Chicago mob.

He continued:

The Left has been engaged in a war against America since the rise of the Children of the '60s. To them, it has been an all-out war where nothing is held sacred and nothing is seen as beyond the pale. It has been a war they've fought with violence, the threat of violence, demagoguery and lies from day one — the violent take-over of the universities — till today.

The problem is that, through these years, the Left has been the only side fighting this war. While the Left has been taking a knife to anyone who stands in their way, the Right has continued to act with dignity, collegiality and propriety. [I remind you that this is Savet's position. Many would differ with him here.]

With Donald Trump, this all has come to an end. Donald Trump is America's first wartime president in the Culture War.[3]

The truth be told, I'm a fighter too, engaged in one conflict or another virtually every day of my life. And I can relate to the famous saying of Jerome (347-420), written concerning the subject of persecution for the faith, "Nothing is more to be feared than too long a peace. A storm puts a man upon his guard, and obliges him to exert his utmost efforts to escape shipwreck."[4] Let the conflicts come!

I *do* believe in fighting, but not the way the world fights. As Paul wrote, "We are human, but we don't wage war as humans do" (2 Corinthians 10:3, NLT). To quote the passage in full, "For though we walk in the flesh, we are not waging war according to the flesh. For the weapons of our warfare are not of the flesh but have divine power to destroy strongholds. We destroy arguments and every lofty opinion raised against the knowledge of God, and take every thought captive to obey Christ" (2 Corinthians 10:3–5, ESV).

So, we *do* fight, but not with fleshly, carnal weapons. And we *do* fight, but not always the same way that Donald Trump fights. And we *do* fight, just not with each other!

He's a street fighter. We're Spirit fighters. He wins by insults. We overcome insults with truth, spoken in love. He looks to start trouble. We look to bring peace and reconciliation. There's quite a difference between being a troublemaker and a peacemaker.

To repeat: This does not mean that we don't have backbone. In fact, one of my mottos is that we need "backbones of steel and hearts of compassion." But courage is not cruelty and determination is not derision. You can have backbone without belligerence and strength without surliness.

For Trump, words like "kindness" and "gentleness" can equal weakness and wimpiness. As he said in a *Playboy* interview in 1990, "I think if this country gets any kinder or gentler, it's literally going to cease to exist."[5] (This was in reference to President George H. W. Bush's call for a "kinder, gentler nation.") For followers of Jesus, words like "kindness" and "gentleness" equal spirituality and maturity.

In the words of Trump, from a 2004 book, "For many years I've said that if someone screws you, screw them back. When somebody hurts you, just go after them as viciously and as violently as you can."[6] In the words of Jesus, from the Sermon on the Mount, "Love your enemies and pray for those who persecute you so that you may be sons of your Father who is in heaven" (Matthew 5:44b-45a, ESV). Or in the words of Paul, from his Letter to the Romans, "Bless those who persecute you; bless and do not curse them" (Romans 12:14, ESV).

He also wrote, "Beloved, never avenge yourselves, but leave it to the wrath of God, for it is written, 'Vengeance is mine, I will repay, says the Lord.' To the contrary, 'if your enemy is hungry, feed him; if he is thirsty, give him something to drink; for by so doing you will heap burning coals on his head.' Do not be overcome by evil, but overcome evil with good" (Romans 12:19-21, ESV with reference to Proverbs 25:21-22).

A Christian writer asked evangelical pastor Robert Jeffress, "Don't you want the president to embody the Sermon on the Mount?" He answered, "I said absolutely not."[7]

For this Pastor Jeffress was roundly criticized, although I do understand his point. If an invading army attacked our nation, you would expect the president to defend us with force, driving the enemy out. You would not expect him to turn the other cheek and let the nation be destroyed. That's what Jeffress meant when he said that he didn't want the president to embody the Sermon on the Mount.

But Pastor Jeffress would certainly say that *we*, the followers of Jesus, should embody the Sermon on the Mount. In fact, that was the Lord's very audience, as Matthew records plainly, "Seeing the crowds, he went up on the mountain, and when he sat down, his disciples came to him. And he opened his mouth and taught them, saying . . ."

(Matthew 5:1–2, ESV). The Sermon on the Mount is for us. And if you say, "I like Trump's way better," than you are following the wrong master.

We Do Fight

To say it again: We *do* fight. We *do* take stands. We *do* refuse to compromise. We *do* push back against ungodliness and sin. We just do it differently than Trump often does. That's because Jesus, not President Trump, is our model.

You might say, "But Jesus drove out the money changers and overthrew their tables. That sounds pretty strong to me. And just look at how He rebuked the religious hypocrites, calling them snakes and vipers and more. That's the example I'll follow."[8]

To be candid with you, if we had the same self-control as the Son of God and we were faced with similar circumstances, and God Himself was leading to take such action, that would be one thing. But we are not Jesus, and more times than we would like to admit, we get in the flesh, reacting rather than responding, lashing out rather than speaking the truth in love, losing our tempers rather than having a holy and righteous indignation. We'd probably end up in a fistfight or in jail or worse, and it wouldn't be to the glory of God. Instead, it would be to our shame, and it would bring reproach to the gospel.

But don't take my word for it. Listen to Peter, the one who was rebuked by Jesus for cutting off the ear of the high priest's servant when the soldiers came to arrest Jesus. At that time, the Lord said to Peter, "Put your sword back into its place. For all who take the sword will perish by the sword" (Matthew 26:52, ESV). Peter, this is not how we advance our cause!

Years later, Peter wrote,

> For to this you have been called, because Christ also suffered for you, leaving you an example, so that you might follow in his steps. He committed no sin, neither was deceit found in his mouth. When he was reviled, he did not revile in return; when he suffered, he did not threaten, but continued entrusting himself to him who judges justly. He himself bore our sins in his body on the tree, that we might die to

sin and live to righteousness. By his wounds you have been healed. For you were straying like sheep, but have now returned to the Shepherd and Overseer of your souls (1 Peter 2:21–25, ESV).

Did you get that? The example that Jesus wants us to follow is the example of sacrificial love, of trusting our cause to the Lord rather than repaying insult with insult, of dying for a sinning world – and thereby saving a sinning world.

Proverbs teaches that, "A soft answer turns away wrath, but a harsh word stirs up anger." And, "With patience a ruler may be persuaded, and a soft tongue will break a bone" (Proverbs 15:1; 25:15, ESV). This is wisdom, not weakness. This is divine pragmatism. (If you think that Proverbs is filled with idealistic platitudes, think again. The book is as real as they come.)

Trump, in contrast, often operates on the principle of, "It's best to use harsh words and stir things up," and it has worked very well for him. The whole world knows his name, and he has the ability, on some level, to bait the media into unwise responses. At the same time, the Trump method has stirred up a lot of junk, some of it very hurtful, much of it very divisive. Is this the heart of God?

But don't get me wrong. My point here is not to bash the president. He is who he is. My point is to say to each of us: *Do* follow his example when it's good, but do *not* follow his example when it's bad. Don't fight *the way* he fights. Be strong and immovable, but based on biblical principles. Stand for what is right, but do it full of the Word, full of the Spirit, full of Jesus. We will never change the world by becoming like the world. We will change the world by becoming like Jesus.

As for fighting with each other, James (Jacob) asked, "What causes quarrels and what causes fights among you? Is it not this, that your passions are at war within you?" (James 4:1, ESV)[9] Quarrels and fights in the Body are bad. Tearing each other up is bad. Exchanging Trumpian insults with each other is bad. Thinking that nastiness is a sign of spirituality is bad. Really bad.

So, it's one thing to vote for Donald Trump, which I did, and I'm glad I did. It's another thing to become like Donald Trump.

We, God's children, should be interceding for him rather than imitating him (in terms of his bad qualities I've outlined). We should be admonishing him, with honor and respect (as in, "Mr. President, do you really think being so nasty is helpful?"), rather than admiring him when he gets in the flesh, as funny as some of his zingers might be. (Be honest: Haven't you laughed at *some* of his nasty, name-calling tweets, at least once or twice?)

In short, it's one thing to elect the president. It's another thing to emulate the president. I'm all for the former, if Trump is the candidate against the left. But I am not for the latter. No way, no how. Jesus, not Trump, is my example. And whereas the president's style caters to the flesh, the Savior's style crucifies it.

Let us, then, step higher. Let love prevail. Let kindness triumph. Let unity rise. To quote Peter once more, "Having purified your souls by your obedience to the truth for a sincere brotherly love, love one another earnestly from a pure heart." And, "Above all, keep loving one another earnestly, since love covers a multitude of sins" (1 Peter 1:22; 4:8, ESV citing Proverbs 10:12).

As my wife Nancy urged in an impassioned FB comment, "If I could, I would BEG all believers to stop biting and devouring one another.....especially over politics and Trump. This is not the heart of God. The attacks and slander.....and hatred that is aimed towards the ones they are commanded to love with all sincerity and purity is so far from everything I know about the Lord, it's difficult to understand how we got here. Jesus said that the world would know we are truly his disciples by our love for one another. How far we have fallen!"[10]

Love one another!

FOUR

Does Character Still Count and Does Morality Still Matter?

David French is a leading evangelical attorney, a graduate of Harvard Law School, and a respected conservative columnist. He is also a prominent Never Trumper. Writing for the *National Review* on December 22, 2016, French said,

> I'm old enough to remember when Southern Baptist leaders really and truly cared about the character of public officials. The year was 1998, Bill Clinton had sullied the Oval Office with a tawdry affair, and the Southern Baptist Convention passed a Resolution on Moral Character of Public Officials. It's a powerful document — an eloquent and true statement of Christian truth.[1]

Evangelical Christians were terribly upset with the moral failings of President Clinton, recognizing that the sins of the nation's leaders, especially those of the president, could affect the country as a whole. As the resolution noted, "character does count in public office." Christians, therefore, should do their best to elect "candidates, who, although imperfect, demonstrate consistent honesty, moral purity and the highest character."

French cited some excerpts from the resolution in his article, but it's worth reading it as a whole, as it remains relevant to this day. The resolution, which was drafted in Salt Lake City, Utah, stated:

> WHEREAS, "Righteousness exalts a nation, but sin is a disgrace to any people" (Proverbs 14:34 NAS); and
>
> WHEREAS, Serious allegations continue to be made about moral and legal misconduct by certain public officials; and
>
> WHEREAS, The Bible calls upon all citizens to submit themselves to their governing authorities as ministers of the Lord (Romans 13:1; 1 Peter 2:13); and
>
> WHEREAS, Scripture further teaches, "Whoever resists authority has opposed the ordinance of God; and they who have opposed will receive condemnation upon themselves" (Romans 13:2); and
>
> WHEREAS, Governing authorities are not themselves exempt from the rule of law and must submit to the nation's statutes, rather than mocking them (Romans 13:1; 1 Peter 2:14; Proverbs 19:28-29; 2 Samuel 12:7; Mark 6:17-18); and
>
> WHEREAS, Some journalists report that many Americans are willing to excuse or overlook immoral or illegal conduct by unrepentant public officials so long as economic prosperity prevails; and
>
> WHEREAS, Tolerance of serious wrong by leaders sears the conscience of the culture, spawns unrestrained immorality and lawlessness in the society, and surely results in God's judgment (1 Kings 16:30; Isaiah 5:18-25); and
>
> WHEREAS, Many public officials and candidates deserve our gratitude and support for their consistent moral character and their uncompromising commitment to biblical principles of right and wrong, resulting in blessing upon their people.
>
> Therefore, be it RESOLVED, That we, the messengers to the Southern Baptist Convention, meeting June 9-11, 1998, in Salt Lake City, Utah, affirm that moral character matters to God and should matter to all citizens, especially God's people, when choosing public leaders; and
>
> Be it further RESOLVED, That we implore our government leaders to live by the highest standards of morality both in their

private actions and in their public duties, and thereby serve as models of moral excellence and character; and

Be it further RESOLVED, That we urge all citizens, including those who serve in public office, to submit themselves respectfully to governing authorities and to the rule of law; and

Be it further RESOLVED, That we urge Southern Baptists and other Christians to fulfill their spiritual duty to pray regularly for the leaders of our nation (1 Timothy 2:1-4); and

Be it finally RESOLVED, That we urge all Americans to embrace and act on the conviction that character does count in public office, and to elect those officials and candidates who, although imperfect, demonstrate consistent honesty, moral purity and the highest character.[2]

In response to this major statement, French wrote: "That was then, when the Clintons were in charge. Now it's time to Make America Great Again. New standards apply."[3] Is he right? Is it true that, in choosing Trump, many evangelical Christians, including a goodly percentage of Southern Baptists, changed their moral standards?

On December 27, 2019, French posted a paragraph from the resolution and tweeted, "Question for Christian followers. Is this statement, from the 1998 Southern Baptist Convention Resolution on Moral Character of Public Officials, wrong? If you believe it's wrong, should those Christians who believed it applied to Bill Clinton repent for their error?"[4] These are fair questions to ask.

Values Voters?

For several years now, evangelical Trump supporters have reminded us that, "We're electing a president, not a pastor (or priest). We're voting for a Commander in Chief, not a spiritual leader."

But is this how we felt in the days before Trump? Did we use this same reasoning when Bill Clinton was president? Weren't we saying that character counted and morality mattered? And haven't we been known as "Values Voters"? What "values" would those be? Didn't we call ourselves the "moral majority"?

The Southern Baptist resolution expressed concern that, "Some journalists report that many Americans are willing to excuse or overlook immoral or illegal conduct by unrepentant public officials so long as economic prosperity prevails." But that is exactly what we hear today from those evangelical Christians who point to Trump's economic success as a valid reason to overlook his moral failings. "After all," we're told, "he's the president, not the Pope."

The resolution stated that, "Tolerance of serious wrong by leaders sears the conscience of the culture, spawns unrestrained immorality and lawlessness in the society, and surely results in God's judgment." Do we still believe that today? Or have our own consciences become seared?

The resolution also affirmed "that moral character matters to God and should matter to all citizens, especially God's people, when choosing public leaders." But today, when concerned Christians point to President Trump's questionable morality, they are called legalists, or shortsighted, or religious, or worse. What has happened to our convictions?

The simplest answer would be this: We still believe that character counts and morality matters, but things have become so extreme in America that we had to elect a streetfighter, someone who would stand up for our cause – not just for our good, but for the good of the generations to come. The battle we are fighting is an existential one, with our most fundamental liberties under attack. Trump, with all his shortcomings, was the best man for the job. As noted by Tucker Carlson, "If you're wondering why so many Christians have been willing to support this president despite his personal life, this is why: It's because whatever his flaws, he's made it clear that he's not the enemy of Christians."[5] Many a Trump supporter would say, "Precisely so!"

In harmony with these sentiments, when Franklin Graham was asked why he talked about politics more than his father did. Franklin responded, "When my daddy was a child, they read the Bible in school."[6] How things have changed!

Approaching this from another angle entirely, Dennis Prager, a respected Jewish thinker, author, and radio host, said this:

> I do not know how to assess a person's character -- including my own
> -- outside of how one's actions affect others. Since I agree with almost
> all of President Trump's actions as president and believe they have

positively affected millions of people, I have to conclude that as president, Trump thus far has been a man of particularly good character.

Of course, if you think his policies have harmed millions of people, you will assess his character negatively. But that is not what never-Trump conservatives or Christians such as the Christianity Today editor-in-chief argue.[7] They argue that his policies have indeed helped America (and even the world), but this fact is far less significant than his character.

Thus, for Prager, "our support for the president is entirely moral."[8] What, exactly does he mean?

Prager lists an impressive number of Trump accomplishments, including: putting pressure on Iran and getting out of President Obama's disastrous nuclear deal; "enabling millions of black Americans to find work," along with helping millions of other Americans find employment and get freed from food stamps; "appointing more conservative judges than any president in history"; moving our embassy in Israel to Jerusalem; and increasing our military budget. All these, to Prager, are "moral issues," which means that our support for Trump *is* moral after all. And, as I have heard Prager say, he does not remember his father telling him when he was a child, "Now, pay careful attention to the president and follow his moral example."[9]

But in fairness to Prager, who is always worth listening to, he was not claiming that adultery disqualified someone from leadership back when we evangelicals were saying that Clinton should be removed. To the contrary, in a 2011 article, in answer to the question, "What does adultery tell us about a person?", Prager noted that, "For many Americans, the answer is: 'Pretty much all we need to know.' This certainly seems to be the case with regard to presidential candidates. The view is expressed this way: 'If he can't keep his vows to his wife, how can we trust him to keep his vows to his country?'"

Prager differed with that view, responding, "I am a religious conservative, but I know this statement has no basis in fact. It sounds persuasive, but it is a non sequitur. We have no reason to believe that men who have committed adultery are less likely to be great leaders or that men who have always been faithful are more likely to be great leaders."

And, he added, "while on the subject of leadership, another question for religious and/or conservative readers who believe that a man who sexually betrays his wife will likely betray his country: Who would you prefer for president? A pro-life conservative who had had an affair, or a pro-choice man of the left who had always been faithful to his wife?"

Prager also pointed to "the American who, perhaps singlehandedly, may have prevented inter-racial war in America, Martin Luther King Jr., committed adultery on a number of occasions."[10] It is, therefore, no surprise that Prager would not have a major problem with Trump's mean-spirited tweets, his exaggerations and lies, or his past immorality when, in Prager's view, Trump is doing so many things of great moral consequence. Which morality matters most to the Lord?

The same cannot be said for many evangelicals, and not just in the Clinton era. One of the reasons I so strongly opposed Trump in the primaries was his sordid past and his questionable present. What kind of man would make derogatory comments about the looks of the wife of another candidate (or, of another candidate herself)?[11] Or claim that the father of another candidate was involved in the assassination of JFK?[12] Or boast about the size of his sexual organ?[13] Or mock a disabled reporter?[14] (Trump always denied mocking the reporter, with possible video support, but at the time, that was my impression.)[15]

Valid Questions About Trump

On November 29, 2015, I asked, "Should evangelical Christians support Donald Trump as the Republican candidate?" This was during the primaries, and in this very same article, I said the question would have to be reassessed if the elections came down to Trump vs. Hillary Clinton. But at that time, I answered, "I do not see how we can if the Word of God is to be our guide and if it's important to us that a candidate have a solid moral compass and a biblically based worldview – and I mean to be our president, not our spiritual leader, since we are electing a president, not a pastor or priest."

I explained, "I'm not just talking about his silly attacks on Megyn Kelly (blood), Carly Fiorina (face), and Marco Rubio (sweat) or his more serious attacks on Mexican immigrants (accusing the many of what the few do) and others. I'm talking about his character assault on Ben Carson, comparing him to a child molester who has pathological problems and, most recently, his apparent mocking of the disability of *New York Times* reporter Serge Kovaleski."

I added, "Is this the man you want to be our president? The warnings in Proverbs are strong: 'Do you see a man who is hasty in his words? There is more hope for a fool than for him' (Proverbs 29:20, ESV). And, 'A fool gives full vent to his spirit, but a wise man quietly holds it back' (Proverbs 29:11, ESV).

"We need a statesman, not an irresponsible flame thrower, and one can be a strong political leader who is cutting and fearless with words – think of Winston Churchill – without making a fool of oneself."

Indeed, I claimed, "But what is undeniable is that he is often irresponsible and reckless in his speech, something that could be utterly disastrous for the president of the United States of America. As noted by Jay Ruderman, an advocate for the disabled, 'It is unacceptable for a child to mock another child's disability on the playground, never mind a presidential candidate mocking someone's disability as part of a national political discourse.'"

Even if Trump did not, in fact, mock the disabled, he has certainly mocked and ridiculed and basely insulted many healthy people since. What do we say to this? I also pointed to Trump's pride, referring to it as "the sin that is often at the root of a host of other sins (Isaiah 14:11-15), the sin which God resists (James 4:6), the sin which leads to destruction (Proverbs 16:18)."

And so, I concluded, "while I do understand why many Americans are behind Donald Trump and while I do believe he could do some things well as president, I cannot understand how evangelicals can back him, especially when we have a number of solid, God-fearing, capable alternatives."[16]

That was written in 2015, and some feel the same to this day. How is that I, along with other evangelicals, voted for him in 2016 and plan to do so in 2020? Have we exchanged godly principles for worldly pragmatism? According to Christian psychologist Chris Thurman, we have.

He writes,

I believe evangelicals who support Donald Trump are being both blind and foolish to do so and that labeling them as such is not sinful but appropriate and necessary. By support, I'm not referring to evangelicals who voted for Trump in 2016. I'm referring to those evangelicals who continue to hold Trump up as a great leader, say he is God's chosen one for the presidency, applaud his appalling words and actions, ignore his glaring moral defects, and enable his dangerous presidency to continue by giving him their time, talents, and treasures.[17]

So, Dr. Thurman is not simply speaking of evangelicals who voted for Trump in 2016, which would include me. Rather, he is speaking of those who are his apologists and defenders, applauding his crude insults rather than cringing over them. At the same time, Thurman saw no way that evangelicals could support Trump in 2020, concluding his article "by challenging those evangelicals who support Trump to humble themselves, admit they made a grave mistake by backing a man so clearly psychologically and morally unfit to be president, and repent of their misjudgment of this man by vigorously opposing his re-election."[18]

Dr. Thurman singles out Ralph Reed, "former head of the Christian Coalition and founder and chairman of the Faith and Freedom Coalition"; Jerry Falwell, Jr., president of Liberty University; Rev. Franklin Graham; and Vice President Mike Pence. All of them, in Thurman's eyes, are guilty of hypocrisy and moral compromise, defending the indefensible and justifying the unjustifiable.

In response, many Trump supporters would say, "Men like French and Thurman are splitting hairs. They are missing the forest for the trees.

"Morality does matter, which is why we support Trump's efforts to save the lives of millions of babies in the womb, even if he can be crude at times. Morality does matter, which is why we stand with the president when he stands for religious liberties, which lie at the foundation of our nation, even if he can play with the facts at times. Morality does matter, which is why we're glad to have a fighter in the White House, someone who will confront Islamic terrorists and speak up for persecuted Christians, even if he doesn't always act 'presidentially.'

"You need to wake up to reality and gets your hands dirty with real life and death issues. Your prissy Christianity doesn't cut it when a nation is being destroyed. Wake up and get behind Trump!"

The only problem with this argument (which is a powerful one to me and explains why I continue to support Trump) is that we need to address our very vocal views from the past, views which stated plainly that the personal conduct and morality of the president are of great concern to the nation and that his character (or lack thereof) affects us all.

It is for good reason that many non-believers ask us how we can support someone like Donald Trump, a man married three times, a man who boasted about his past affairs, a man whose wife once appeared topless in a photo shoot, a man who made money off of casinos (one of which had a giant strip club), a man who spoke freely about groping women, and a man who said he had done nothing for which he needed to ask God's forgiveness.

I do believe we have answers to these questions, questions that are valid and understandable. But all too often we fail to feel the weight of these concerns, making us appear superficial and hypocritical, not to mention giving the appearance that we are hungrier for political power than for moral and spiritual purity. And all too often we *are* hypocritical. Never Trump evangelical Ben Howe does a great job of laying this out in his book *The Immoral Majority*, pointing to evangelical statements about character regarding President Clinton.

Are We Being Inconsistent?

I noted, above, that Dr. Thurman called out Ralph Reed, Franklin Graham, Jerry Falwell, Jr., and Mike Pence for their wholehearted support of Trump. Yet Howe notes that,

> Ralph Reed, James Dobson, Pat Robertson, Jerry Falwell Sr., and scores of other evangelicals took the position in light of the increasing evidence for a lack of moral character on the part of Bill Clinton that he should resign the presidency for the good of a nation already desensitized to moral depravity.
>
> They believed that there would be a long-term cultural consequence if he were to stay in office, and that the decline of

expectations of character or the acceptability of adultery and hedonism, already something they viewed as a growing problem in the culture, would steepen the downward trajectory of American values.[19]

Should this give us pause for thought?

Howe quotes Dr. James Dobson at length, since he had very strong opinions when President Clinton's adulterous behavior was exposed, challenging the idea that the ends justifies the means. He said:

Because the economy is strong, millions of people have said infidelity in the Oval Office is just a private affair—something between himself and Hillary. We heard it time and again during those months: "As long as Mr. Clinton is doing a good job, it's nobody's business what he does with his personal life."

That disregard for morality is profoundly disturbing to me. Although sexual affairs have occurred often in high places, the public has never approved of such misconduct. But today, the rules by which behavior is governed appear to have been rewritten specifically for Mr. Clinton.[20]

Indeed, Dr. Dobson was concerned about the *moral example* of Clinton, writing,

At any given time, 40 percent of the nation's children list the President of the United States as the person they most admire. What are they learning from Mr. Clinton? What have we taught our boys about respecting women? What have our little girls learned about men? How can we estimate the impact of this scandal on future generations? How in the world can 7 out of 10 Americans continue to say that nothing matters except a robust economy?

As George Washington said in his presidential farewell address, "Of all the disposition and habits which lead to political prosperity, Religion and morality are indispensable supports . . . And let us with caution indulge the supposition, that morality can be maintained without religion . . . reason and experience both forbid us to expect that national morality can prevail in exclusion of religious principle."[21]

But when *Christianity Today* editor-in-chief Mark Galli called for the removal of President Trump, Dr. Dobson wrote:

I have read a new editorial published by Christianity Today that promotes impeachment of President Donald Trump. The editors didn't tell us who should take his place in the aftermath. Maybe the magazine would prefer a president who is passionately pro-abortion, anti-family, hostile to the military, dispassionate toward Israel, supports a socialist form of government, promotes confiscatory taxation, opposes school choice, favors men in women's sports and boys in girl's locker rooms, promotes the entire LGBTQ agenda, opposes parental rights, and distrusts evangelicals and anyone who is not politically correct. By the way, after Christianity Today has helped vacate the Oval Office, I hope they will tell us if their candidate to replace Mr. Trump will fight for religious liberty and the Bill of Rights? Give your readers a little more clarity on why President Trump should be turned out of office after being duly elected by 63 million voters? Is it really because he made a phone call [meaning, the Ukraine phone call] that displeased you? There must be more to your argument than that. While Christianity Today is making its case for impeachment, I hope the editors will now tell us who they support for president among the Democrat field. That should tell us the rest of the story.[22]

On the one hand, I agree with Dr. Dobson that Galli was quite wrong in his call for Trump's removal (see Chapter Eleven), although I would question the idea that Galli was suggesting that a liberal Democrat take Trump's place.[23] And I stand with him in pointing to the good that President Trump has done. On the other hand, it would only be fair to ask if there appears to be any contradiction between Dr. Dobson's stance in 1998 and in 2019.

On August 19, 2109, I posted a poll on Twitter, asking: "Were evangelicals too idealistic in the past when we said that, when it came to our political leaders, character was very important? Or do we now say (re: President Trump) that character counts, but other factors are more important." Only 16.3 percent said we were "too idealistic," compared to 48.4 percent who said, "No, we were right" and 35.3 percent who said that "other factors [were] now bigger."[24]

I believe it is imperative, then, that we address the issue of President Trump's character and morality, given our strong stances in the past. (I have barely scratched the surface of relevant evangelical quotes during the Clinton scandal. For years we have had a lot to say about the moral character of our leaders.) Have we changed our tune or not? Have we sold our souls for political power or not? Are we Christian first and American second, or the reverse?

Preserving Our Integrity and Witness

In my opinion, the big problem for us in terms of our reputation and witness is not that we voted for Trump, as it's clear that the same leftist media that urges us to abandon the president is the same leftist media that despises our religious values and wants to see him defeated. By no means do I think for a split second that, if I were say, "I will not vote for Donald Trump again," that the leftist media would say to me, "Dr. Brown, now we see that you're a reasonable person and not a religious fanatic. Please do explain to us why you oppose abortion and do not recognize same-sex 'marriage'." Not a chance.

So, I'm not suggesting that we let the left or the media or the world dictate our actions and words. But I am suggesting that the left and the media and the world have some very valid concerns about our integrity and our consistency. Does our faith really and truly impact our lives?

How, then, do we respond to those who question how we can cry out "Character counts" in 1998 and then vote for Donald Trump in 2016 or 2020? (There are plenty of fine Christians who ask this question as well.)

First, we need to say, "That's a great question! We do believe character counts, and that's why so many of us had a real problem with Donald Trump. That's also why we still get upset over some of his words and actions. We are not his apologists, and we have no desire to whitewash his very evident shortcomings.

"Not only so, but we believe that he is often his own worst enemy and that, with all of his marketing genius and ability to self-promote, he frequently alienates people unnecessarily. This means that his character failings *do* have negative consequences, and that does concern us."

Addressing this head-on, with honesty, will go a long way to refuting the charges of hypocrisy.

Second, we can point out that Trump has shown no evidence of promiscuity or sexual misbehavior in the White House. We hear no rumblings of secret affairs (for which President John F. Kennedy was infamous) and nothing remotely resembling the Clinton-Lewinsky scandal. And, contrary to popular opinion, candidate Trump *did* apologize for his lewd comments captured on tape from more than 10 years earlier. He said, "I've never said I'm a perfect person, nor pretended to be someone that I'm not. I've said and done things I regret, and the words released today on this more than a decade-old video are one of them. Anyone who knows me knows these words don't reflect who I am. I said it, I was wrong, and I apologize . . . . I pledge to be a better man tomorrow and will never, ever let you down."[25]

Melania also issued this statement: "The words my husband used are unacceptable and offensive to me. This does not represent the man that I know. He has the heart and mind of a leader. I hope people will accept his apology, as I have, and focus on the important issues facing our nation and the world."[26]

Third, we can point to Trump's strong character qualities, which include keeping his word to evangelical Christians in ways that no president before him has done. That is very positive and very moral. He is also loved by his children, which certainly speaks well of him. Perhaps he is not as ugly a character as he is made out to be? Although I cannot explain the difference between his public persona and his private persona, I can say that everyone I know who has spent time with him one on one has told me how humble he was face to face, how attentive he was, and how he seemed to genuinely fear God and respect Christians.

As to the larger question of his character failings, Professor Wayne Grudem took issue with Mark Galli's description of Trump's tweets as "a near-perfect example of a human being who is morally lost and confused." Grudem wrote:

The expression "near-perfect example" suggests that something like

90% or 95% of his tweets reflect morally evil choices. But, after reading these tweets, it seems to me that Galli has made a false accusation. The most objectionable thing that I see in these tweets is that Trump labels his political opponents with derogatory nicknames (Crazy Nancy Pelosi, Cryin' Chuck Schumer, and Adam Shifty Schiff), but that impoliteness is a comparatively trivial matter that comes nowhere close to being a "near-perfect example of a human being who is morally lost and confused."

I see in these tweets a president who is rightfully proud of a healthy economy, a stronger military, and the appointment of 187 federal judges who are committed to judging according to what the law says and not according to their personal preferences. Such accomplishments are *morally good* benefits for the nation as a whole, and they have been accomplished by Trump in the face of relentless opposition from Democrats. Far from being "morally lost and confused," Trump seems to me to have a strong sense of justice and fair play, and he is (I think rightfully) upset that the impeachment process in the House was anything but just and fair.[27]

This is not to minimize or excuse Trump's often inappropriate language. But it is to say, "Let's not blow it out of proportion either."

Personally, I do believe that the Trump presidency has contributed to a further degrading of our country. We seem more vile. More profane. More free to attack each other in the harshest of terms. But I'm also aware that, as a culture, we were already quite vile and profane and ugly. The Trump presidency has only added fuel to the fire. So, he has added to an existing problem and, at the same time, helped make a major shift in the right direction, as noted in Prager's next point.

Fourth, in keeping with Dennis Prager's points, we emphasize that Trump has done a tremendous amount of moral good which, in our view, much more than compensates for the damage he has done. Put another way, do you really think that babies saved from abortion will grow up to say, "I would rather have been killed in the womb than see Donald Trump insult a political opponent"? I seriously doubt it. Or do you think a Christian in Syria saved from death at the hands of ISIS will say one day, "I would have rather ISIS killed me and my family

than seen a nasty man like Donald Trump drive ISIS out of our land."
Hardly!

Saving babies is a good, moral thing. Fighting terrorism is a good,
moral thing. Pushing back against oppression is a good, moral thing. As
Grudem also explained:

> My response is that is not correct for Galli to say that character
> "doesn't really matter" to evangelical Trump supporters, for we have
> roundly and universally condemned his past immoral behavior.
> Character matters. But the moral character that Trump has
> demonstrated while in the White House, his unswerving commitment
> to his campaign promises, his courage, and his sound judgment on
> one policy issue after another, are commendable.
>
> And the future of the nation also matters. It matters a lot, not only
> for ourselves, our children, and our grandchildren, but also for the rest
> of the world, for whom a strong United States is the primary bulwark
> against tyranny and oppression. And it matters for the future of the
> church, for which freedom of religion remains a precious benefit not
> shared today by Christians in numerous other countries.

And he concludes, "On issue after issue, President Trump is
changing the direction of the country for the better. When I weigh
these results against his sometimes imprecise and coarse speech, there is
no comparison."[28]

As stated in a tweet by a man named Jonathan, "Humm, prison
reform, against abortion, illegal immigration, religious liberty, no new
wars, more jobs, should I keep going? President isn't a God, but this
president has done more to implement Godly principles than never
trumpers or dems."[29] Or, in the words of Ryan on my Facebook page,

> I was one of the Christians that was horrified about the evangelical
> support for Trump, and I absolutely hated the way Christianity
> became intertwined with politics in America. After going to UNCC
> [the University of North Carolina Charlotte] and seeing how ungodly
> and far left things have become, and seeing how Academia
> indoctrinates my generation, my views about Trump have completely
> changed. I will definitely be voting for Trump in 2020. He is a

necessary force against the insanity that's being peddled not only in the universities, but also in media and the workforce.[30]

You say, "But Trump is putting children in cages! And Trump is a racist! And Trump is taking health care from the poor!"

A Trump supporter would respond that we do have real problems at our borders, but that is nothing new.[31] And Trump has been working together with Hispanic leaders and others to come up with a viable plan for immigration reform.[32] As for Trump being a racist (especially a supporter of neo-Nazis and the like), that too is based on either exaggerations or outright misrepresentations.[33] As for taking health care from the poor, his policies have actually helped many poor people get jobs, and his goal is to come up with positive, health care reform.[34]

Do I believe that he has made some bad decisions? Of course. Which president hasn't? Do I believe that his own mouth is responsible for many of the negative perceptions about him (including that he is a racist)? Absolutely. In fact, at my only meeting in the White House so far (not with the president but with some of his team), together with about twenty other evangelical leaders, I brought up this very issue, noting that he takes three steps forward with his policy decisions but then takes two steps back with his tweets. I also explained that his comments and behavior sometimes made it difficult for us to support him.

So, to repeat, I am not deaf to these concerns. But I do have responses to them. And this brings me to the final reason why we are not being hypocritical to support him.

Fifth, America needed a man with unusual backbone to push back against forces that were poised to destroy our nation as we knew it. We needed a political outsider who was not beholden to the system and would genuinely try to drain the swamp. We needed someone who would stand up to international tyrants. The positive is that we have found that man in Donald Trump. The negative is that when you are a human wrecking ball, as he is, there is a lot of collateral damage. As I've said before, a wrecking ball is great for demolishing an old building. It is *not* great for renovating a room.

Some Wise Words from Professor Robert George

So, we get the good with the bad in very pronounced ways with President Trump, and weighing things in the balance, without compromising our consciences, we have voted for him and are glad we did. Princeton law professor Robert P. George summed things up well in a Facebook post dated December 27, 2019:

> Whatever one thinks of Donald Trump (and my own views about the President's delinquencies are well known) surely it's not hard to understand why large numbers of Evangelicals and Catholics favor him over any of the Democrats seeking their party's nomination (despite the fact that many Evangelicals and Catholics aren't happy about the President's character, coarse rhetoric, and some of his polices). There is the fealty of every single one of the Democratic nominees--every single one--to the abortion and sex lib lobbies. If you believe, as Evangelicals and Catholics believe, that abortion is the unjust killing of innocent and defenseless members of the human family, then it is nigh impossible to imagine circumstances under which one could support a politician who pledges to work night and day to deny unborn children any legal protection against the lethal violence now visited with impunity upon nearly a million of them each year. And that is precisely the pledge every Democratic candidate makes to Planned Parenthood, NARAL, and the entire base of their party. But that's only for starters.

So, Prof. George clearly recognizes the weaknesses of our president (he actually calls them "delinquencies") but points to his moral actions when it comes to defending the lives of the unborn. This is major.

George continues:

> Evangelicals and Catholics have watched as Democrats and progressives across the country have worked to shut down Catholic and other religious foster care and adoption agencies because, as a matter of conscience, these agencies place children in homes with a mom and a dad. They have watched as cake bakers, florists, caterers, wedding planners, and others (even the pizza shop-owning O'Connor

family and the software designer Brendan Eich) have been harassed in efforts to drive them out of business and deprive them of their livelihoods because of their beliefs about marriage and sexual morality. They have watched as the Democratic and progressive mayor of Atlanta terminated the employment of Kelvin Cochran, the city's Fire Chief, for the same reason--he had published a book upholding Biblical teaching on marriage and sexual morality. They have watched as Democrats and progressives have tried to "cleanse" entire fields of medicine and healthcare of Evangelicals, Catholics, and other pro-life people by imposing on them requirements to implicate themselves in the taking of innocent life by abortion. They watched as Beto O'Rourke proposed--over no truly meaningful opposition from his fellow Democratic presidential aspirants--to selectively yank the tax exempt status from churches and other religious organizations that refused to fall in line with progressive ideological orthodoxy on sex and marriage.

I could go on.

This is a moral issue of great importance – the issue of preserving our most fundamental liberties as Americans – and here too, President Trump is on the right side of this issue.

Back to Prof. George:

Now, none of this is to deny that there are some Evangelicals and Catholics (and other Trump supporters) who seem entirely to overlook Donald Trump's faults and failings. They see nothing but good in the man. But at least in my experience these Evangelicals and Catholics are in the minority. Most recognize his faults and failings and wish he were better. Their support for him is based on a prudential judgment that the overall situation for the common good would be made much worse if he were to lose to one of the Democrats. And they fear--with justification--that the consequences for themselves and their religious institutions would be dire if such a thing were to happen. In this respect, their position is formally like that of their anti-Trump co-religionists who favor a Democrat because their prudential judgment is that, though a Democratic president would do great harm to values they cherish (such as the sanctity of human life, and religious liberty and the rights of conscience), the harm would be less than the harm Trump will do to those values and others in the long run.

I'm not sure he is entirely right about the proportion of Christian Trump supporters who entirely overlook his "faults and failings." There might be more of these than we care to admit, and that continues to concern me. But very few Christian leaders that I know personally overlook these deficiencies. They simply believe, as stated repeatedly here, that the real good Trump is doing far outweighs the bad.

George concludes with this:

> My point here is not to try to adjudicate this dispute. (For what it's worth, I think that it's a more complicated business than most people on either side suppose. I may say more about that on another occasion after I've reflected on it a good deal more.) It is simply to say that no one should be surprised that many Evangelicals and Catholics (including some like my pal Keith Pavlischek who refused to vote for Trump in 2016) support the President over the Democratic alternatives. Whether one assesses and weights the reasons as they do or not, they do have reasons.[35]

Jim Daly, who succeeded James Dobson as the head of Focus on the Family, in his response to *Christianity Today*, seemed to suggest that, perhaps in the past we *were* too idealistic in our position, failing to recognize how far everyone falls from God's standards. He wrote, "Looking at the data and talking to thousands of people, I believe many conservative Christians realized – perhaps for the first time – that we will not find a man or woman who is committed to strong social policies who is also capable of perfectly fulfilling the Ten Commandments.

"In reality, this has always been the case."

And that's why so many evangelicals support Donald Trump. Hence, his question for *Christianity Today*: "As a Christian, I would ask Christianity Today this: What is more important? A president who talks smoothly and statesman-like but accelerates the killing of innocent human life? Or perhaps a president who supports the deconstruction of religious freedom and undoes societal norms for the sake of the few to feel included?"[36]

As Prof. George said, we "do have reasons" for supporting Trump. Some in our camp, to be sure, are guilty of hypocrisy, condemning ungodly behavior when they see it in their political opponents but excusing it when it comes to the president. And, to say it once more, the president's failings do have negative consequences. The Book of Proverbs explains clearly and forcefully that our behavior and our words have positive or negative effects. But there is no question that a strong, moral argument can be made *in favor* of President Trump, not just here in America but on a global scale as well.

Andrew T. Walker, Associate Professor of Christian Ethics at The Southern Baptist Theological Seminary and Executive Director of the Carl F. H. Henry Institute for Evangelical Engagement, summarized things well in a *National Review* article published February 10, 2020. He noted first that,

> Critics, whether secular or religious, are right to note the odd relationship between religious conservatives and Donald Trump. The refrain is familiar: To anyone with a conscience, Trump is both lewd and prurient, a man whose life has involved adultery, misogyny, racial insensitivity, vainglory, profanity, deceit, sexual aggression, divorce, fornication, casinos, and porn. Religious conservatives should not accept these vices, but rather denounce them. With Trump, it's easier to find what offends the religious-conservative conscience than to find what does not.

Indeed, he added,

> Here was a man whose career and persona typify all that religious conservatives have protested in American culture. Or, lest we overlook recent history, a persona that religious conservatives spent the late 1990s imputing to President Bill Clinton. Critics of religious conservatives correctly point out what seems a glaring contradiction: Some religious-conservative leaders ignore or downplay moral indiscretions when it is their political party in power. Though religious conservatives don't believe morality is relative, the moral outrage directed at Clinton is notably absent with Trump.

How, then, have so many evangelicals, including major leaders, gotten behind Donald Trump? Prof. Walker notes that,

> an event on October 10, 2019 explains the odd-couple relationship of religious conservatives and Donald Trump. That evening, during a CNN townhall on LGBTQ issues, the now-former Democratic presidential candidate Beto O'Rourke proclaimed that churches failing to toe the line on gay and transgender rights would lose their tax-exempt status in his administration. O'Rourke's comments represented a high-water mark of a culture that has jettisoned anything resembling a Christian moral ecology.[37]

This, then, was illustrative of the unexpected alliance between Trump and Christian conservatives. It typified why so many "morality first" voters could vote for such an immoral man, and it helped explain why these strange bedfellows became such close coworkers.

A major poll conducted by Pew Research, released in March, 2020, underscores these conclusions. It found that, "Fully eight-in-ten white evangelical Protestants say that the phrase "fights for what I believe in" describes Trump 'very well' or 'fairly well,' including roughly half who say this describes him 'very well.'" In addition, "white evangelical Protestants overwhelmingly feel that the Trump administration has helped (59%) rather than hurt (7%) the interests of evangelical Christians. And three-quarters of white evangelicals say they agree with the president on 'many,' 'nearly all' or 'all' important issues facing the country." At the same time,

> While white evangelical Protestants generally see Trump as standing up for them, they are less convinced that he personally lives a moral and ethical life or conducts himself admirably. Just 15% of white evangelicals say the phrase "morally upstanding" describes Trump very well, and about a quarter say "honest" is a very good descriptor of the president (23%). About one-third of white evangelicals (31%) say they like the way Trump conducts himself as president (aside from his positions on the issues). Fully two-thirds either have "mixed feelings" about his conduct (44%) or say they don't like it (22%). And only

about one-in-eight white evangelicals (12%) think Trump is a very religious person.[38]

This is hardly an example of blind, cult-like devotion or of sticking our heads in the sand. Instead, it is a matter of recognizing and regretting the president's moral weaknesses while appreciating the pro-evangelical stands he has taken.

We can therefore say that, in the end, character does count and morality does matter. And that's why, when faced with a vote between President Trump and a radical leftist candidate, many of us can support Donald Trump. Some of us do it with reluctance and concern, others with confidence and enthusiasm, but either way, we can look at the world without shame and we can look at the Bible without shame and say, "We voted our conscience, we are not compromised, and we have made a deal with the devil."

FIVE

The 'Cult of Trump' vs. 'Trump Derangement Syndrome'

Does Donald Trump use proven cultic techniques to manipulate and control his followers, and do some of them follow him with a cult-like devotion? Does their loyalty to him and esteem for him go far beyond what is acceptable (or even logical)? In January, 2016, candidate Trump (in)famously said, "You know what else they say about my people? The polls, they say I have the most loyal people. Did you ever see that? Where I could stand in the middle of Fifth Avenue and shoot somebody and I wouldn't lose any voters, okay? It's like incredible."[1] This is not just "like incredible." It's downright dangerous, and, given the loyalty of some fervent Trump, it hardly feels like an exaggeration.

It's one thing to be an enthusiastic Trump supporter, like this gentleman named Howard, who tweeted after the president's State of the Union address in February, 2020, one day before his expected acquittal: "Shalom Dr Brown, as you know, God has raised Donald Trump up for this time to do a work, and after He's Acquitted today, He will be re-elected, Roe v Wade will be overturned, and Donald Trump will finish the work that God sent him to do!!"[2]

It's another thing to have an almost religious devotion to him, to defend his every word and deed, to reverence him as a savior figure, to see him as called by God so much and raised up so much "for such a time as this" that to criticize him is to criticize the Lord. This certainly concerns me.

In the first chapter, I cited some tweets from progressive Christian activist Shane Claiborne where he brought serious accusations against both Trump and his evangelical supporters. He said:

Trumpevangelicalism is a cult.
Let us rebuke it... in the name of Jesus.[3]

And,

I love Jesus.
And it is precisely my love for Jesus that creates my outrage at Trump.
When I look at the things Jesus said and compare them to the things Trump says... it is impossible to reconcile the two.
I don't know how any Christian can defend Trump.[4]

He also said:

He could shoot someone in the middle of Fifth Avenue...
And some Christians would still defend him.
But the resistance is growing.
Every generation has its own revolution.[5]

The "Cult of Trump"?

In 2019, Steven Hassan, a mental health professional with extensive background in the cults, published a book titled, *The Cult of Trump: A Leading Cult Expert Explains How the President Uses Mind Control.*[6] During the primaries, Hassan was surprised by "the intensity of Trump's support, especially from evangelical Christians," given Trump's history and character. "How," Hassan wondered, "could he possibly gain enough support among the conservative Christians who would be so important for him to be elected?" But as he watched Trump pick off one Republican contender after another, he realized that Trump was exploiting certain "psychological and social techniques" to great effect.[7]

For Hassan, who had been a member of the Rev. Moon cult in the 1970s, this was a cause for real concern, especially after he had his déjà vu moment. He writes:

I had a bizarre kind of déjà vu. It struck me that Trump was exhibiting many of the same behaviors that I had seen in the late Korean cult leader Sun Myung Moon, whom I had worshipped as the messiah in the mid-seventies. Moon had promised to make America—indeed the entire world—great. He promised a re-creation of the Garden of Eden. No wars, poverty, crime. Everyone would live in harmony together in God's paradise on earth. Moon, of course, was not a messiah, nor were his aims beneficent. That is the case with many cult leaders—they promise something that people want to believe in but that they can never actually deliver. They do so by utilizing a set of influence techniques that can be likened to a cult leader's playbook.

I now believe—and it is the argument of this book—that Trump has gotten where he is today in large part because he has exploited that same playbook. Trump's air of absolute confidence, his grandiosity —"Only I can fix this"—his practice of sowing fear and confusion, his demand for absolute loyalty, his tendency to lie and create alternative "facts" and realities, his shunning and belittling critics and ex-believers —these are the same methods used by Moon and other cult leaders such as L. Ron Hubbard, David Koresh, Lyndon LaRouche, and Jim Jones, to name just a few high-profile ones.[8]

Does this sound extreme? Hassan points out that he is hardly the first to make these accusations. He notes,

On June 7, 2018, the *New York Times* ran an editorial, "The Cult of Trump," describing how the Republican Party was obediently, almost blindly, rallying around the president in a cult of personality. Former Tennessee Republican senator Bob Corker was quoted in the *Washington Post* as saying, "It's becoming a cultish thing, isn't it?" In 2019, Maryland Democratic representative Jamie Raskin said, "The Republican party is almost like a religious cult surrounding an organized crime family. That's the mentality." Former White House staffer and Apprentice contestant Omarosa Manigault Newman ends her book, Unhinged, with these memorable words: "I've escaped from the cult of Trumpworld. I'm free."[9]

Is Hassan on to something here? Or is he projecting his own experience onto others – onto to people who have had it with weak politicians who promise one thing and do another and are simply glad to have a no-nonsense, get-things-done leader like Trump? Is there really a "Cult of Trump," or did Trump simply have the ability to tap into the frustrations and concerns of tens of millions of Americans and to become their champion? In other words, could it be that, rather than bringing people under his power by creating fears, he was savvy enough to fight for what was important to his tens of millions of Americans?

Critics of Hassan's book were not impressed with his arguments, with one reader, named Jesef, writing:

> Dear Steve, I've really admired your work as it pertains to undue influence (cults), particularly high-demand religious/spiritual cults. But I think you've let your political views get the better of you in producing this. While there's no question that DJT is a megalomaniac & a narcissist, and the current/temporary/default leader of the Republican party, the only organization over which he holds absolute power is his administration - where he has power to hire/fire people. And this is time-limited. He does not hold this power over Congress or the Supreme Court justices, Republican party members, or the citizenry. He is not and cannot be a tyrant, outside of that small Executive branch circle of influence - or he is severely limited and easily rebuffed elsewhere anyway. He is being impeached right now, for crying out loud. He cannot pass legislation on his own - USMCA has been sitting on the Speaker's desk for close to 10 months now. Does the POTUS have power? You've often said that a cult is hard to leave, but it is not hard to "leave Trump" or even his administration. He fires people and people quit all the time - he's had more turnover than probably any POTUS in history. Now I wouldn't disagree with his use of manipulative undue influence techniques. But you've really shown your political bias to apply this to him and by extension Republicans and not to the Democrats and their propaganda media outlets. CNN, MSNBC, ABC, NBC, CBS, etc. - all of them

demonstrably parrot the same DNC-authored talking points, show after show, all day every day. So, if you're going to point out "political" undue-influence/cults, at least apply it equally to both sides. I think you've left your wheelhouse and shown your bias with this book. Why didn't you write "Cult of Obama" or "Cult of Clinton" books? Sorry, huge fan of your work, but this one left me scratching my head at its blatant political bias.[10]

Yes, what about the "Cult of Obama"? Was he not labeled the "Chosen One"? Did not *Newsweek* magazine run a cover story on January 18, 2013, as the beginning of Obama's second term, titled "The Second Coming"?[11] As noted by Joseph Curl in the *Washington Times* on April 30, 2019,

> Yes, Mr. Trump is harsh — even immature — about the press and its coverage of him. He has thin skin and he's never grown out of the name-calling phase of his snot-nosed youth. Mr. Trump's a talker — often a whiner — but he's never really done anything to the media, which are flourishing despite his supposed efforts to thwart them.
>
> But President Obama — celebrated as The Chosen One and beloved by the media — stomped on the freedom of the press like no other president since Tricky Dick.
>
> Mr. Obama, who pledged "the most transparent administration in history," was deemed "the least transparent and the most antagonistic toward the media since the Nixon administration" by The San Diego Union-Tribune, which summed up him efforts to control the media in a single paragraph.[12]

Wouldn't Obama's behavior, then, be more cult-like and dangerous? And wasn't he greatly revered by his supporters? Yet even if Obama was all but deified by his followers, there did not seem to be the same cult-like *loyalty* to him that there is to Trump, especially among evangelicals. Nor does it explain the degree to which Trump's supporters will believe him – no matter how impossible or false his claims – and brand all opposing information as "fake." Those are the parts of the "Cult of Trump" that need to be examined. And without a doubt, accusations of the "Cult of Trump" abound.

In August, 2019, Utne.com ran an article by Miguel A. De La Torre, author of *Burying White Privilege*.[13] It was titled, "Christianity and the Cult of Trump." According to De La Torre, "Eurocentric Christianity has legitimized a patriarchy where authoritarian men rule at home, rule in the church, and rule in public." Adding to this is "the way in which whiteness expanded the authoritarian model by feminizing men and women of color, thus placing their fate under the benevolent masculine hand of the white, male overseer who knows what is best for inferior people. Christianity in the United States is simply simpatico with a political model designed to justify white supremacy."

And this, according to De La Torre, explains the "Cult of Trump":

> When authoritarian figures can do no wrong, the problem is not so much with the leader but with the followers, who, like followers of religious cults, willingly drink the proverbial Kool-Aid regardless of how high their IQ may actually be. Seeing their unearned, privileged positions threatened by merit-based concepts such as equality, they embrace cult leaders who present themselves as the only solution to their downward-spiraling predicament, or as Trump proclaimed while mounting the Republican National Convention stage: "I am your voice. I alone can fix it."[14]

Trump, then, should be compared to political leaders like Hitler, Mussolini, Stalin, Mao, and Castro or to religious leaders like Jim Jones or David Koresh.

On February 4, 2019, progressive pastor John Pavlovitz posted his "Cult of Trump" article, claiming, "America is in a cultic crisis, and Trumpism is the cult. There is no other way to approach these days." He writes,

> When you believe one man above Science, above our Intelligence agencies, above former CIA directors and retired generals and revered journalists—when you believe that one man above even your own eyes and ears—you are fully indoctrinated.
>
> This hasn't happened by accident, but by sickening design. Cult leaders prey upon emotionally vulnerable people, leveraging their loneliness, their disenfranchisement, their disconnection. They

bombard their targets with a steady stream of misinformation, incendiary rhetoric, and chaotic prophecy—and into the swirling confusion created inside their heads, they come promising safety and security, while having no concern for them at all. They start a fire—and rush in with a bucket of water.[15]

Indeed, like Big Brother of 1984 or Kim Jong Un of North Korea, Pavlovitz believes that Trump, the cult leader, manufactures new crises every day, spews a steady stream of misinformation, and then presents himself as the one and only savior, to the delight of his brainwashed, dependent minions.

But it is not just Hassan and De La Torre and Pavlovitz who share these concerns. As noted by Benjamin E. Zeller in *Religion and Politics* on October 29, 2019:

The number of commentators, news outlets, and public figures who have compared Trump to a cult leader and his political movement to a cult is ever-growing. The *Utne Reader* wrote of the "Cult of Trump," while the *National Journal* warned of "Trump's Cult" overwhelming the Republican party. References to Trumpism as a cult or Trump as a cult leader litter the pages of *The Washington Post*, *The Economist*, *Los Angeles Times*, *GQ*, and *Vanity Fair*, not to mention online media such as *Salon* and *The Daily Kos*. Many of these are liberal or politically moderate publications, but conservatives have gotten in on the act too. Tennessee Republican Senator Bob Corker called Trump's leadership a "cultish thing," and the GOP in a "cult-like situation." Even Donald Trump, Jr., responding to Corker's criticism, seemed to accept the comparison of his father's leadership to a cult. "You know what? If it's a cult, it's because they like what my father's doing," he told Fox & Friends.[16]

Questioning the "Cult of Trump"

But Zeller, who is an associate professor of religion at Lake Forest College and the author of *Heaven's Gate: America's UFO Religion*, is not entirely happy with the "Cult of Trump" language. He writes,

Granted that many individuals voted for Trump while holding their noses, or out of shrewd political calculation, yet still millions are committed followers. How to explain that? The reason cannot be brainwashing or mind-control, disputed pseudoscientific concepts that lack any empirical support. His success rates are actually vastly higher than any cult or NRM. The actual reasons for his political success require careful analysis by political scientists, not pseudoscientific concepts such as mind-control. Personally, I think Trump's rise must be assessed by the way he appeals to the power of tribalism, and with it the fears of others benefiting at America's expense. It's a simultaneous appeal to the communal solidarity of patriotism and American exceptionalism, and the resultant desire for isolationism and retrenchment of Us against the menacing Them. Others view Trump's appeal differently, but the fact is, it's not mind-control or brainwashing. However, it does parallel the sort of dualistic worldview of us/them, good/evil, insider/outsider seen in many new religions.[17]

So, it is not so much Trump's alleged mind-control tactics and cult-like leadership that explain his wide-ranging influence and the loyalty of his followers. Rather, it is his shrewd political ability to appeal to the fears and concerns of millions of Americans and to convince them that he's their man, the only one who will really stand up for their cause.

Following Zeller's lead, a January, 9, 2020 article on *The Conversation* was titled, "Why It's Wrong to Refer to the 'Cult of Trump.'"[18] According to the author, Sharday Mosurinjohn, Assistant Professor, Cultural and Religious Studies, Queen's University, Ontario, "suggestions that supporters of U.S. President Donald Trump are exhibiting cult-like behaviour isn't helpful in an era of significant political polarization."

She notes that alleging a "cult of Trump" only "substitutes a value judgment in place of a sorely needed argumentative analysis of how voters generate their own political feelings, fantasies and attachments. And this feeds the cycle of polarizing political identities and political institutions."

And, while Prof. Mosurinjohn is critical of many of Trump's policies, she also says of his followers that,

To dismiss such people as being under the sway of a cult misses what Trumpism offers them. It therefore makes it harder to understand Trump's power. It also makes it more difficult to understand the circumstances of Trump supporters' lives. It makes other people's feelings seem foreign, when they may be fundamentally common.

In conclusion, while there are many legitimate ways to critique Trump, demonizing his voters doesn't help us understand why they are attracted to him, how their worldview has developed and how to do something about it.[19]

Personally, I do believe that there are many Trump supporters (including evangelicals) who seem to have a cult-like devotion to him, passionately defending him no matter what. (See above, Chapter Four). And, as much as I differ with many of Pastor Pavlovitz's assessments, I too have seen evangelical supporters of Trump change before my eyes, becoming almost rabid in their devotion to him and seeming to exalt nationalism over the kingdom of God.

On the other hand, there are *plenty* of Trump supporters who are anything but cult-like in their support of him. They freely express their differences with him. They publicly bemoan his tweets and comments. They wish he would not shoot himself in the foot so often. And they make clear that they are voting *against* the radical left more than they are voting *for* him. As Southern Baptist professor Andrew T. Walker rightly observed on *The National Review*,

> In my experience, huge numbers of religious conservatives are not proud about voting for Trump. They don't need any more hot takes denouncing them as irredeemable hypocrites. Their consciences bear a discomfort governed by their love for America and the reputation of their faith. But if these religious conservatives have to choose between the dueling dumpster fires of either Trump or a possible Bernie Sanders presidency, they will vote overwhelmingly for Trump. And anyone who misunderstands this will continue projecting onto religious conservatives the usual tired bromides that refuse to reckon with a complicated situation.[20]

Exactly. Tens of millions of Americans voted for Donald Trump for pragmatic, rational, defensible reasons, recognizing the clay feet of their candidate and assessing him to be the best man for the job. There's nothing cult-like about it, and to refer broadly to the "Cult of Trump" is to insult many millions of people.

A Very Different Perspective

Surprising confirmation for this comes from Karlyn Borysenko, self-described as a twenty-year Democrat who "was one of those Democrats who considered anyone who voted for Trump a racist. I thought they were horrible (yes, even deplorable) and worked very hard to eliminate their voices from my spaces by unfriending or blocking people who spoke about their support of him, however minor their comments."[21] And Borysenko wanted to see Pete Buttigieg elected as president.

But when she saw so much hatred coming from the left – especially from some of her "social justice" circles – she decided to listen to the other side. To her shock,

> The more voices outside the left that I listened to, the more I realized that these were not bad people. They were not racists, nazis, or white supremacists. We had differences of opinions on social and economic issues, but a difference of opinion does not make your opponent inherently evil. And they could justify their opinions using arguments, rather than the shouting and ranting I saw coming from my side of the aisle.[22]

Finally, she decided to attend a Trump rally, fearing the worst. In fact, when she shared at an MSNBC taping that she was on her way to the rally, fears were even expressed for her safety. She was actually nervous as she headed over to the convention center.

But when she arrived there ninety minutes before the doors were to open and four hours before Trump was scheduled to speak, the line was already one mile long. She writes:

> As I waited, I chatted with the folks around me. And contrary to all the fears expressed, they were so nice. I was not harassed or intimidated, and I was never in fear of my safety even for a moment.

These were average, everyday people. They were veterans, schoolteachers, and small business owners who had come from all over the place for the thrill of attending this rally. They were upbeat and excited. In chatting, I even let it slip that I was a Democrat. The reaction: "Good for you! Welcome!"[23]

This doesn't sound cult-like to me. Not only so, but there was a stark contrast between the Democrat rally she had attended with all the candidates in attendance and the Trump rally:

With Trump, every single person was unified around a singular goal. With the Democrats, the audience booed over candidates they didn't like and got into literal shouting matches with each other. With Trump, there was a genuinely optimistic view of the future. With the Democrats, it was doom and gloom. With Trump, there was a genuine feeling of pride of being an American. With the Democrats, they emphasized that the country was a racist place from top to bottom.

And what was her overall assessment?

Now, Trump is always going to present the best case he can. And yes, he lies. This is provable. But the strength of this rally wasn't about the facts and figures. It was a group of people who felt like they had someone in their corner, who would fight for them. Some people say, "Well, obviously they're having a great time. They're in a cult." I don't think that's true. The reality is that many people I spoke to do disagree with Trump on things. They don't always like his attitude. They wish he wouldn't tweet so much. People who are in cults don't question their leaders. The people I spoke with did, but the pros in their eyes far outweighed the cons. They don't love him because they think he's perfect. They love him despite his flaws, because they believe he has their back.[24]

To be sure, these are the observations of one individual. But this individual identifies with the left, not the right. And this individual is a Democrat. And a woman. She is hardly mesmerized by the cult-leader Trump and is anything but a member of the "Cult of Trump." That's what makes her observations all the more telling. Yes, Trump's supporters "love him despite his flaws, because they believe he has their back."

In many ways, it is just that simple. To call this a cult is to miss the forest for the trees.

The "Trump Derangement Syndrome"?

But there's another side to this discussion, a totally opposite side, and it is one which we must factor into the question of the alleged "Cult of Trump." I'm speaking of what is commonly called "Trump Derangement Syndrome." As defined quite dispassionately on Wikipedia, **"Trump derangement syndrome (TDS)** is a term for criticism or negative reactions to United States President Donald Trump that are alleged to be irrational and have little regard towards Trump's actual positions or actions taken."[25]

Writing in *Psychology Today*, psychiatry professor Rob Whitely notes that, among the varied discussions of TDS is

> a notion that the everyday activities of President Trump trigger some people into distorted opinions, extreme emotions and hysterical behaviors. Well-known writer Bernard Goldberg gives supposed behavioral examples of TDS among Trump's political opponents, including fainting, vomiting, students retreating to "safe spaces" and others demanding "therapy dogs." Political commentator Justin Raimondo focuses on opinions, language and cognition, writing in the *LA Times* that "sufferers speak a distinctive language consisting of hyperbole [leading to] a constant state of hysteria... the afflicted lose touch with reality."[26]

I even wrote an article in May, 2018, asking the question, "Am I Tuning In At the Wrong Times, or Does CNN Really Have Trump Derangement Syndrome?" As I noted, no matter when I happen to tune in to CNN, it seems that every host is hammering the same theme over and again:

They're breathlessly discussing President Trump and the latest alleged scandal. They're examining the newest dirt in fine detail. They're talking about chaos and upheaval and crisis. They're talking about Trump melting down. Things are really bad, and they're getting worse by the moment!

> Watching CNN, you're surprised when you hear the president utter a single sane word. You'd think he was out of his mind!
>
> Watching CNN, you're shocked to see that his administration survived another day. And you can hardly believe that Trump and Melania are still together.
>
> Through the lens of CNN, the White House sky seems to be falling multiple times a day, as crisis after crisis comes crashing down. At least that's how CNN's reporting sounds in my ears.[27]

And that was back in 2018, before we got into the heart of the Mueller investigation, before the impeachment hearings, and before Trump's alleged mishandling of the coronavirus crisis. In fact, a friend of mine who was an avid CNN viewer switched over to Fox News one day, and, while noting Fox's evident biases, said to me, "I didn't realize there was other news going on in the world. CNN only reports on Trump." And, I should add, CNN seems to do so without even an attempt at being balanced and fair. Donald Trump is a maniac and a menace. Donald Trump must go.

Already in January 2016 (yes, that far back), Charles Hurt spoke of DTDS (the D standing for "Donald") and noted with literary aplomb,

> Beware the latest nasty virus sweeping the East Coast, particularly the most elite citadels of New York City and Washington, D.C.
>
> It is a fast-moving disease, highly contagious and attacks the nervous system. Early stages are inexplicable, fast eye-blinking, light palsy, stammering and overbearing snobbery. Sometimes redness of the face and shortness of breath accompany.
>
> Later stages include total delusionment, dementia, inability to think clearly and, ultimately, a madness that cannot be contained.[28]

He ended his article with this:

Sadly, researchers do not have the slightest hope of a cure for those in advanced stages of the disease. The only known Hail Mary prescriptions have been to either send them to Syria as DTDS refugees or allow them to sneak across the Mexican border before the Trump Wall and Casino is built.

Scientists, meanwhile, are hurriedly developing an 8-year, slow-release Ambien that can be taken now so that the patient wakes up in the final months of the Trump administration, once America has been Made Great Again.[29]

It would seem, then, that the sword cuts both ways. There is irrational behavior on both sides of the Trump divide. Some of his supporters revere him with cult-like devotion. Some of his critics revile him with maniacal obsession. And it is here, I believe, that we find the core of the problem: we live in a deeply divided nation and Donald Trump is a deeply divisive leader. He appeals to some of our loftiest values and reveals some of our basest attitudes.

In other words, Trump knows how to push our buttons, for better or for worse. He knows how to make himself the focus of the news cycle. He knows how to rally a crowd. He knows how to sell his own product. He knows how to produce outrage. He knows how to foster loyalty.

As a result, some people, including evangelicals, show him cult-like loyalty to the point of becoming irrational in their support. Others, including evangelicals, treat him with such disdain to the point of becoming irrational in their opposition. Thus, Trump, simply by being himself, contributes to both the "Cult of Trump" and "Trump Derangement Syndrome." At the same time, many others simply make pragmatic choices for or against Trump, without being part of a cult and without being deranged. It's really that simple.

We must also remember that the American political system is extremely polarized, with just two major political parties. Contrast this with Israel, which has *more than twenty* parties competing for votes and *more than a dozen* winning enough votes to gain seats in the Knesset. Italy has at least five major parties, as do Germany and a number of other countries. And while political friction may be just as intense in America as in, say Israel, the divide is not as simple and stark.

Not only so, but believers do not tend to polarize as deeply in other countries over the elections as they do in America. As some German Christians shared with me, they were surprised to see how politically divided the churches were in the States, with one explaining, "We can have a friendly discussion over coffee about who we voted for, and no one gets upset."

It is into this unique, American political environment that Donald Trump has entered, and it is here that he has made his mark. To point to the "Cult of Trump" or to "Trump Derangement Syndrome" tells us even more about ourselves than it tells us about him.

SIX

Did God Uniquely Raise Up Donald Trump?

At 12:09 AM, April 30, President Trump tweeted, "Lyin' Brian Williams of MSDNC, a Concast [sic] Scam Company, wouldn't know the truth if it was nailed to his wooden forehead. Remember when he lied about his bravery in a helicopter? Totally made up story. He's a true dummy who was thrown off Network News like a dog. Stay tuned!"[1]

Fourteen minutes later, at 12:23 AM, he wrote, "I must admit that Lyin' Brian Williams is, while dumber than hell, quite a bit smarter than Fake News @CNN 'anchorman' Don Lemon, the 'dumbest man on television'. Then you have Psycho Joe 'What Ever Happened To Your Girlfriend?' Scarborough, another of the low I.Q. individuals!"[2]

Yes, these were the words of the forty-fifth president of the United States, Donald J. Trump, words which I would not expect from my 13-year-old granddaughter, let alone from my 19-year-old granddaughter, let alone from an older, mature adult, let alone from the most powerful man on the planet. How is it, then, that so many evangelicals believe that Trump has been uniquely raised up by God? And how could I, after opposing him so vigorously during the primaries, pen an article the day after his 2016 election titled, "Donald Trump, President of the United States by the Sovereign Intervention of God"?[3]

On November 5, 2018, Ben Parker, Stephanie Steinbrecher, and

Kelsey Ronan posted an article with a compelling headline: "Lest We Forget the Horrors: A Catalog of Trump's Worst Cruelties, Collusions, Corruptions, and Crimes. the Complete Listing (So Far). Atrocities 1-546."[4] Those are very serious charges! Even if many items on their list are false or exaggerated, if other items on the list were true (and I say "if"), they would portray Trump as a monster. Yet many evangelicals see the hand of God on Donald Trump in a unique and special way. How can that be?

As of April 14, 2020, the *Washington Post* claimed that, "President Trump made 18,000 false or misleading claims in 1,170 days."[5] Again, even if the many items on this list prove to be bogus (in other words, Trump did not lie or mislead), many other items on the list certainly are not. In fact, a book was self-published in June, 2017, just six months into the Trump presidency, titled *Liar-in-Chief: The Lies of President Trump*,[6] and evangelicals universally agree that lying is sinful. How, then, can we claim that Trump is "anointed" by the Lord?

Bishop Talbert Swan, an outspoken African American leader, tweeted this on November 4, 2019: "Calling a Black POTUS married 25 yrs to 1 wife with 2 children, no mistresses, affairs or scandals, 'the antichrist' but a white POTUS married thrice, 5 kids by 3 women, mistresses, affairs & scandals, 'God's anointed,' proves your religion is white supremacy, not christianity [sic]."[7]

To be sure, Bishop Swan is not a stranger to extreme and even bigoted statements himself, tweeting in January, 2018 (with reference to white evangelical Republicans), "Frankly, if heaven is going to be full of American evangelicals, I'll take my chances on hell."[8] But putting aside his own racism and his charges of "white supremacy," Swan raises the same question many others have raised: How can we possibly call Trump "God's anointed"?

Trump and the Politics of Fear

John Fea is an evangelical scholar who teaches American history at Messiah College. He is the author of *Was America Founded as a Christian Nation?*[9] and also the author of *Believe Me: The Evangelical Road to Donald Trump*,[10] a scathing critique of President Trump and the evangelical leaders who closely and openly support him. Fea brands them "court evangelicals," comparing them to the compromised court advisers of kings of old. "Like the members of the kings' courts during the late Middle Ages and the Renaissance," he writes, "who sought influence and worldly approval by flattering the monarch rather than prophetically speaking truth to power, Trump's court evangelicals boast about their 'unprecedented access' to the White House and exalt the president for his faith-friendly policies."[11]

In an article published December 19, 2019, Fea challenged these evangelical leaders, asking, "Hey Court Evangelicals, What's Wrong with Mike Pence?"[12] After listing all of Pence's bona fides, Fea wrote:

Pence is no different than Trump on the issues that are important to conservative evangelicals. But with Trump, conservative evangelicals also get:

- A pathological liar
- An adulterer
- A narcissist
- A nativist
- A person who separates families at the border
- A crude and vulgar leader who lacks character
- A person loved and adored by white supremacists
- A misogynist
- A man who degrades the human dignity of his enemies

Fea then asked, "So why didn't evangelicals support impeachment? Why don't they support Trump's removal from office? If conservative evangelicals really have a contractual relationship with Trump, wouldn't this be a good time to end the contract? Future historians will forever connect evangelical Christianity with this man and his presidency."[13]

Of course, Trump supporters would push back on a number of items on Fea's list. But no one would argue that, when it comes to being a solid, committed Christian, Pence is far ahead of Trump. Why, then, didn't evangelicals seize the moment to drop Trump and let Pence inherit the White House?

Fea wondered aloud: "Maybe conservative evangelicals really do believe that Trump is God's anointed one (as opposed to Pence) and to remove him would violate God's will." Was that the reason they didn't support his removal?

Oddly, Fea failed to recognize the first and most obvious reason Trump supporters did not back his impeachment: They did not believe he was guilty. They did not think for a second that he committed an impeachable offense. That's why they didn't support his impeachment. They saw it as a political hit job. But were others willing to look the other way because of their deep faith that Trump was uniquely raised up by God? Did they do this as part of an evangelical power grab, compromising their values in exchange for political clout? After all, as Fea notes in *Believe Me*, more evangelicals voted for Trump in 2016 than for Romney in 2012, McCain in 2008, and George W. Bush in 2004 and 2000.[14]

So Fea asks, "How did a crude-talking, thrice-married, self-proclaimed philanderer and ultra-materialistic businessman who showed virtually no evidence of a Spirit-filled life win over evangelicals in a field of qualified GOP candidates who self-identified—in one way or another—with this form of conservative Christianity?"[15] In a word, according to Fea, Trump appealed to "fear," something, Fea claims, came right out of the standard, white evangelical playbook. Thus, "with their fears now stirred to a fever pitch, not enough evangelicals believed that [Ted] Cruz, [Marco] Rubio, or [Ben] Carson could protect them from the progressive social forces wreaking havoc on their Christian nation. The evangelical candidates stoked fears of a world they seemed unfit to tame. Desperate times called for a strongman, and if a strongman was needed, only Donald Trump would fit the bill."[16]

Fea points to talk a September 2016 lecture at Messiah College, where

conservative New York Times columnist Ross Douthat told a packed audience that in a post-Christian age, evangelicals might find themselves relying more heavily on political strongmen to shield them from rushing secularization. In one of the more stinging lines of the talk, Douthat suggested that evangelicals seem to need Trump, a man with no real Christian conviction to speak of, to protect them in the same way that Syrians needed the brutal dictator Bashar al-Assad to protect them against the threat of ISIL.[17]

For evangelicals (especially white evangelicals), this man was Donald Trump:

> Here, then, was someone who sounded like a *real* strongman, whose tough talk made him seem to many to be strong enough to stand up to the terrors of the age. He quickly found the perfect approach. Despite his wealth and power, Trump presented himself as an embattled outsider—as many evangelicals now saw themselves—who always rose triumphant over the myriad forces trying to bring him down. He was a "winner," and he managed to convince American evangelicals that he could score a culture-war victory on their behalf.[18]

The Exaltation of Donald Trump

As much as I differ with Prof. Fea on a number of points in his book, I agree with him on others, in particular: 1) the danger of fear-based politics (although this tactic is used on both sides of the political divide, and some of the fears are justified); 2) the failure to recognize America's checkered past (in other words, we have been Christian, but how Christian?), which colors what we mean by "Make America Great Again"; 3) the real possibility of compromising our convictions (or, at the least, silencing those convictions) for a seat at the table of power; 4) the danger of putting our trust in a man; and 5) the damage we do to our Christian witness by associating too closely and totally uncritically with President Trump.

There is also the very troubling tendency which I pointed to in Chapter Two, wherein Christian supporters of Trump seem more loyal to him than to the Lord, as if it were their sacred responsibility to defend "God's man." (In a June, 2016 article, Fea took aim at David Barton, considered by conservative evangelicals to be an expert in early American history but who is rejected by critics as a political hack. Barton referred to Trump as "God's guy.")[19]

Writing from Canada in November, 2019, news correspondent Neil MacDonald asked, "Donald Trump, anointed of God – seriously?"

Indeed, he opined, "It is no exaggeration to say many evangelicals consider Trump an anointed figure; a clearly venal man somehow chosen by their God to rescue America from venality. Eighty-one per cent of white evangelicals voted for him in 2016 . . . ."

And, speaking of Trump's large rallies, MacDonald noted that, "Paul Hunter of the CBC's Washington bureau attended one in Tupelo, Miss., recently where the opening prayer declared to God: 'It is you that has appointed him, ordained, anointed him to be our great leader.'

"I don't imagine they said that about Barack Obama, whom Trump in any case declared was a Muslim."[20]

In this same spirit, a June, 2019 editorial in *Church and State Magazine* was titled, "God And Trump: The Offensive Notion Of Divine Anointment." The article provided a who's who list of Christian leaders who pointed to Trump as being appointed by God, citing his campaign manager, Brad Parscale, who tweeted on April 30, "There has never been and probably never will be a movement like this again. Only God could deliver such a savior to our nation, and only God could allow me to help. God bless America!"

The editorial closed with these scathing words:

> The idea of Trump as God's chosen leader probably alternately amuses and horrifies atheists, but the people it really ought to alarm are Christians. The claim verges on blasphemy.
>
> It's also dangerous. After all, if Trump is God's vessel, how dare we mere mortals criticize him, his policies or his actions?
>
> The phrase "God works in mysterious ways" is not found in the Bible. It's apparently taken from a Christian hymn text written in 1773 by William Cowper called "God Moves in a Mysterious Way." Regardless of the phrase's origins and its veracity, one thing should be pretty clear: A god who would anoint someone with the morals of Trump to be his representative isn't just "mysterious." It is offensive to believers and non-believers alike.[21]

Again, I have witnessed this dangerous mentality on social media, where Christian supporters of Trump recoil at any criticism of "God's anointed man." In fact, they will quickly turn and attack you, as if your faith in Jesus was now questionable because you dared to question

God's servant in the White House. As for Trump, it's as if he can do no wrong in their eyes, as if any disapproval of his words or decisions is part of a demonic attack against him, as if the man is somehow sacrosanct, not merely elected by the people but installed by the Lord Himself.

At the same time, when Christian leaders began to talk about Trump being "anointed," it was in the full light of his evident failings (especially his ugly past). This is also part of why I felt that the ultimate reason he became president was because of the sovereign intervention of God. In other words, it took God working in an unusual way, beyond normal electoral patterns and beyond God's normal interaction with the world, to get a man like Trump in office. To be sure, that sword cuts in many directions (God may have many different reasons for the Trump presidency, which we'll discuss below, in Chapter Seventeen). But I believe there *is* something to the idea of Trump being specially anointed by God, just not in the way either the critics or the hyper-loyalists see it.

A Very Short History of the Trump Prophecies

In April 2020, James A. Beverley, a research scholar and long-time professor at Tyndale University in Canada, published a full collection of all the significant Trump prophecies, along with relevant articles and commentaries. The book, compiled with the help of Larry N. Willard, was titled *God's Man in the White House: Donald Trump in Modern Christian Prophecy*, and it amounts to almost 100,000 words.[22] (The title does not indicate Beverley's own position; rather, it speaks of the viewpoint of the Trump prophecies.)

Beverley writes:

> It is widely reported that Kim Clement, one of the most famous Christian prophets, announced Trump's presidency in 2007. Mark Taylor—firefighter turned prophet—has become famous for his 2011 announcement that Trump was to be commander in chief, though Taylor originally thought that prophecy was for the 2012 election. Other prophecies about Trump can be traced to the summer and fall of 2015, when Jeremiah Johnson, Lance Wallnau, and Lana Vawser

(Australia) made known their belief that God was going to use Trump for divine purposes. (Remarkably, they came at a time when most Evangelical leaders were supporting Ted Cruz or Marco Rubio—and Donald Trump was doing very poorly in polling.) Prophecies about Trump increased with a frenzy during 2016, leading up to the November election. Prophets also issued divine warnings about Barack Obama, Clinton, and the Democrats in general.[23]

On April 4, 2007, Clement declared,

The Spirit of God said, this is a moment of resurrection. For the Spirit of God says, honor Me with your praise and acceptance of this that I say to you. This that shall take place shall be the most unusual thing, a transfiguration, a going into the marketplace if you wish, into the news media. Where Time Magazine will have no choice but to say what I want them to say. Newsweek, what I want to say. The View, what I want to say. Trump shall become a trumpet, says the Lord! No, you didn't hear me. Trump shall become a Trumpet. Are you listening to me? I will raise up the Trump to become a trumpet and Bill Gates to open up the gate of a financial realm for the Church, says the Spirit of the Living God![24]

On April 28, 2011, Mark Taylor prophesied (but with the assumption this applied to the 2012 elections):

The Spirit of God says, I have chosen this man, Donald Trump, for such a time as this. For as Benjamin Netanyahu is to Israel, so shall this man be to the United States of America! For I will use this man to bring honor, respect and restoration to America.

America will be respected once again as the most powerful and prosperous nation on earth, (other than Israel). The dollar will be the strongest it has ever been in the history of the United States, and will once again be the currency by which all others are judged.[25]

There is more to both Clement's and Taylor's prophecies, and all of their words need to be carefully judged and evaluated. But it turns out that these words, which got limited publicity before 2015, were only the first among many others, and it was the prophecies of Jeremiah Johnson and Lance Wallnau that got my attention, since I know both of them personally.

Johnson, who is a young man cut out of the old prophetic mold (meaning, a very intense, God-fearing man who weeps over the words he delivers) knew very little about Donald Trump when he posted this word on July 15, 2015. Significantly, he likened Trump to an ancient Persian king named Cyrus, whom we'll discuss in a moment.

Here is the post in full. It quickly went viral when it appeared on a popular charismatic website:

> In His great wisdom throughout the course of human history, God has chosen not only to fulfill His plans and purposes through men and women who have yielded to the sound of His voice, but He has also chosen to accomplish His will through men and women who have ignored and rebelled against Him. One such man was King Cyrus mentioned in Isaiah 45.
>
> Isaiah prophesied of Cyrus and speaks as a mouthpiece of the Lord when he declared, "I have even called you by your name [Cyrus]; I have named you, though you have not known Me. I am the Lord and there is no other; there is no God besides Me. I strengthen you, though you have not known Me, so that they may know from the rising of the sun and from the west that there is no one besides Me. I am the Lord, and there is no other" (Is. 45: 4–6).
>
> What a powerful and profound prophetic declaration to a man who did not know or serve the Lord! Could God not use the wicked and ungodly to bring about His plans and purposes thousands of years ago and can He not still do the same thing again, especially in the midst of the crisis that we find America in today?
>
> I was in a time of prayer several weeks ago when God began to speak to me concerning the destiny of Donald Trump in America. The Holy Spirit spoke to me and said, "Trump shall become My trumpet to the American people, for he possesses qualities that are even hard to find in My people these days. Trump does not fear man nor will he allow deception and lies to go unnoticed. I am going to use him to expose darkness and perversion in America like never before, but you must understand that he is like a bull in a china closet. Many will

want to throw him away because he will disturb their sense of peace and tranquility, but you must listen through the bantering to discover the truth that I will speak through him. I will use the wealth that I have given him to expose and launch investigations searching for the truth. Just as I raised up Cyrus to fulfill My purposes and plans, so have I raised up Trump to fulfill my purposes and plans prior to the 2016 election. You must listen to the trumpet very closely for he will sound the alarm and many will be blessed because of his compassion and mercy. Though many see the outward pride and arrogance, I have given him the tender heart of a father that wants to lend a helping hand to the poor and the needy, to the foreigner and the stranger."[26]

Like Clement, Johnson said that "Trump would be a trumpet." But here, Johnson noted how God can use people who do not know Him (such as King Cyrus), men who even ignore Him and rebel against Him, men who were wicked and ungodly. Cannot God, Johnson asked, do the same with Trump? Yes, he will be "like a bull in a china closet"; and yes, many will see "the outward pride and arrogance," although God had given him a tender heart.

"Could it be true?", I wondered when I read Jeremiah's words. Could I also be judging by outward appearance? Honestly, I was having a hard time getting beyond the "outward pride and arrogance," especially when we had so many other, fine Republican candidates from which to choose, with Ted Cruz being highest on my list. What were to make of this prophecy?

Then there was the word from Lance Wallnau, who has a business background as well as a ministry background and often thinks outside of the traditional Christian box. On October 12, 2015, during a TV interview, he said,

Donald Trump is anointed in this season to break things open. Like Jeremiah of old he has an assignment to tear down and to uproot and to plant. He has broken up a demonic cartel of political correctness and now it is up to you and me, each of us to move forward in our own sphere and knock down the obstacles that are silencing us and holding us back from what we are called to say and do.[27]

Wallnau had been to an earlier meeting at Trump Tower on September 28, 2015 with a number of evangelical leaders and was positively impressed by Trump. Wallnau recalled:

> Trump scanned the room and said: "I think we had such a long period of Christian consensus in our culture and we kind of got… spoiled. Is that the right word?" Then he turned the tables on us and said something shocking: "Every other ideological group in the country has a voice. If you don't mind me saying so, you guys have gotten soft." Ouch! That's the line I won't forget. Then in a moment of reflection he corrected himself, "I mean, we, myself included, we've had it easy as Christians for a long time in America. That's been changing."[28]

Then, sometime later, back at home, the Spirit led him to Isaiah 45, the passage about God raising up Cyrus.

> The Spirit impressed upon my mind "read Isaiah 45."
>
> To be honest, I didn't recall what the chapter was about. I opened a Bible and began to read, "Thus sayeth the Lord to Cyrus whom I've anointed." Cyrus, I thought? Who is he in relation to all this? I recalled that he was a heathen king who was indispensable to the protection of the Jews but was frankly confused as to what God was saying.
>
> With 15 candidates running, many who were clear conservative evangelicals, why would God be talking about Cyrus? I quickly looked up the number of the next president. I confirmed that Barack Obama is number 44. The next president will indeed be number 45. I kept reading Isaiah 45.[29]

Subsequently, on November 30, 2015, at a meeting with black evangelical leaders and Trump at Trump Tower, Wallnau felt led to read the words from Isaiah 45 out loud to Trump, including this verse: "For Jacob My servant's sake, And Israel My elect, I have even called you by your name; I have named you, though you have not known Me" (Isaiah 45:4, NKJV). So, in the presence of Donald Trump and other Christian leaders, Wallnau felt God saying to him that He was raising this man up to accomplish His purposes, *even though Trump did not know the Lord.*

There were other prophecies of interest, including those of Lana Vawser, who is based in Australia. (I do not know Lana personally.) On October 11, 2015, without any political agenda in her heart, she posted this word:

> *I had a dream recently where I was in a political arena and I saw Donald Trump and he was passionately putting forward his policies. In this dream I could not "hear" what he was saying, I just remember seeing him speaking with great passion.*
>
> *Suddenly, I was lifted above the United States of America and I saw the nation as if I was looking at a map. Written across the United States of America was the word "TRUMP" in big letters.*
>
> *As I looked at this word suddenly the letters began to rearrange and the word went from "TRUMP" to "TRIUMPH."*
>
> *I then heard the Lord speak loudly in my dream "TRUMP SHALL LEAD THE UNITED STATES OF AMERICA INTO TRIUMPH!!!"*[30]

She also delivered this urgent message on October 9, 2016, one of several Trump-related prophecies, again making clear that it was not a political word (meaning, not based on political policies or agendas). She also emphasized that her prophecies should not be taken as condoning sin, referring in particular to the sin in Donald Trump's past.

Vawser reported seeing a horde of demons that were being released against the body of Christ in the USA. They were coming, she said,

> to blind people to the truth that I have anointed Donald Trump and Mike Pence and the people of God need to hear this so that they keep pressing in for discernment despite what the media and the 'natural world' says. Things are going to continue to escalate and pressure intensify to push Donald Trump out, but My people need to take their place and stand with Me to see My purposes come to fruition."
>
> The sense surrounded me that this is a very strategic moment, a time of urgency and a time to pray even more fervently. The sense of 'laying down agenda(s) and simply seeking the heart of God for this new season for the nation of America that is approaching.[31]

There was much more to her prophecy, but again, the theme was similar: There was a larger, divine purpose in view, and Donald Trump was to play a unique role in shaping America's future. He was the man, the highly unlikely man, God was choosing for this hour. What were we to make of words like these?

I remember the day when I got on my knees in prayer, telling the Lord, "I respect Jeremiah. And I respect Lance. But I just don't see what they're seeing." At that time, I was still solidly in Senator Cruz's corner and strongly opposed to Donald Trump, writing and speaking against his candidacy and issuing warnings to my evangelical friends. Yet I also realized that sometimes God comes in the back door rather than the front door, that appearances can be deceiving, and that what seems to be the worst-case scenario ends up being a platform for greater good.

Looking back, I can say that some of the warnings I issued about Trump and his behavior proved accurate. Yet some of the other warnings I issued, specifically, as to whether he could be trusted to keep his campaign promises to evangelicals, proved inaccurate.

For the record, throughout the primaries, I said that I hoped I was wrong about Trump and, should it come down to Hillary Clinton vs. Donald Trump, I would reevaluate my position, since I could not vote for her. Yet, the more I saw Trump win and the more I saw him supported by solid Christian friends of mine, the more I questioned my opposition to him. Were all my friends that wrong? Did they all suddenly lose their moral bearings? Were they all that unspiritual? Were they all power hungry, hyper-nationalists? Was there something else going on that I was missing?

Anointed to Be "God's Chaos Candidate"

Returning to Lance Wallnau, he not only prophesied about Trump but he wrote a book on the subject of Trump's candidacy, published shortly before the 2016 elections. It carried this intriguing title: *God's Chaos Candidate: Donald J. Trump and the American Unraveling.*[32] As Wallnau explained, "When Jeb Bush referred to Donald Trump as 'the chaos candidate,' he may have been tapping into something more prophetic than he was aware. America is already in chaos and heading into what I am referring to as the Fourth American Crucible."[33]

Amazingly, although this was Wallnau's first book, and although he did very little advertising and had no major publisher or PR firm behind the book, it suddenly became a bestseller, jumping up the charts on major booksellers like Amazon. What was he tapping into? Why did he believe Trump was being "anointed"?

Wallnau wrote of Trump:

> The moment he began speaking the entire conversation shifted. Trump gave nervous evangelicals a gift that many of them lacked—the gift of boldness. Here was a man who had opinions. He didn't speak in the calculated talking points of a politician. His delivery, with a slight accent from Queens, NY, was simple and direct. His emergence is such a destabilizing threat to the vast deal making machinery embedded in both parties that he has the unique distinction of being rejected by both liberal Democrats and establishment Republicans at the same time.[34]

In his mind, there is a liberal, progressive agenda that has been growing in power and destructive influence for decades, and Trump is uniquely positioned to take it down. Yes, he wrote, "No one in American history has been better poised to set back the progress of progressives and tear through the web than the wrecking ball himself."[35]

Indeed, according to Wallnau,

> America is unraveling at the seams because a powerful group of Americans—the "shadow cabinet"—want it to. They are a group of billionaires and millionaires, politicians, consultants, academics and activists. This is not a very large group. It is a small number of people exerting a great deal of influence. This can't be emphasized enough. This is a minority of people who are succeeding in bullying the majority of the people in this country. This little group does not represent all liberals, but their access to media and academia intimidates those who would like to push back against them.[36]

Now, some of this is reminiscent of Rodney Howard-Browne's warning about the alleged agenda One World Order (or, New World Order),[37] and it is easy to shout, "Conspiracy theory!" and dismiss this

DR. MICHAEL L. BROWN

without further thought. As I have often stated, I am very slow to believe such theories, and I have no interest in flailing against the wind. At the same time, I have no doubt that there are powerful influencers on the left who have a major agenda, and their vision for what is best for America is very different than mine.

Either way, the point in all this is that Wallnau and others believe that Donald Trump has been raised up precisely because he *is* so abrasive and strong-willed and stubborn, a "wrecking ball to the spirit of political correctness."[38] And that means there will be a lot of collateral damage. As I have often said, a wrecking ball is great for demolishing a building but not for renovating a room. And so, with Trump, the wrecking ball president, a lot is being exposed and demolished, but with much collateral damage along the way. That's what happens with a "chaos president," but one, many believe, who was appointed by God.

Wallnau also made this important observations (remember that his book was published in the fall of 2016, so, more than four years before the COVID-19 pandemic), explaining that America had experienced three previous crucibles, with a fourth closely on the way:

- **The first crucible** involved the founding of our nation and we know it as the American Revolution, 1775-1783.
  - **The second crucible** was the Civil War, 1860-1865. Abraham Lincoln writes of civil war as a "testing whether that nation, or any nation so conceived and so dedicated, can long endure."
  - **The third crucible** was the Great Depression, 1929-1939, and World War II, 1939-1945. It was a test of our survival as a nation.
  - **The fourth crucible is upon us**.

We are already witnessing the first phase of the "unraveling"—race wars, class wars, and religious wars as Islamic terror incidents at home add to the combustion. All of this is the intentional destabilizing prelude to the great economic "reset." The trigger for this fourth crucible could come from any number of global incidents, but whatever the cause, it will most likely manifest in regional social upheavals and a national economic meltdown. It can be swift or prolonged. It can be very severe or less severe. Much depends on the governing philosophy that enters the White House in 2016. This factor more than any other will shape America and the world for better or worse.[39]

For Wallnau and others, Trump resembled King Cyrus of Persia precisely *because* he was an outsider (Cyrus being a non-Jew and Trump, at least in his past, being far from Christian). Yet, just as God anointed an idol-worshiping foreigner, He anointed a worldly, self-centered billionaire playboy.

Look at what Cyrus said about himself in what is called the Cyrus Cylinder, discovered in 1879 and written in 539 BC:

> I am Cyrus, king of the universe, the great king, the powerful king, king of Babylon, king of Sumer and Akkad, king of the four quarters of the world, son of Cambyses, the great king, king of the city of Anshan, grandson of Cyrus, the great king, ki[ng of the ci]ty of Anshan, descendant of Teispes, the great king, king of the city of Anshan, the perpetual seed of kingship, whose reign Bel (Marduk) and Nabu love, and with whose kingship, to their joy, they concern themselves.[40]

Does that sound a little grandiose? A little self-exalting? And what of his adoration of different deities especially Marduk, whom Cyrus hails as "lord of the whole heaven and earth"? Cyrus declared, "Marduk, the great lord, bestowed on me as my destiny the great magnanimity of one who loves Babylon, and I every day sought him out in awe." Yet this was the man chosen by the Lord and even called *mashiach*, anointed one – the Hebrew word for Messiah!

In the Cyrus Cylinder, Marduk was given the credit for raising him up, taking him by the hand and calling him by name: "[Marduk] searched everywhere and then he took a righteous king, his favorite, by the hand, he called out his name: Cyrus, king of Anšan; he pronounced his name to be king all over the world."[41] God's Word, the Bible, has something else to say. Cyrus and his people may have thought Marduk raised him up, but Isaiah and his people knew otherwise. It was the Lord, Yahweh, who took Cyrus by the hand and called him by name:

This is what the LORD says to his anointed, to Cyrus, whose right hand I take hold of to subdue nations before him and to strip kings of their armor, to open doors before him so that gates will not be shut: I will go before you and will level the mountains; I will break down gates of bronze and cut through bars of iron. I will give you hidden treasures, riches stored in secret places, so that you may know that I am the LORD, the God of Israel, who summons you by name. For the sake of Jacob my servant, of Israel my chosen, I summon you by name and bestow on you a title of honor, though you do not acknowledge me. I am the LORD, and there is no other; apart from me there is no God. I will strengthen you, though you have not acknowledged me (Isaiah 45:1–5).

I repeat: it is in this context that the concept of Trump being "anointed" first arose, a context that compared him to an idol-worship king who did not know the very Lord who raised him up. So, rather than this pointing to evangelical blindness, it pointed to evangelical awareness. A rough and tumble man with a very checkered past was being raised up by a holy God to help the nation and to stand with God's people, just like Cyrus of old.

Wallnau rightly points out that, "No politician can do the task that has been given to the American church—the task that we alone have the authority to carry out. The gates of hell will not yield an inch just because of a ballot box. In this American unraveling we need both a unified church and a Cyrus leader in government who is built to navigate the chaos—*a chaos candidate.*"

And, he adds,

I believe Trump is the chaos candidate who has been set apart by God to navigate us through the chaos coming to America. I think America is due for a shaking regardless of whom is in office. I believe the 45th president is meant to be an Isaiah 45 Cyrus. With him in office, we will have authority in the Spirit to build the house of the Lord and restore the crumbling walls that separate us from cultural collapse. Yet even then, this national project is likely to be done as Daniel prophesied: *"in troublous times"* (Daniel 9:25)[42]

So, Trump functions like a wedge in the door, giving breathing room for the church to do what only it can do. And, Wallnau claims,

More than any other candidate in history, Donald Trump is receptive to what the church can do. If you think about it, no candidate other than Trump would even risk the political liability of promoting a faith-based solution to a problem, especially if they ran as an evangelical Christian. Can't you see them jumping all over President Cruz or Huckabee if one of them started pushing "faith based" initiatives? With Trump it's a different story. No one thinks he's a Christian so nobody suspects him of trying to push religion on people.[43]

Not only so, but as the wrecking ball, Trump has exposed the radical agenda of the left, the deep biases of the media, the evil intent of countries like China, and, some would claim, the clandestine goals of the "Deep State" and the One World Order.[44] (We'll look at this in more depth in Chapter Fourteen.) At the same time, there has been a lot of collateral damage. Will the close association of key evangelicals with Trump end up hurting our gospel witness more than it helps advance some of our major Christian issues? Or will our votes for Trump help push back a disastrous agenda that would have destroyed our nation as we know it? That is the tightrope we must walk.

Anything Is Possible!

On February 5, 2017, I published an article titled, "The Election of Donald Trump Tells Us That Anything is Possible."[45] I noted that John Zmirak, a conservative Catholic columnist who holds a Ph.D. in English from Louisiana State University and is a senior editor of The Stream, told me[46] that when he was a student at Yale, his professors uniformly praised communism, making clear that it was communism, not capitalism, that was the key to the world's future success. They were quite confident that this socialist system was here to stay, with its sphere of influence growing by the decade.

Who would have imagined how dramatically and quickly it would collapse around the globe? And, Zmirak asked, who would have believed that the principal players who would help topple communism would be a former Hollywood actor (Reagan!), a female Prime Minister in England, the daughter of a lay preacher and grocer (Thatcher!), a shipyard worker who became the head of a Polish trade union (Walesa!) and a Polish pope (John Paul II!). Yes, who would have believed this?

I closed the article with these lines:

> Today, it is a wealthy, former playboy, real estate tycoon and reality TV star who is shaking up the political scene and exposing the biases of the mainstream media.
>
> If this, then, is actually happening, why is it so hard to imagine that God will send a massive spiritual awakening to our nation?
>
> Why not?[47]

Some have likened Trump to Winston Churchill (although none would compare Trump's oratory skills with Churchill's), noting that Churchill had a way of ruffling people's feathers. He was also a prodigious cigar-smoker, a heavy drinker (although not considered an alcoholic), and quite an eater. He also had an acerbic tongue with which he humiliated his political enemies.

An article posted by Bruce G. Kauffman on the History Lessons website titled "Winston Churchill's Many Vices" said this:

> Of his drinking, he said, "I believe I have taken more out of alcohol than alcohol has taken out of me." Of his eating he said, "All the food faddists [healthy eaters] I have ever known have died young after a long period of senile decay." Of his cigar smoking, he said, "I smoke cigar after cigar. That is why I am in two-hundred-percent form."
>
> Winston Churchill, drinker, smoker, prodigious eater — and the man upon whose shoulders the survival of Great Britain and Europe rested during World War II — died this week (Jan. 24) in 1965. He was 90 years old.[48]

Of course, Churchill was not accused of being a serial womanizer or of constantly lying, just to mention a few ways that he does not compare to Trump. But he was certainly God's man – anointed, you could say – to stand up to Hitler, and Christians who voted for him cast the right vote for the right man. Could it be the same with Donald Trump, an even unlikelier candidate than Churchill, a man likened by some to a pagan king named Cyrus? Stranger things have happened in the past, and I would not put it past God to do something like this again today.

Without question, we can view Trump as "anointed" in in a wrong and dangerous sense, as if nothing he says or does can be questioned. We dare not challenge God's anointed! And we can certainly compromise our witness by turning a blind eye to his failings and flaws. At the same time, with spiritual eyes, we can see how God raised up someone like him, a chaos candidate and a wrecking ball of a man, for such a time as this.

Our job, then, is to do our job, namely, by being the church and doing the work of the church while we pray that the good Trump does will outweigh and outlast the bad. That is exactly why some of the evangelical leaders whom Fea decries have stayed close to Trump. Some of them are anything but yes men, speaking the truth to power and even calling the president on the carpet when he does wrong. (This has been shared with me directly by a man who has spent hours alone with Trump, often speaking to him very firmly and in very strong terms.)

Perhaps, then, there really is something to the idea that God uniquely raised up Donald Trump, especially when, right until the night of the 2016 elections when the vote counts were coming in, it seemed beyond unlikely that he would win. For me, it is much easier to find a supernatural explanation for his presidency than a natural one. And the fact that it was Donald Trump, not Bill Clinton and not George W. Bush and not Barack Obama, who finally moved our embassy in Israel to Jerusalem makes the modern day Cyrus comparison all the more interesting. As the prophet Isaiah declared more than 2,500 years ago:

> This is what the LORD says-- your Redeemer, who formed you in the womb: I am the LORD, the Maker of all things, who stretches out the heavens, who spreads out the earth by myself, who foils the signs of false prophets and makes fools of diviners, who overthrows the learning of the wise and turns it into nonsense, who carries out the words of his servants and fulfills the predictions of his messengers, who says of Jerusalem, "It shall be inhabited," of the towns of Judah, "They shall be rebuilt," and of their ruins, "I will restore them," who says to the watery deep, "Be dry, and I will dry up your streams," who

says of Cyrus, "He is my shepherd and will accomplish all that I please; he will say of Jerusalem, 'Let it be rebuilt,' and of the temple, 'Let its foundations be laid.'" (Isa 44:24-28)

And did I mention the coins that were minted in Israel, depicting both Cyrus and Trump, and that in Israel, Trump is extremely popular, especially when compared to his predecessor, Barack Obama?[49] Sometimes truth is stranger than fiction.[50]

SEVEN

Does a Vote for Trump Really Hurt Our Witness?

In early 2019, Jarod, a graduate from our ministry school, was standing in line waiting to get into an event when he struck up a conversation with the man standing in front of him. Soon enough, the conversation turned spiritual, and Jarod began to share his faith in Jesus. The man then asked him, "Did you vote for Donald Trump?" When Jarod said yes, the man stopped talking with him. The conversation was over. There would be no more discussion about the Lord.

How often does something like this happen today in America? How often does the name of Trump come up when we are seeking to share the gospel with non-believers? I posed this very question in a Twitter poll on August 14, 2019, asking, "When you talk to non-believers about your faith in Jesus, do you find them bringing up President Trump and how you voted?"[1] The results were striking.

Five percent answered, "I don't talk about faith." Forty-eight percent responded, "Never." But 33 percent answered with "sometimes" and 15 percent with "often." In other words, *48 percent* of those polled said that when they are sharing the gospel with non-believers, either sometimes or often, people ask them if they voted for Trump.

That is a staggering statistic, and I can't imagine that this was the case with past presidents, at least on this level. It's possible that evangelicals associated with George W. Bush were challenged about our war with Iraq, but, again, that was certainly not a common objection when we shared our faith. And I don't recall being challenged if I voted for Reagan when talking to people about Jesus during his tenure in the White House.

Yet the question of, "How did you vote in 2016?" or, "How will you vote in 2020?" is becoming somewhat of a litmus test for true Christian faith these days. And if you say, "Trump has my vote," many will instantly brand you a hypocrite – if not much worse. In fact, according to some, you are a xenophobic, misogynist racist if you voted for Trump. Therefore, in their minds, a vote for Trump hurts the cause of Christ.

But what if it's actually the leftwing media that is driving this narrative? What if it's their hatred of Trump that is fueling these fires? After all, the idea that you're a racist if you voted for Trump comes straight from the talking points of the left. As expressed in a tweet by CNN contributor Joe Lockhard, "Anyone who supports a racist or a racist strategy is a racist themselves. 2020 is a moment or reckoning for America. Vote for @realDonaldTrump and you are a racist. Don't hide it like a coward. Wear that racist badge proudly and see how it feels."[2]

Over at MSNBC, host Donny Deutsch opined "that every Trump voter 'owns' the entire Trump presidency and that swing voters have to be 'shamed' into understanding that you can't disagree with President Trump on some things without also 'own[ing] the racism.'" He continued, "I think that's the message that's got to get out there: 'You own it. You own the blood that happens. You own Charlottesville. You can't do it. You get the whole package."[3]

How extraordinary. If you voted for Trump in 2016, then you are personally responsible for the tragic death of a young woman in Charlottesville at the hands of an alt-right protestor. Her blood is on your hands. And the left is preaching this volatile message to national, viewing audiences.

No wonder, then, that there is such hostility towards Trump. No wonder, then, that evangelicals who voted for Trump are branded as immoral hypocrites by the left. And it is often the left that brings that very accusation, presented as if with concern. To paraphrase, "The evangelical Church has lost its standing in society by supporting Donald Trump."

But do you think the leftwing media actually cares about our standing? When they warn us that we cannot be taken seriously as Christians if we support Trump, is it because they want our gospel message to be heard or because they want Trump to lose? And why should it be so hard for someone to understand that there's a lot we do *not* like about Trump, both past and present, but that we prefer his policies to those of the radical Democrats?

On the other hand, while the leftwing media is definitely stoking the anti-Trump fires, there are many Americans who genuinely *do* find our support of Trump to be utterly incomprehensible, especially when major evangelical leaders sing his praises. Perhaps we are at fault after all?

In response to one of my articles from August 2019 (an article completely unrelated to Trump), an angry, anti-Christian reader named Eric wrote, "If you try to preach to me I might punch you in the face. I don't walk up to strangers and try to tell them they are evil because they don't believe in ludicrous millennia old myths and parables. You are all insane for thinking anyone wants to hear your childish nonsense. Religion is fading and the world will be better for it."

Another reader asked him, "I'm curious, why do you harbour so much animosity and anger?"

Before continuing his anti-religious rant, Eric responded, "Lately it's because Christians support Donald trump, a man who might actually be the Antichrist and has proclaimed himself 'the chosen one', with 3 wives. 17 sexual assault accusations, and the least functional brain in American political history."[4]

Granted, this is extreme rhetoric, in particular, comparing Trump to the Antichrist. But the overall sentiment is shared by many other Americans today. "If you claim to be a Christian, you cannot support Donald Trump. The two are incompatible."

I Lost an Old Friend Because of My Support for Trump

Growing up in a small Jewish community on Long Island, most of my best friends were also Jewish. And like the majority of American Jews, most of those old friends are now liberal Democrats. And a few of those old friends – or neighbors – are my Facebook friends.

That means they see my many posts about controversial cultural issues, like abortion and LGBT activism, and they do not unfriend me. Others, not surprisingly, did unfriend me along the way, which I fully understand. We weren't super close, and they didn't appreciate my views. All clear.

But one in particular, whom I had known since elementary school, somehow stuck around, and every so often he'd post a nice comment to a family update or the like. Unfortunately, the day came when my support for the President on a particular issue was more than he could take, and that was the end of that. I hated to see it happen.

More recently, another childhood friend, named David, posted this in response to one of my Trump-related articles:

> How can any Christian support such an immoral and divisive man? He's broken every commandment and has committed all Seven Deadly Sins. Ask yourself two questions....would Jesus support such behavior? Would Jesus treat illegals the same way?
>
> The answer is no to both questions and I question your commitment to Jesus if you support Donald Trump.
>
> Instant redemption is bull as Trump never seems contrite in his poor decisions.

Have you encountered comments like this from friends and family and co-workers? It's becoming more and more common. The question is: how do we respond?

It appears that the order of the day is to fight fire with fire, offense with offense. You blast me and I blast you. Forget about substance. About content. About details and facts. And forget about conducting ourselves in a godly manner. Not a chance. Fire away! But the Book of Proverbs has a relevant word for us here: "A gentle answer deflects anger, but harsh words make tempers flare" (Proverbs 15:1, NLT).

I knew that David's life experience and faith perspectives were very different than mine, and personally, I was glad to see he was still a Facebook friend, despite our differences. So, I wrote back,

> You definitely represent the concerns of many others, especially non-Christians. Here's the short answer: 1) Donald Trump is NOT our

Savior, and for many of us, he was the last choice of the Republicans running for office. But a vote for him was a vote against Hillary, who we believed would be a disaster for our country. 2) While the issue of migrant children is a serious one and needs to be addressed, for us, slaughtering one million babies in the womb [each year] is a massively bigger issue. The brutal and horrific slaughter and torture and displacement of millions of Christians in the Middle East by ISIS and other Islamic militants is a massively bigger issue. The possibility of Iran getting nuclear weapons to attack Israel fits in this same category. And these are just some of the biggest issues to us. That's why we voted for Trump. We felt Hillary would be on the wrong side of all of these. As for immigration, remember that Obama deported far more illegals, at this time in his presidency, than Trump, and the problem of separating children from parents has existed for years before Trump. Christian supporters of Trump simply need to make clear that we want something done that is compassionate and fair. 3) When we excuse Trump's sinful behavior, we discredit our own witness. I agree. But we do NOT compromise our Christian witness when we say, 'We deplore his past, playboy lifestyle, and we hate his crude and ugly attacks against others, but out of the choices for president in 2016 (or, potentially in 2020), we believe he's the better choice.' I encourage you to think this through. God bless!"

And how did David respond on Facebook? He wrote,

Michael, thanks for the answer. As you know, we have many issues facing us as a country and as religious groups. There are no easy answers. I'm not sure if prioritizing our response based on religious views is the answer.

It saddens me to see not one of the responses I got from people here address my two questions about Jesus approving of Trumps actions. I see a herd of Trump apologists who cherry pick their Christian values.

Michael, I admire you as a person, you serve a very important role in today's world. Keep up the good work you do! Be well!

I responded, "Thanks for the kind words. This is the kind of interaction we all need. Much appreciated! And keep raising your voice when you want to weigh in. I always welcome respectful differences of opinion."

As of today, David and I are still Facebook friends. But the point of me posting this is not to say, "Look at how wise my interaction was!" The point, instead, is this. We need to do our best to communicate. To interact substantively rather than be reactionary. To make a real effort to hear the heartfelt concerns of the opponents of Trump. And then, rather than dismissing those concerns as if they were baseless – is that how we want our concerns treated? – we share our point of view with clarity and grace. In the end, rather than losing friends over views about Trump, we just might gain some. But at the least, seeing that many people truly feel that faith in Christ is incompatible with support for Trump, we need to engage them in substantive and respectful dialogue rather than push them away or build our own walls.

After all, isn't our greatest goal to glorify the Lord and reach those who do not know Him? Isn't winning a soul more important than winning an argument? And isn't it a good sign that, for these critics, Christianity is associated with ethical behavior and strong morals? In other words, the reason these people can't see how a Christian could support Trump is because they have a high view of Christian ethics and a low view of Trumpian ethics. Why not start, then, with an affirmation of their positive view of Christian morals? Why not appreciate their respect for Christians? From there, you might be able to help them see why your support for Trump is not a violation of your faith.

Don't Underestimate How Much the Leftist Media Is Fueling the Fires

I'm aware, of course, that Trump is often his own worst enemy. I'm aware that he sometimes makes it very difficult for his evangelical supporters to stand with him. But let's not underestimate just how much the leftist media fuels the fires of Trump hatred. It is a drum they beat incessantly.

On October 2, 2017, NPR reported, "Compared to other recent presidents, news reports about President Trump have been more focused on his personality than his policy, and are more likely to carry negative assessments of his actions, according to a new study from the Pew Research Center's Journalism Project."[5] One year later, the *Investor's Business Daily* website reported, "To say that the big networks haven't exactly had a love affair with Donald Trump, as they plainly did with President Obama, is an understatement. An October 2018 survey shows that not only is coverage of Trump overwhelmingly negative, but the president's biggest accomplishment — the roaring economy — gets almost no attention." Specifically, the in-depth study, done by Media Research Center (the MRC), found that, "Over the summer, the broadcast networks have continued to pound Donald Trump and his team with the most hostile coverage of a president in TV news history — 92% negative, vs. just 8% positive."[6] That's one reason for the extreme hostility towards Trump. He is constantly demonized by the left.

As media watcher Brent Bozell noted in January, 2019, "Month after month going back to the start of his campaign, without interruption, his coverage on evening newscasts has hovered around 90% negative."[7] And once the impeachment hearings began, it was even worse, as a Fox News headline announced: "Broadcast news slams Trump with 96 percent negative coverage since impeachment inquiry began, study says."[8] Ninety-six percent! Tell me that doesn't color opinions about Trump. Tell me that doesn't distort the picture of who he really is. And overseas, some of the coverage has been ever more hostile. Seriously![9] Don't forget that when addressing critics of the president.

Christian Support for Trump Is Not the Main Reason Churches Are Losing Members

It's also important that we don't fall into the trap of blaming Trump for everything that is going wrong in the church, as in, "Churches in America are losing millions of members, and record numbers of people, especially young people, are identifying as 'nones,' meaning, they have no religious affiliation. This is because of Donald Trump! Evangelical devotion to Trump is directly related to the rise of religious nones."[10]

But is this true? Hardly. Church attendance in America was on the decline long before Trump came on the political scene. The same can be said of the rise of the "nones." Their numbers were increasing long before Trump. In fact, a similar phenomenon can be found in Europe and Canada, where church attendance has been on the decline and religious "nones" have been on the rise for a couple of decades, at the least.

Not only so, but the churches in America that are the most committed to the historic message of the gospel (as opposed to the more modern, progressive version – which is not the gospel at all) are the ones that are either sustaining their numbers or growing in numbers. And while I certainly believe that the hyper-politicization of American evangelicals has driven many away from the gospel, I'm quite sure that this is only part of a much larger issue.

To illustrate the point, on March 15, 2020, I did a Google search for "rise of the religious nones." The oldest article that came up was dated to March 12, *2012*, in other words, it was dated to right in the middle of the Obama presidency.[11] To repeat: the rise of the "nones" is not a new, Trump-related phenomenon. Even more interesting was this: the newest article that came up was dated to February 12, 2020, and it was titled, "US decline in religious affiliation may be slowing: researchers." Yes, "The much-documented decline in religious affiliation among United States citizens may finally be slowing down, according to recent research."[12] So, three years into Trump's first term in office, this negative trend may be reversing itself. Be careful, my friend, for blaming everything on Donald Trump. You make a big mistake when you do.

Let's also consider that the churches that are bleeding members the most, on average, are "liberal" (or "mainstream" or "progressive") churches. They have been in serious decline for years.[13] And they the members of these churches vote overwhelmingly Democrat. What do you know! Not only so, but these churches are often losing more young people than any others. Are you going to blame that on Trump?

In sharp contrast, *Newsweek* reported on January 6, 2018, that, "None of America's 100 largest churches are LGBT-affirming and almost all of them are led by white men, according to ChurchClarity.org, an organization that reports churches' LGBT policies and rates congregations based on their level of clarity."[14] Yet, for the most part, members of churches like this would be likely to vote Republican, and they are the churches that are growing.[15]

Of course, a Trump critic would say, "Yes, it's the racist, homophobic, xenophobic churches that are growing. Of course their brand of Christianity would not be hurt by a vote for Trump."

Still, that would fail to explain: 1) why these churches are not experiencing an even higher dropout rate, since, we are told, the younger generation has had it with this form of Christianity; and 2) the rise of the religious "nones" is most pronounced in liberal, pro-LGBTQ, pro-abortion, pro-Democratic churches.

I could also point out that, if you got to know many of these churches firsthand, you would find that they are highly engaged with their local communities and have excellent track records of compassionate, holistic, Christian service. They are known for their good deeds and for making a difference where their people live, breaking the racist, hateful stereotyping of their critics.

Not only so, but where God is moving powerfully, young people are flocking to the meetings. Politics is not the issue. Jesus is the issue. Encountering the Lord is the issue. Being touched by the Spirit is the issue. Being part of a loving community is the issue. And this is happening both in local church settings and in large corporate gatherings.

To cite one example among many, an article posted on the Fox News site December 31, 2019, began with these words:

> It's not your typical college New Year's party — more than 65,000 young Christians gathering in an Atlanta stadium to kick off a new decade with worship, prayer and Bible teaching.
>
> While a Pew Research Center survey shows the "nones" or religiously non-affiliated Americans are increasing, with a decline in Christians over the last decade, the sold-out conference Passion 2020 seems to be outright defying that.[16]

But of course. This has been the pattern for years now. And, with rare exception, those attending these gatherings lean conservative in their social values and religious beliefs. That's why it is no surprise to read that, as of March, 2019,

> The fact that evangelicals' share of the population remains relatively stable over the last decade is striking given the continued rise of the

nones. Evangelicals have been able to replace losses as fast as they are occurring, at least for now. Recent survey evidence has found that nearly 95 percent of born-again Christians stayed that way from 2010 to 2014, compared to just 85 percent of those who said that they were Protestant but not born-again. In addition, a significant portion of "nothing in particular" respondents do make their way back to evangelical churches.[17]

As to the larger question of the rise of the religious "nones," while speaking in Vancouver, British Columbia (Canada) in 2019, I did a little research, since this is one the least Christian-identified cities in North America. I learned that, "Only 41 per cent of Metro residents are Christian, compared to a national [Canadian] average of 67 per cent. B.C. [British Columbia] has the fewest Christians on average of any province or territory." Accordingly, "Even while the city has grown in population, the total number of Christians in Metro has actually dropped by four per cent in the past decade, to 950,000."

Not only so, but,

Even though Christians as a whole continue to make up by far the biggest single religion in the region, there is an equally large group in B.C. and Metro Vancouver who express no religious affiliation.

More than 41 per cent of Metro Vancouver residents, or 945,000 people, told Statistics Canada they have no religion.

That is a far higher proportion than in any other major city in Canada — or, for that matter, North America.

Across Canada, the proportion who claim no religion has risen to 24 per cent from 16 per cent in 2001. In Toronto, the figure is just 21 per cent.[18]

Need I point out the obvious? This has nothing to do with Donald Trump. Instead, it is part of a larger, global phenomenon, one that existed long before Trump came on the scene.[19] (According to a 2018 Pew Research Center report, "Young adults around the world are less religious by several measures.")[20]

So, while I agree that our unconditional, seemingly blind support for President Trump can hurt our Christian witness, I'm also confident that: 1) if we build relationships and put the gospel before politics, our outreach can be as effective as ever; 2) we can justify our balanced support of the President, feeling free to differ with him when called for; and 3) Trump is not primarily to blame for the rise of the religious "nones."

To be sure, an argument can be made that, to the extent the "moral majority" was perceived as an appendage to the Republican Party, that weakened our gospel witness.[21] And to the extent we make political affiliation a major platform of our church position, we alienate people unnecessarily. (Friends of mine who pastor multi-ethnic churches will educate their congregants on the issues but steer clear of any political affiliation.) Yet this, too, was a problem long before Trump came on the scene. Let's not allow any negative feelings for the President cloud our judgment. And let's not be pawns of the media, be it the leftwing media or the right. Instead, let's be Word-based, Jesus-centered, Spirit-empowered, neighbor-loving Christians. That's just what a hurting world needs.

As for Donald Trump, we pray for him and support him, but he is not the love of our lives or the theme of our songs. That honor belongs to one alone: our Savior and Redeemer, the Lord Jesus. Let the whole world know!

EIGHT

Did We Vote Our Pocketbook or Our Principles?

According to evangelical, Never Trump author Ben Howe, the main reason evangelical Christians supported Donald Trump in 2016 was money, not morality.[1] In other words, they did not vote for him primarily because of moral issues like abortion or Supreme Court appointees. Rather, they voted for him because they felt he would do a better job with the economy than Hillary Clinton. Is this true? If it is, then, in my opinion, Howe would have good reason for calling such voters hypocritical.

After all, it would be one thing if these voters (which include me) said, "We don't like Trump's past, and we certainly don't look to him today as a serious Christian or a paragon of moral virtue. But the unborn are being slaughtered, and our religious freedoms are under attack. And because Hillary is pro-abortion and even opposed to our religious liberties, we'll vote for Trump, albeit with some reservation. Just putting the right people in the Supreme Court will be reason enough to vote for him."

That, in my opinion, is a defensible choice for evangelicals, one that is even based on morality and Christian principles. It is a choice in harmony with our values. As evangelical theologian Wayne Grudem explained in July, 2016,

It isn't even close. I overwhelmingly support Trump's policies and believe that Clinton's policies will seriously damage the nation, perhaps forever. On the Supreme Court, abortion, religious liberty, sexual orientation regulations, taxes, economic growth, the minimum wage, school choice, Obamacare, protection from terrorists, immigration, the military, energy, and safety in our cities, I think Trump is far better than Clinton . . . . Again and again, Trump supports the policies I advocated in my 2010 book *Politics According to the Bible.*[2]

But it would be another thing if we said, "We don't like Trump's past, and we certainly don't look to him today as a serious Christian or a paragon of moral virtue. But our number one issue is financial prosperity, and we believe he can do a better job of strengthening the economy than Hillary, so we'll vote for Trump, albeit with some reservation."

That, in my opinion, would be a carnal choice, even a hypocritical choice. Yet according to Howe, that is exactly why most evangelical Trump voters supported him. Not his pro-life position. Not his stance on behalf of religious freedoms. Not his solidarity with Israel. Not his pushing back against radical LGBT activism. Not his commitment to nominate conservative judges. No. It was primarily a money-based vote.

Where does Howe get this idea? From the polls. Writing in September, 2019 on the *Christian Post,* Samuel Smith noted that, "Americans with evangelical beliefs are more likely to care politically about healthcare and economic issues than they are about issues typically associated with evangelical political engagement such as religious liberty and abortion, a new survey found."

Smith continued,

"Our respondents surprised us by how little they appeared to care about stereotypically evangelical causes," Georgetown University professor Paul Miller wrote in a white paper analyzing the survey's findings published by the Southern Baptist Convention's Ethics & Religious Liberty Commission.

LifeWay Research released a new poll this month sponsored by the ERLC exploring the views of American evangelicals on politics, social civility, media consumption and their engagement with those who have opposing political ideas.

The survey was conducted last November and included responses from 1,317 evangelical respondents who were screened to distinguish between respondents with evangelical beliefs (933) and respondents who self-identified as evangelical Christians (1,001).

The respondents were specifically asked to identify three public policy concerns that "are most important to you."

The top answer for both self-identified evangelicals and respondents with evangelical beliefs was "healthcare" (51 percent). The second-most common answer (49 percent for self-identified and 46 percent of those with evangelical beliefs) was "the economy."

In contrast,

Just 33 percent of both self-identified evangelicals and respondents with evangelical beliefs highlighted "religious liberty" as an issue of importance for them.

Twenty-nine percent of evangelicals by beliefs highlighted "abortion" as an issue of importance to them while 28 percent of self-identified evangelicals said the same.

Only four percent of both sets of respondents identified "LGBT rights" as a political issue that is important to them. [3]

Based on this data, Howe concludes,

It seems to say that while the reasonable desire to have a prosperous economy and a credible expectation of safety may be fine, for these supporters, a prosperous economy and a credible expectation of safety are far more important than their stated desire to save human life in the womb. By a lot.

The notion of religious liberty is not nearly as important to evangelical voters as the stock market surging or 'finally' having a president who's willing to threaten to use nuclear weapons on our adversaries. Whether religious liberty is truly in danger or not is irrelevant to the point.[4]

Of course, one could argue that combatting terrorism also saves lives and therefore should not be contrasted with combatting abortion. But even so, how do we explain so few evangelical Trump voters stating that abortion was a major factor for them? I'm not arguing with the general (and astute) observation of conservative leader Peter Wolfgang that, "America's real religion is capitalism, not Christianity."[5] But is capitalism more important to evangelicals than Christianity? That's what I wonder about.

What About Those Polls?

It's tough to argue with the polls, especially when one of the polls was conducted by LifeWay Research. We can't simply dismiss the polling data as "fake news." And yet I must argue with the polls for two simple reasons: First, as one who lives in the world of conservative evangelicalism, I have yet to meet (or hear from) an evangelical whose *main reason* for voting for Trump was economic.

I'm not denying that such voters exist. I'm simply saying that I have not encountered them. Not face to face. Not in my speaking engagements and during Q&A sessions. Not on my radio show. Not in online interaction.

Second, almost every evangelical I know who voted for Trump did so because of his pro-life, pro-religious liberties position. Or, directly related to this, they voted for him because of potential Supreme Court and federal court appointees. Some also voted for him because of his pro-Israel position, which tied in with his anti-terrorist position.

In harmony with this, many voted for him simply as a vote against Hillary Clinton, whom they perceived to be on the very wrong side of these issues. Otherwise, with a more moderate Democratic candidate, they might have sat out the elections. This was confirmed by polls I conducted on Facebook and Twitter on August 28, where I asked these same questions.

On Facebook, where I could only offer two choices, I asked, "if you voted for Trump in 2016 (and only if you voted for him), between these two issues, which was more important to you? Did you vote for Trump mainly to fight against abortion or mainly to improve the economy?"[6]

Out of the 2,057 who responded, 83 percent said abortion and only 17 percent economy.

On Twitter, I posted two consecutive polls, giving a total of 8 options asking, "If you voted for Trump, what was your primary reason of voting for him?"[7] The results were just as pronounced:

- Anti-Hillary: 33 percent
- Abortion: 25.3
- The courts: 14.7
- Economy: 8.3
- Pro-Israel: 6.5
- National security: 6.3
- International issues: 3.7
- LGBT concerns: 1.8

Obviously, these polls are not scientific, and, at best, they reflect the views of those who follow me on social media, and I do have a fairly substantial social media following (at present, 590,000 followers on Facebook, 40,600 on Twitter, and 109,000 YouTube subscribers). Yet they confirm everything I thought to be true before I did the polling based on more than two years of interacting with Trump supporters and detractors. Did we, then, compromise our convictions for the sake of a better economy? Perhaps some did, but to my knowledge, most did not.

This is a representative sampling from commenters on Facebook:

- Rob McCormick: Definitely not true for me, nor can I imagine for any true Born Again Christ follower.
- Sheldon Cote: Not me, #1 abortions is why voted Trump n will again
- Scott Cheatham: I voted BECAUSE of the SCOTUS appointments. Absolutely.
- Claire Jopo: The economy means nothing compared to killing our children.
- Debbie Barton: I voted for President Trump because of his support of religious liberty, stance against abortion, concern for the justices appointed to the Supreme Court. We don't need activists on the high court pushing an agenda for

spiritual bankruptcy like we've seen recently. I also voted for him because of his love for Israel, and I definitely didn't like all the corruption in the government.

- Kim Fitzsimons: NO, that is not true!!! We care MORE about the BABIES being murdered than we do about the economy!!!!!!!!!!!!! ABORTION IS MURDER!!!!
- Alyssa White: Abortion is always my top voting issue. I WILL not vote for anyone who is in favor of abortion.
- Phillip G. Bradshaw: Obviously, the abortion issue was the only reason Christians voted for Trump. Certainly not for his example of morality or business mind demonstrated with his operating in bankruptcy.
- Brandon Butler: Not true for me. I voted for Trump because I knew Hillary would be an unmitigated disaster for the Supreme Court at the very least.

In fact, out of many hundreds of responses to my Facebook polls and related articles, I found precious few evangelicals who said they voted for Trump because of the economy rather than abortion. In keeping with this, an old friend of mine, Alastair Geddes, who is a staunch Never Trumper, commented, "I agree, I have never met an evangelical who voted for Trump because of the economy!"

Not surprisingly, some of the most "liked" comments on Facebook included these:

- Bob Anderson: I will NEVER EVER vote for a pro-choice candidate. I will not have the blood of the innocent on my hands.
- Rita Gilmore Cruse: Not true. My primary concern was the Democratic Party platform which promoted late term abortion to be paid for with taxpayer funds...my money being used to kill babies up to the moment of birth. I will not be able to stand before my God blameless at judgement if I have willingly abetted murder of the preborn.
- Nathan Schleis: My wife & I voted for Trump for reasons that have nothing to do with $$$. He vowed to protect the unborn...and he is doing so. He vowed to appoint

conservative Supreme Court Judges...and he has done that. He vowed to actively protect religious freedom...he is doing so. Our next vote for Trump will once again have absolutely nothing to do with money.

- Josh Olar: The main reasons for me and everyone I know was because of abortion and the courts. It was his appointment of Gorsuch that rallied people behind him. Never Trumpers sold their soul to the media.
- Dava Watson: I voted for Trump for several reasons and the economy was at the bottom of the list. He pledged to protect the unborn and he is doing so. He promised to appoint conservative Supreme Court Judges - and he has kept that promise.. He promised to protect religious freedom...and again he is doing what he said.

Over on Twitter, A Losen San Miguel wrote, "Howe is categorically wrong on his view and you are correct. Taken my own poll on this over the last three years. Results support Dr. Brown."[8] Tim Hairston commented: "I set out the 2016 first time since the 80's. But I'm voting for @realDonaldTrump this time. Economy is good but not my main reason. Abortion and the courts to combat the lawlessness now in the USA."[9] Comments like this, which, again, are just a representative sampling, confirmed what I understood to be the case: evangelical Christians did not put money over morality.

Interestingly, if we fast forward to January 30, 2020, CNN's religion editor Daniel Burke tweeted, "What's the top issue for religious groups in 2020? It's not religious freedom, abortion, judges, jobs, foreign policy or the economy. It's health care,"[10] with reference to a poll released earlier that month on the PRRI (Public Religion Research Institute) website.[11] Specifically, for white evangelicals polled, their top three issues were terrorism, immigration, and health care.

This, in turn, confirmed a survey released in September, 2019, which indicated that,

Americans with evangelical beliefs are more likely to care politically about healthcare and economic issues than they are about issues typically associated with evangelical political engagement such as religious liberty and abortion, a new survey found.

"Our respondents surprised us by how little they appeared to care about stereotypically evangelical causes," Georgetown University professor Paul Miller wrote in a white paper analyzing the survey's findings published by the Southern Baptist Convention's Ethics & Religious Liberty Commission.[12]

More specifically,

The respondents were specifically asked to identify three public policy concerns that "are most important to you."

The top answer for both self-identified evangelicals and respondents with evangelical beliefs was "healthcare" (51 percent). The second-most common answer (49 percent for self-identified and 46 percent of those with evangelical beliefs) was "the economy."

Forty percent of those with evangelical beliefs identified "national security," while 43 percent of self-identified evangelicals did the same. Forty-one percent of self-identified evangelicals identified "immigration" as an issue of importance to them, while 39 percent of respondents with evangelical beliefs said the same.

Just 33 percent of both self-identified evangelicals and respondents with evangelical beliefs highlighted "religious liberty" as an issue of importance for them.

Twenty-nine percent of evangelicals by beliefs highlighted "abortion" as an issue of importance to them while 28 percent of self-identified evangelicals said the same.

Only four percent of both sets of respondents identified "LGBT rights" as a political issue that is important to them.[13]

Making Sense of the Differing Data

How, then, do we reconcile these polling results, which differ so deeply from my own? First, we can see that there is significant variation between the polls, as economic issues did not make it into the top three categories in the PRRI survey for eight of the nine groups surveyed. Second, the PRRI poll didn't even list "abortion" as a category. How then could respondents list it as one of their concerns? Third, issues like terrorism, immigration, and healthcare are moral issues, but without having more information in front of us, we don't where, exactly, white evangelicals stood on these issues. Fourth, and perhaps most importantly, neither of these polls asked the question we are asking here, namely, if you voted for Trump, why did you vote for him? So, it's very possible that the same evangelicals who responded to these polls as they did would have responded differently had they been asked a Trump-related question.

Another possibility is that the circles in which I travel represent a more devout, Scripture-based evangelicalism, one that puts greater emphasis on abortion and religious liberty and the like. In that case, the more committed evangelicals are putting religious issues first while the less committed evangelicals are putting economics first. This would seem to be confirmed by Pew Research poll released March, 2020, mentioned earlier, in Chapter Four.

According to this poll,

U.S. adults prize a president who lives a moral and ethical life more than they care about having one who is religious. More than six-in-ten Americans say it is "very important" to them to have a president who personally lives a moral and ethical life. By comparison, just one-in-five say it is very important for a president to have strong religious beliefs, and even fewer respondents think it is vital for the president to share their own religious beliefs.

However,

Two-thirds of white evangelicals say it is very important to have a president who stands up for their religious beliefs, about double the share who say it is very important for a president to have strong religious beliefs. And white evangelicals say Trump fits the bill: Fully eight-in-ten white evangelical Protestants say that the phrase "fights for what I believe in" describes Trump "very well" or "fairly well," including roughly half who say this describes him "very well."

In addition, "white evangelical Protestants overwhelmingly feel that the Trump administration has helped (59%) rather than hurt (7%) the interests of evangelical Christians. And three-quarters of white evangelicals say they agree with the president on 'many,' 'nearly all' or 'all' important issues facing the country."[14]

It is true that this survey does not address the issue of the economy, but it does indicate the extent to which white evangelicals believe that Trump is fighting for the causes that matter most to them, specifically, for their religious beliefs. And this confirms what I have been saying. Our vote for Trump is not immoral.

There's one more angle to consider, namely, that a vote for a strong economy can be a morally based vote, since a strong economy allows more people to get the health care they need. This was drilled home to me by Prof. Jay Richards when I interviewed him on March 24, 2020.[15] He explained that, for example, an elderly couple on very tight finances would be more reluctant to go to the doctor or get necessary medications, thereby endangering their lives. In keeping with this, economist Richard Smith noted that: "A decade ago, Columbia University's Mailman School of Public Health found that poverty was the *underlying* cause of 172,000 U.S. deaths, or 4.5% of total deaths. 'Social causes can be linked to death as readily as can pathological and behavioral causes,' states Dr. Galea, the leader of the research team and Gelman Professor of Epidemiology.'"[16] Prof. Richards also noted that, when surveys are done, voting for a healthy economy is often seen as a moral choice rather than a merely selfish choice.

That being said, I don't doubt that many people do vote based on their own pocketbook. In other words, their vote is self-centered more than God-centered or morally-centered. Yet a good economy is good for all, and those who want to see national thriving know that this requires a healthy economy. That's why some evangelicals could put a healthy economy high on their list of priorities without making a moral compromise.

The bottom line for me, though, remains the same: within my own circles and within the circles of those I can reach online, the vast majority of evangelicals stand with Trump for moral and religious reasons, despite his many flaws and weaknesses. They do not stand with him primarily for personal financial gain.

NINE

Responding to a Passionate Plea from 'Progressive' Christians

On January 18, the Global Center for Religious Research (GCRR) posted, "An Open Letter to Evangelicals of Moral Conscience." The subtitle read, "Help us end the cult-like determination to ignore, excuse, and justify Mr. Trump's blatant and obvious moral depravity!" The letter began with this appeal:

Dear American Evangelical Friends,

It is with great sadness that we, the undersigned faith leaders, biblical scholars, philosophers, and other academics, many of whom began our walks of faith in the evangelical tradition, hereby call on all American evangelical Christians of moral conscience who recognize and regret the corrupting and corrosive influence of Donald J. Trump, to join us in repudiating those evangelical leaders and institutions that have politically entangled themselves with him. We believe this action to be an urgent moral imperative because these leaders and institutions, which have unfortunately become the dominant voice of modern American evangelicalism, have shown themselves to be obstinately bound to the control of influences overtly opposed to the gospel of Jesus Christ and have resisted repeated pleas to disentangle themselves.[1]

Those are strong words. Have evangelical supporters of Trump really "shown themselves to be *obstinately bound* to the control of influences *overtly opposed to the gospel of Jesus Christ* and *have resisted repeated pleas to disentangle themselves*"?[2] It is often said that it's not a good idea to insult the jury when making appeal to the jury, but that's exactly what these leaders have done, right out of the gate. For me, that immediately raises some concerns.

There's something else that gets my attention. The writers state that "many of [them] began [their] walks of faith in the evangelical tradition," which means they are no longer part of the tradition, presumably because they found something they felt was better or because they had a problem with their evangelical roots. Either way, this raises a question: as an evangelical, why should I pay special attention to a moral appeal – really, a moral rebuke – from former evangelicals? If I had left the Catholic Church in favor of the evangelical tradition, on what grounds could I make a special appeal to Catholics as Catholics?

Someone might say, "But you're missing the point here. This letter is not addressing evangelicals who voted for Trump in 2016 or who plan to do so in 2020. It's calling on evangelicals to repudiate 'those evangelical leaders and institutions that have politically entangled themselves with him.'"

True, but the devil is in the details. What, exactly, do they mean by this? What of your everyday evangelical Christian who believes that Trump is doing far more good than harm? Should they be repudiated as well? A related blog post on the GCRR website posted by Dr. Darren M. Slade was titled, "Open Letter to Conscientious Evangelicals: Your Silence is Complicity! End the Trump Cult!"[3] So, unless you actively speak out against these other evangelicals, you are complicit in Trump's sins as well.

Accompanying the blog post was an offensive cartoon picturing a slickly-dressed, faux-sincere, evangelical leader (with a bolo tie, no less, and halo over his head) standing next to a devil-like Donald Trump, red, with horns, and in flames, with 666 inscribed on his left shoulder. And these are the Christian leaders who are rebuking evangelical supporters of Trump for their alleged unchristian alliances? The cartoon, penned by political cartoonist David Fitzsimmons, has the evangelical leader speaking these words to (or, about) Trump: "As long as he's pro-life we can overlook some minor character issues."

So, Donald Trump is the devil incarnate, the antichrist. And evangelicals who feel that fighting for the life of the unborn is more important than being nice, are in union with the evil one. Really?

How Bad Is Donald Trump?

The Open Letter certainly pulls no punches when it comes to its view of President Trump. It speaks of his "corrupting and corrosive influence" and notes:

> The image of Christ as a voice of love is tarnished when evangelical followers actively support someone who has repeatedly and openly bragged about being a womanizer, sexually assaulting unsuspecting women (not just in the infamous Access Hollywood tape but in decades of on-air interviews), and entering the dressing rooms of teenage beauty pageant contestants, as well as someone who has been credibly accused of sexual assault, sexual harassment, and sexual misconduct over twenty times since the 1980s, and has made sexually inappropriate remarks about pre-teens and even his own daughter.

The article also cites *Christianity Today* editor Mark Galli's call for the removal of President Trump (see Chapter Eleven) – actually, Galli's name occurs eleven times in the letter – and cites his reference to Trump's "grossly immoral character" and speaks of him as "a human being who is morally lost and confused." And the letter cites the damning assessments of Trump's character from Southern Baptist leaders Russell Moore (from September 17, 2015)[4] and Al Mohler (from October 11, 2016), the latter who opined that we would not want our children around Trump, who referred to him as a "sexual predator," and who stated "we wouldn't want this man as our next-door neighbor, much less as the inhabitant of 1600 Pennsylvania Avenue."[5]

Linked to the Open Letter is "Addendum B: A *Short* List of Mr. Trump's Immoral and Corrupt History," consisting of fifty-nine items, some of them quite serious.[6] Trump supporters will immediately note that many of the items are quite specious and subjective,[7] but even if half of them (or even more) could be dismissed out of hand, what of the rest?

The Open Letter then notes how 200 evangelical leaders reaffirmed their support of President Trump after Galli's call for his removal, branding these evangelical leaders and their institutes as "corrupt." Indeed, the letter states, "Just as the underground Confessional Church separated itself from the German Evangelical church in the 1930s, by way of the Barmen Declaration which declared that current political convictions should not influence church teachings, we call on evangelicals to end the cult-like determination to ignore, excuse, and justify Mr. Trump's blatant and obvious depravity." Standing with Trump, then, is just as immoral as standing with the Nazis. And it is all the more evil and dangerous when we claim that God has somehow raised up or appointed Trump to the presidency. As I said, this Open Letter pulls no punches.

And so, these leaders write:

> To refuse to call out Mr. Trump's immoral actions (as detailed in Addendum B) is to lose moral authority, integrity, and to become complicit in them. Indeed, moral and legal complicity in such actions is why certain Trump officials have left the Trump administration (Addendum C), why many of his associates have renounced him (Addendum D), and why the plethora of Trump associates, who have already been indicted for or convicted of criminal activity, reflect so badly on Mr. Trump and those who continue to support him (Addendum E).

Then, after citing former evangelical leader Brian McLaren, the Open Letter builds to a climax with great passion:

> Ours is not a call to adopt or reject any theological doctrine, to abandon the term "evangelical," or to abandon the practice of evangelism. Rather, our hope in issuing this call is that a mass movement of Christians of good conscience, repudiating in one voice the corruption of evangelical leaders and their institutions, and calling them to turn away from their adulation of the Golden Idol they have

made of Mr. Trump, might become the genesis of a more healthy evangelical revival.

And then this, in bold:

Until such time as those evangelical institutions and leaders disentangle themselves from the corrupting power and privilege that their complicity with Mr. Trump is providing them, we call upon Christians of good conscience to disentangle themselves from them, join us in repudiating them, and be prepared to explain why. We know it won't be easy. We know it may take different forms for different people. But we believe that to heal our individual consciences, to heal the conscience of our country, and to heal the conscience of American evangelicalism, it must be done.[8]

You Make Some Valid Points, But . . .

What should we make of this letter? To be completely candid, there's a lot I agree with in the critique, putting the rhetorical flourishes aside. In fact, that's one reason I wrote this book (along with my earlier compilation, *Donald Trump Is Not My Savior*)[9] – to address this very quandary. And that's why one chapter in this book – a key, thematic chapter that makes up the longest in the book – is titled, "Does Character Still Count and Does Morality Still Matter?" I *do* have a problem with the over-exaltation of Trump as a savior figure. I *do* have a problem when we look the other way at his obvious, moral failings. I *do* have a problem when we excuse behavior in his life that we would have condemned in the life of a Democrat or liberal. That's why I asked in my previous book, is our relationship with Donald Trump a match made in heaven or a marriage with hell?

To be sure, the leaders who wrote the Open Letter do not help their cause by accusing Trump's evangelical supporters of making him into a Golden Idol, or by posting the Fitzsimmons antichrist cartoon, or by speaking of Trump's "obvious moral depravity." A little restraint would have gone a long way towards changing hearts and minds.

But that's not my big issue with the Open Letter. Rather, it is the blatant hypocrisy of the letter that is so disturbing to me. For example, Addendum A cites the comments of leftwing evangelical leader Jim Wallis, founder and editor of *Sojourners* magazine, excerpted from his July 18, 2019 article, "Who Will Call Out the President's Racism?"[10] (We'll return to the question of Trump's alleged racism in Chapter Ten.)

Yet Rev. Wallis was closely associated with President Barack Obama and openly campaigned for the Democratic Party, frequently lauding Obama and never openly speaking against his militant, pro-abortion positions or his open support of same-sex "marriage." Yet *we* are hypocritical for supporting Trump?

Just weeks after Obama finished his second term, Wallis wrote an article in *Sojourners* titled, "The Legacy of Barack Obama," with the subtitle, "The Obama presidency marked a historic era in the movement to undo white supremacy and privilege."[11] And the article, which was short, did not contain a negative syllable about the president's legacy. Even while referencing Genesis 1:26-27, which Wallis rightly said "establishes the foundational value of every human as being made in the image of God (*imago dei*)," Wallis ignored Obama's deep violation of this principle when it came to the unborn. Aren't they created in God's image? And don't they have "foundational value"?

And where, pray tell, is Wallis's moral outrage for Obama's record of voting against the Born Alive Protection Act, which would demand that medical care be given to a baby that survived abortion?[12] And, since Genesis 1 and 2 plainly describe marriage as the unique and lasting union of a man and a woman for life, where was Wallis's moral outrage for Obama apparently deceiving Americans by saying he opposed same-sex "marriage" in 2008, only to endorse it in 2012?[13] Little wonder that a June 25, 2008 article by Greg Mitchell on the *Huffington Post* was titled, "Jim Wallis, Evangelical Leader, Defends Obama, Rips Dobson."[14] (Yes, this was back in 2008.)

This is not to say that I differ with Wallis at every point. To the contrary, there are many social concerns, such as compassionate for the poor, that the Bible clearly emphasizes and that should be important to all believers. (See below, for more on this.) It is, again, his hypocritical rebuke to evangelical Trump supporters while himself being a supporter of President Obama.

Alan Beam, one of the first signers of the Open Letter, posted an article on the Friends of Justice website by Charles Kiker on the subject of "Homosexuality, Abortion, and Political Ideology."[15] The author of the article writes,

> I do not think society should deny people of homosexual orientation who live in a committed relationship the legal rights and privileges which are granted by the state(s) to heterosexual couples. I would prefer that this be called "civil union," or some such term. Restrict the terminology of "marriage" to religious groups or to local congregations where there is no religious hierarchy (a la Churches of Christ, Baptists and some others).

This is his conclusion as one "who seeks to follow in the Way of Jesus."

As for abortion, he writes, "I am troubled by abortion. I think the intentional ending of a pregnancy is troubling in any case, even in the case of rape, incest, or when the mother's life is in danger. I do not say I want to make it illegal in any case, but that I am troubled by it. I think most people are." Yet, Kiker concludes, with a call for respect with those who differ, "Given the state of humanity as it is, not as we wish it might be, I will stand with the Clintons (and others) in the position that abortion should be legal, safe, and rare."[16]

So, Alan Beam approvingly posts this article, which in no way affirms a pro-life position and instead approves of the Clintons' position on abortion. Yet Dr. Beam, who serves as the Executive Director of Friends of Justice, and who doubtless stands for many good causes, signs a letter calling pro-life evangelicals who stand with Trump hypocrites. Do you see why this troubles me?

Can Christian Supporters of Same-Sex "Marriage" Stand on Morally Higher Ground?

The Open Letter cites Rev. Brian McLaren, who in 2012 presided over the gay "marriage" of his son.[17] He is also one of the fifty-eight listed signers. Yet we are the hypocrites? The Open Letter also cites Pastor John Pavlovitz, who in December, 2018, tweeted, "When hopelessly phobic people of faith like @DrMichaelLBrown claim that God is against 'homosexual practice.'"[18] And again, "This is the kind of fearful, Jurassic understanding of sexuality that is getting people killed. Someone else's gender identity, sexual orientation, marriage, or sexual activity are none of your business."[19] I'm sorry, but I have a hard time taking the moral outrage of men like this seriously, however sincere they may be.[20]

Again, Revs. McLaren and Pavlovitz are accusing evangelicals of hypocrisy because we feel President Trump is a better choice than Hillary Clinton (or any of the current Democratic candidates). Because we feel he is doing better job at stopping the slaughter of the unborn. Of combatting world terrorism. Of fighting for religious liberties. Of opposing LGBT extremism. Of standing with Israel. We could even argue that Trump is doing a better job of helping the poor, not to mention working harder for prison reform. But no, if we support him, we are the hypocrites. My apologies for being blunt, but you might want to look in the mirror again before lashing out at us.

Another signer is The Very Reverend Penny Bridge, who has earned her own page on the San Diego LGBT Pride website.[21] Among her many accomplishments is "offering blessings at events including three Harvey Milk Diversity Breakfasts" and serving "as spiritual advisor to the Imperial Court's Queen Mother of the Americas, Empress Nicole the Great." In other words, she has embraced LGBTQ activism hook, line, and sinker. And they accuse Trump of "moral depravity"?

The webpage notes that, "Penny is deeply grateful for the many gifts that our LGBTQ citizens bring to St. Paul's and the wider faith community. She currently has a dream of raising funds to purchase niches in the cathedral columbarium to house the ashes of LGBT individuals whose families have never claimed them. Penny is proud to be known as a stalwart ally of the community." And, to repeat, she is one of the signers of this Open Letter, rebuking those of who stand with President Trump.

Of course, from Rev. Bridge's perspective, standing with the marginalized, with the outcast, with the hurting, with the oppressed, with the misunderstood. And to a certain extent, that does reflect the heart of Jesus. But affirming homosexual behavior and relationships does not represent His heart. And, to repeat, it is the height of hypocrisy for an ordained minister to support LGBT activism – in some fairly extreme forms, at that – while deploring the morals of evangelical Trump supporters. She is pointing to the Bible to criticize Trump and his supporters while discarding (and/or rewriting) what the Bible says about sexuality and marriage.

Another signer was Mike Clawson, Ph.D., who in April, 2011, posted an article on the Friendly Atheist website titled, "Support (Finally!) for Gays at the 'Harvard' of Christian Colleges."[22] Aside from *where* he posted his article (the Friendly Atheist blog?), *what* he had to say was equally eyebrow-raising as he celebrated an open letter by Wheaton students and alumni who openly identified as LGBTQ.

Clawson wrote,

> As a former conservative Christian who actually became much more progressive and open minded about my faith during my time at Wheaton (despite the best efforts of its administration), I am thrilled by the efforts of my fellow alumni and proud to be a small part of this effort. It also reminds [me] why I bother to still keep a foot in that evangelical world rather than simply washing my hands of the bigotry often found in those circles. Despite all the ugly and unjust things that are perpetrated in the name of Jesus by many conservative Christians (things that anger and disgust me as a follower of Christ just as much as they anger and disgust my atheist friends), I continue to hold out hope that change is possible. In my past thirty years as an evangelical (and now post-evangelical), I have seen a real and positive shift in attitudes on a whole range of important social issues among that particular tribe of Christians, including the "gay" issue.[23]

And Dr. Clawson is rebuking us? Dr. Clawson is taking the higher moral ground by urging evangelicals to repent of upholding biblical standards of sexuality? And this is just a random sampling of the positions of just a few of the fifty-eight signatories.

Have We Sold Our Souls for a Seat at the Table?

One of the document signers is Rev. Dr. Randall Balmer, who has also served as a contributing editor to *Christianity Today*. On the one hand, I can agree with his sentiments (quoted by Prof. Scot McKnight) that,

"Christianity operates best from the margins of power, not in its center."[24] At the same time, I recognize that, already in 2006, when George W. Bush was president, Prof. Balmer wrote the book, *Thy Kingdom Come: How the Religious Right Distorts the Faith and Threatens America: An Evangelical's Lament.*[25]

I actually bought this book in 2006 and can say "Amen" to much of its contents. At the same time, Prof. Balmer's opposition to Trump can hardly be seen in a vacuum. This was the inevitable trajectory of his personal evangelicalism. Accordingly, the Open Letter repeatedly cites Mark Galli's rightly-criticized *Christianity Today* editorial (for which, see again, Chapter Eleven),[26] and in harmony with his position, states, "When confronted with statements of Mr. Trump that are racist, misogynistic, xenophobic, or known falsehoods, they occasionally critique his 'word choices' but almost never address the underlying prejudicial nationalism behind it."

Again, I have faulted some of my colleagues for their tepid responses to some of the president's more egregious words. But what if we do not feel he is a racist? Or misogynistic (at least, not so today)? Or xenophobic? Rev. James Robison has told me that he has spoken with every adult member of the Trump family, and all of them have expressed their concern for the wellbeing of all Americans, especially the poor and downtrodden. Perhaps that should carry some weight in our assessments as well? Perhaps there is something inherently Christian in their attitude?

Ironically, the Open Letter ends with reference to "**the corrupting power and privilege that their complicity with Mr. Trump is providing them**" but fails to mention how "progressive" Christians have worked side by side with liberal Democrats for years. Somehow, though, when the shoe is on the other foot, there is no "corrupting power and privilege." It is only when conservative evangelicals work with a sitting president that this exists.

I should also emphasize that the evangelicals I work with are not seeking special power or privilege. Rather, we are fighting to preserve our essential, Constitutional freedoms. And we are fighting, above all, for the lives of the unborn, the most innocent and vulnerable among us. I'm sure that some in our larger camp seek political power and influence, just as some religious leaders do in every political camp. But that is not the spirit or goal of those whom I personally know who support Trump today.

To Repeat: I Too Reject Blind Loyalty to Trump

To say it again, along with many of my evangelical colleagues who support Trump, I hate the damage he does with his words. I deplore his attacks on individuals. And I believe that, in some ways, he has degraded the office of the president. In fact, it is rare that I write an article in support of Trump without adding in these caveats, to the point of sounding like a broken record, both in my articles and within this book. (For the record, evangelical leaders close to Trump do not celebrate his shortcomings. Rather, they seek to be godly influences in his life, for which they should be commended.)

And so, over and again, I have stated that, as followers of Jesus, our identity must be found first and foremost in solidarity with the Savior, to whom we owe our very souls. The president simply gets our vote, and at this point, President Trump will have my vote in 2020.

But that is not enough for the writers of this Open Letter. To satisfy their concerns, we must separate from President Trump and renounce him completely. Yes, this is how we are supposed to repay the man who has taken up evangelical causes and concerns in a way that is unprecedented in modern times. Sorry, but I don't think so. In fact, to do so would be quite unchristian.

Had the Open Letter raised nuanced concerns about aspects of evangelical loyalty to Trump, or worse still, evangelical over-exaltation of Trump, I would have offered my hearty agreement. But it is so overstated, not to mention riddled with its own hypocrisy (which I only sampled here), that it has disqualified itself.

And so, to the scholars and religious leaders of the Global Center for Religious Research, I say this: I do not doubt your sincerity and I certainly do not demean your scholarship.[27] I simply ask you to look in the mirror once again, Bible in hand (as I often seek to do), and see if you find some beams in your own eyes that need to be removed (Matthew 7:1-5).

TEN

What Would Bonhoeffer Do?

Let me remove all suspense and answer the question head-on. I cannot say what Dietrich Bonhoeffer would do if he were an American citizen, alive today. I do not know how he would respond to the Trump presidency, I am not a Bonhoeffer scholar, and, while I am certainly a Bonhoeffer admirer, I am hardly a serious student of his life.

Then why do I have an entire chapter devoted to this question? It's because the International Bonhoeffer Society (IBS) issued a major statement, claiming to be true to the spirit of Bonhoeffer, that finds Trump's presidency to be dangerous. As the headline in the flagship, left-leaning, evangelical publication *Sojourner* announced in January, 2020, "International Bonhoeffer Society Calls For 'Ending Donald Trump's Presidency' In 'Statement Of Concern.'"[1] The statement echoes sentiments raised in a February, 2018 article in the *Sojourner* by two professors (and members of the IBS) who asked the question, "Is This a Bonhoeffer Moment?"[2]

So, while I must leave it to the Bonhoeffer aficionados to argue their respective points as to what, exactly, he would do, I can respond to the specific, important concerns that they raise. (My good friend Eric Metaxas, himself the author of a major, bestselling Bonhoeffer biography and a strong Trump supporter, would surely differ with these scholars on some critical points.)[3] Is today, indeed, "a Bonhoeffer moment"? Are there dangerous parallels between Trump and Hitler, between America today and pre-Nazi Germany? As outlandish as these questions may seem to some, others feel they are serious, weighty, and relevant. How should we respond?

The IBS cited a number of Bonhoeffer quotes in support of their call for ending Trump's presidency, specifically:

- He spoke of God's freedom and human freedom as "freedom *for* others" not "freedom *from* others." (1932)
- He preached that the gospel is "the good news of the dawning of the new world, the new order ... God's order," and therefore it is good news for the poor. (1932)
- He warned that leaders become "misleaders" when they are interested only in their own power and neglect their responsibilities to serve those whom they govern. (1933)
- He warned that when a government persecutes its minorities, it has ceased to govern legitimately. (1933)
- He reminded Christians that the church has an "unconditional obligation toward the victims of any societal order, even if they do not belong to the Christian community." (1933)
- He wrote, "For peace must be dared. It is the great venture. ... The hour is late. The world is choking with weapons. ... The trumpets of war may blow tomorrow. For what are we waiting?" (1934)
- He believed that Jesus's commands in the Gospels - like love your neighbor as you love yourself, welcome the stranger, and love your enemies - are to be obeyed in the social and political realm. He wrote: "From the human point of view there are countless possibilities of understanding and interpreting the Sermon on the Mount. Jesus knows only one possibility: simply go and obey." (1936)
- He wrote, "Behold God become human ... God loves human beings. ...Not an ideal human, but human beings as they are. ... What we find repulsive ... namely, real human beings ... this is for God the ground of unfathomable love." (1941)

- He wrote from prison, "... one only learns to have faith by living in the full this- worldliness of life. ...then one takes seriously no longer one's own sufferings but rather the suffering of God in the world. Then one stays awake with Christ in Gethsemane. And I think this is faith; this is [metanoia/repentance]. And this is how one becomes a human being, a Christian. ... How should one become arrogant over successes or shaken by one's failures when one shares in God's suffering in the life of this world?" (1944)
- He wrote from prison, "How do we go about being 'religionless-worldly' Christians, how can we be [ecclesia/church], those who are called out, without understanding ourselves religiously as privileged, but instead seeing ourselves as belonging wholly to the world?" (1944)

How, then, do these quotes support ending Trump's presidency? The IBS statement begins by noting that,

> In 2017, we issued a statement expressing our grave concerns about the rise in hateful rhetoric and violence, the rise in deep divisions and distrust in our country, and the weakening of respectful public discourse ushered in by the election of Donald Trump. We articulated the need for Christians to engage in honest and courageous theological reflection in the face of the threat posed by his leadership. Over the last three years, the need for such discernment has grown more urgent.[4]

To be sure, Donald Trump, both as candidate and president, has deepened these divisions and weakened respectful discourse. But he hardly "ushered" them in. For example, there was tremendous hostility from the left towards President George W. Bush, in particular after his invasion of Iraq. He was blasted as racist and sexist and likened to Hitler, and there were even calls for his death, and not just from some unknown loonies.

As Hollywood icon Harry Belafonte said to Venezuelan dictator Hugo Chavez during the Bush presidency, "No matter what the greatest tyrant in the world, the greatest terrorist in the world, George W. Bush says, we're here to tell you: Not hundreds, not thousands, but millions of the American people ... support your revolution."[5] In a similar spirit, "Antiwar protester and mother of fallen soldier Cindy Sheehan became a brief media sensation for camping out near Bush's Crawford ranch—a status not considerably diminished when she followed Belafonte's lead by calling President Bush 'a bigger terrorist than Osama bin Laden.'"[6] In addition, "Nobel Peace Prize Winner Betty Williams of Northern Ireland gave the keynote speech to the International Women's Peace Conference in Dallas" and said, "Right now, I could kill George Bush, no problem. No, I don't mean that. I mean—how could you nonviolently kill somebody? I would love to be able to do that."[7]

Writing for the *Daily Signal* on October 30, 2009, Rory Cooper noted that,

Liberal icon Gore Vidal, while on the CNN Headline News Show, "The Joy Behar Show" on October 22 said of President Bush: "But I couldn't jump into the screen fast enough to kill him off. That's one murder that I missed not committing." Did host Joy Behar ask him to clarify why he wished he had murdered a U.S. president, or tell him how deplorable that statement was? No. She laughed and said: "Well, it's too late anyway." Wow.[8]

Not only so, but, "President Bush was also the target of a liberal film called 'Death of a President' depicting his assassination while he was still in office shortly after Air America radio host Randi Rhodes said he should be killed off like Fredo in 'Godfather Part II.'"[9]

This is just a tiny sampling of the venomous, even murderous anti-Bush rhetoric. And the IBS claimed that Trump "ushered" in the "the weakening of respectful public discourse"? That he is responsible for "the rise in hateful rhetoric and violence, the rise in deep divisions and distrust in our country"? Could it be these scholars are more biased than they realize?

Think of the ridiculous attacks on Mitt Romney when he ran for president, including the time when "Sen. Joe Biden told an audience which included hundreds of African Americans that Republican economic policies would 'put y'all back in chains.'"[10] Yes, this was said about Romney.

Or consider the level of animosity from those on the right towards President Obama. Writing in the *Washington Post* August 26, 2016,

Carlos Lozada notes that Obama was called, among other things: "Secret Muslim. Socialist. Amateur. Anti-American. Criminal." And he writes,

> Selecting a representative set among dozens and dozens of titles in the Obama hatred literature is not easy. Do you go with "Impeachable Offenses" or "The Manchurian President"? "Divider-in-Chief" or "The Obama Nation"? "Culture of Corruption" or "The Roots of Obama's Rage"? A sample of such books, spanning 2008 to 2016, shows that, while the anti-Obama canon can be predictable, it is by no means static. The aversion to the president is always growing, and the nature of that aversion is always evolving toward harsher conclusions.[11]

There was hardly widespread "civil discourse" in America before Trump's election, and to suggest that was the case is to stick one's head in the sand. (Shall we also go back to the right's attacks on President Bill Clinton, especially after his affair with Monica Lewinsky was revealed? Were the criticisms against him civil and respectful? Was our nation anywhere near united?)

On the flip side, in the eyes of his critics, President Obama was a master of identity politics, opening old wounds and deepening historic divides, all for his political benefit.[12] Trump may have deepened those divides, but it can be argued that Obama helped rip them open. If we're going to be Christian, then let's face the facts, meaning, all the facts. Truth cuts both ways.

The IBS statement next argues that, "The policies of the Trump administration both threaten and disempower the most vulnerable members of our society, including people of color, members of the LGBTQ communities, Muslims and other religious minorities, immigrants, refugees, the poor, the marginally employed, and the unemployed. Moreover, Donald Trump has now taken ill-advised military action that raises the specter of war."

Where the Statement Falls Short

But here, too, the statement falls short. First, it can easily be argued that many of Trump's policies have been of genuine help to the poor and to minorities.[13] As expressed by Jerome Hudson, himself an African American, on May 22, 2020, "President Trump celebrated record low black unemployment in January on Martin Luther King, Jr. day. Trump has also allocated more money to historically black colleges and universities than any other president in U.S. history."[14]

To be sure, his critics believe he has made decisions that have had the opposite effect.[15] But the reality is that there is a vigorous debate over this, just as there is a vigorous debate over the efficacy of many economic policies, generally speaking. In that light, it is highly exaggerated to claim that Trump's policies "both threaten and disempower the most vulnerable members of our society." Some would claim the charge is patently false.

Second, Trump has also taken major strides when it comes to prison reform, most notably, the First Step Act, which was passed in December 2018. Of this, Trump stated, "The First Step Act gives nonviolent offenders the chance to reenter society as productive, law-abiding citizens."[16] (Need I say that the vast majority of prisoners in our jails and penitentiaries come from poor backgrounds, including non-violent offenders?) According to Vox.com, this "is the most significant criminal justice reform legislation in years."[17] Doesn't this demonstrate genuine concern for victims of societal inequities and even outright injustice?

Third, it is beyond odd to find scholars of Bonhoeffer arguing for the cause of LGBTQ activism, as if he would have supported men "marrying" men and women "marrying" women, or as if he would have been fine with biological males sharing bathrooms and locker rooms with biological females. (Yes, President Trump has pushed back against this outrageous school policy, which President Obama had previously mandated.)[18]

Fourth, while some critics believe strongly that Trump's policies have indeed "threatened" or "disempowered" people of color, his supporters, including nationally recognized people of color, would differ. To be sure, The IBS statement would agree with assessments like this one, which claimed early in the Trump presidency that, "In just two months, the Trump Administration has already made it harder for African Americans to buy a house, to vote, to enjoy clean air and water, and to retire with dignity."[19] And there are claims that Trump heartlessly removed needy recipients from the Food Stamp program, with shocking headlines like this: "Trump Is Cutting Food Stamps During a Pandemic. More than half a million SNAP recipients are on the edge of losing access to the crucial food safety net—just as they need it most."[20]

On the flip side, Trump supporters argue that food stamp enrollment has gone down primarily because employment has gone up. Thus, as Breitbart reported on February 15, 2020, "Approximately 6.1 million individuals dropped off the food stamp rolls since President Donald Trump's first full month in office in February 2017, according to the latest data from the U.S. Department of Agriculture (USDA)."[21] So, there is debate here too.

That's why Trump supporters can point to a September 10, 2019 headline in the *New York Times* that announced, "Trump Focuses on Black Economic Gains and Support for Historically Black Colleges." And, the *Times* reported, "Since the beginning of Mr. Trump's presidency, the administration has, in fact, made an effort to support historically black schools, increasing investment in their programs by 14.3 percent."[22]

Not surprisingly, a March 4, 2020 op-ed piece in the *Times* discussing a major survey of 40,000 black voters (from March-December, 2019) indicated that "Trump's favorability rating among black voters overall increased from 7 percent in 2016 to 18 percent in 2019, with a large gender gap; Trump's favorability rating among black men in 2019 was 23 percent and 14 percent among black women."[23] Again, this would suggest that, at the least, the IBS charges against Trump are highly exaggerated. At the most, they are largely false.

It's also fair to ask why Trump has the strong support of a number of key black leaders, including pastors, educators, athletes, entertainers, businessmen, and others, why he has been called the "first black president,"[24] and why he has a black Surgeon General (Dr. Jerome Adams) and a black Cabinet member (Dr. Ben Carson). Certainly, his cabinet and senior leadership is far less diverse than that of President Obama (or, even the overall ethnic and racial diversity of America),[25] but it is also anything but racist.[26]

This is underscored by a widely-published photograph of black Christian leaders laying hands on the president and praying over him while he sits with his head bowed.[27] Could you imagine a photograph of, say, German Jews praying over Adolph Hitler? Or even a picture of

Bonhoeffer, together with godly German pastors, praying over Hitler like this? There's also a viral video of an Ethiopian immigrant leading in prayer[28] at a 2019 Young Black Leadership Summit at the White House following the president addressing the packed room of young black leaders.[29] Watch the videos for yourself and ask yourself if those present would agree with the IBS Statement.

Fifth, while Trump may have engaged in some strategic sword rattling with foreign leaders, he has actively worked to get American troops off foreign soil, most recently in Afghanistan. In fact, he was widely criticized, even by many of his staunchest evangelical supporters, for pulling some of our troops from Syria.[30]

Sixth, and finally, when it comes to Trump's immigration policies, he certainly has appealed to American nationalism and drawn attention to weak border control. And some of his statements (regarding Muslims and Mexicans) could have been articulated with much great clarity (although his critics have done their part in exaggerating his words). And I don't know anyone who is comfortable with putting people in cages, especially children. At the same time, only the most radical leftists would argue that we don't need secure borders, and Trump supporters have opposed illegal immigration vs. legal immigration.

The question, then, is how to go about making the borders secure while at the same time ensuring compassionate immigration policies. When it comes to "putting children in cages," some Trump supporters have argued that: 1) this was the continuation of an Obama policy (so said President Obama's ICE chief);[31] 2) the amount of children separated from their parents (while it was being determined that these really were their parents) was highly exaggerated; and 3) most all of this is a thing of the past.[32] But even if the worst case scenario proved true, there is no evidence that Trump wanted children "put in cages" or that he made this a goal of his policies or that his supporters liked the idea. Certainly not.

It has also been claimed that, "President Donald Trump's border security policies contributed to a lowering of deaths from opioid overdoses in 2018 relative to 2017, said Dr. Nicole Saphier, author of *Make America Healthy Again: How Bad Behavior and Big Government Caused a Trillion-Dollar Crisis*, linking the reduction in overdose deaths to a broader increase in life expectancy across the same timeframe."[33] So, once again, the debate goes both ways, meaning that some of the main concerns of the IBS could well reflect political bias (or, simply political perspective) rather than concrete indictments, making it quite presumptuous to speak on Bonhoeffer's behalf.

And what would the IBS have to say about Trump's unprecedented actions on behalf of the unborn, little ones for whose plight I imagine Bonhoeffer would have had great sympathy. Put another way, would Bonhoeffer been cheering President Trump when he spoke at the 2020 March for Life, the first sitting president ever to do so? Or would he have been jeering with the pro-abortion protesters? Or has the IBS lurched so far to the left they are do not support the rights of the unborn? (This is an honest question, not an attempt to provoke.)

The Danger of Equating Nationalism with the Kingdom of God

Having said all this, I do believe concerns could be raised in connection with the larger issue of nationalism, patriotism, and the empowering of a strong-handed leader by Christian leaders. Hitler's theme could well have been, "Make Germany Great Again," and there were hordes of professing Christian leaders who compromised their biblical convictions out of fealty to the Fuhrer. Are there parallels with American Christians and Trump?

In both cases, there was a close association between nationalism and the Christian faith. In Germany, this dated back to the influence of Martin Luther, because of which, in 1933, "Almost all Germans were Christian, belonging either to the Roman Catholic (ca. 20 million members) or the Protestant (ca. 40 million members) churches. The Jewish community in Germany in 1933 was less than 1% of the total population of the country."[34] (I would qualify this to state that "Almost all Germans professed to be Christian.") And, tragically, this "Christian" legacy was tainted by historic, Church-based antisemitism, which made the Nazi's unapologetic antisemitism all the more acceptable.[35] Thankfully, in that regard, there is virtually no parallel today with American evangelicalism and Trump today.

But there was more than Nazi antisemitism that resonated with many professing German Christians. As noted in the online Holocaust Encyclopedia:

The attitudes and actions of German Catholics and Protestants during the Nazi era were shaped not only by their religious beliefs, but by other factors as well, including:

- Backlash against the Weimar Republic and the political, economic, and social changes in Germany that occurred during the 1920s
- Anti-Communism
- Nationalism
- Resentment toward the international community in the wake of World War I, which Germany lost and for which it was forced to pay heavy reparations

These were some of the reasons why most Christians in Germany welcomed the rise of Nazism in 1933.[36]

Hitler would make Germany great again after the humiliation of World War I, but to do so would require making the Church of Germany into his puppet. As pointed out by Metaxas, "Hitler was moving ahead with his own plans for the church. He knew quite well how to deal with these Protestant pastors. 'You can do anything you want with them,' he once remarked. 'They will submit . . . they are insignificant little people, submissive as dogs, and they sweat with embarrassment when you talk to them."[37] Hitler also had plans for the Catholic leaders, whom he also felt could be put into the palm of his hand.[38]

What Would Bonhoeffer Say?

In a letter to his grandmother in 1993, Bonhoeffer wrote, "It has become ever more evident to me that we are to be given a great popular national Church, whose nature cannot be reconciled with Christianity, and that we must prepare our minds for the entirely new paths which we shall then have to follow. The question is really: Christianity or Germanism? And the sooner the conflict is revealed in the clear light of day the better."[39]

To quote the Holocaust Encyclopedia again,

Historically the German Evangelical Church viewed itself as one of the pillars of German culture and society, with a theologically grounded tradition of loyalty to the state. During the 1920s, a movement emerged within the German Evangelical Church called the Deutsche Christen, or "German Christians." The "German Christians" embraced many of the nationalistic and racial aspects of Nazi ideology. Once the Nazis came to power, this group sought the creation of a national "Reich Church" and supported a "nazified" version of Christianity.[40]

Certainly, this will seem very foreign to twenty-first century, American evangelical Christians. (Note that in Germany, "Evangelical" was and is a synonym for Lutheran, so its meaning was not the same as "evangelical" in America today). As evangelical believers, we are utterly repulsed by Nazism and by Hitler, and we are, for the most part, strongly pro-Israel. At the same time, because of America's strong Christian roots, we often confuse "Make America Great Again" with "Thy kingdom come, Lord," and there is often a strong overlap between patriotism and the kingdom of God. And just as German Christians looked to an uncouth strong man named Adolph Hitler, contemporary Christians are looking to an uncouth strong man named Donald Trump. And hasn't Trump made strong appeals to nationalism and to America first, to the point that he has been called xenophobic? And hasn't the alt-right rallied around these cries?

To be sure, white supremacists and hyper-nationalists have rallied around calls to make America great again, putting their own particular spin on this concept. But that doesn't mean that Trump himself adheres to alt-right ideology (he clearly does not). Even less does it mean that Trump's evangelical supporters would back such unchristian thinking. And there is no evidence that Trump views evangelical leaders the way Hitler viewed the Lutheran church leaders in his day ("they are insignificant little people, submissive as dogs"). To the contrary, it was because he was so impressed with these leaders and their causes that he pledged himself to stand with them. And to this day, some of these leaders are not afraid to speak truth to power, confronting him (with respect for his office) when called for.

And sometimes that confrontation is even public, as when the president announced he was pulling our troops out of Syria, thereby endangering the Kurds, who had been our faithful allies. An October 9, 2019 headline in *New York Magazine's* Intelligencer carried the headline, "Why Trump's Evangelical Allies Are Enraged Over His Betrayal of the Kurds."[41] This was echoed by similar stories in major, leftwing news outlets including the *New York Times*[42] and NPR.[43] The articles cited quotes from leaders like Pat Robertson, who warned that Trump could lose his mandate from heaven, and Franklin Graham, who publicly called for prayer for the Kurds. And, the Intelligencer article, written by Ed Kilgore, adds, "Perhaps most strikingly, Christian Right journalist David Brody, co-author of a hagiographical "spiritual biography" of Trump, retweeted this assessment by right-wing controversialist Erick Erickson: 'President Trump has committed an egregious act of betrayal in what he is doing to the Kurds. Shame on him.'"[44] Can you imagine what these leaders would do if Trump abandoned his pro-life stance or stopped fighting for our religious liberties or turned his back on Israel? They would be anything but "insignificant little people, submissive as dogs."

But the differences between Christian support for Hitler and Christian support for Trump are far greater than this, since Hitler was a truly evil, murderous madman. No sane critic of Trump can make such a comparison. Not only so, but years before World War II began, the real anti-Christian spirit of Nazism had been laid bare. As Eric Metaxas notes, shortly after Germany voted to leave the League of Nations in November, 1933, the Nazis held a large rally for the "German Christians" (meaning, the pro-Nazi "Christians"), with 20,000 in attendance. There, a high-school teacher named Reinhold Krause, who was the leader of the German Christians, addressed the exultant crowd:

> In coarse, crude language, Krause demanded that the German church must once and for all divest itself of every hint of Jewishness. The Old Testament would be first, "with its Jewish money morality and its tales of cattle merchants and pimps!" The stenographical record notes that "sustained applause" ensued. The New Testament must be revised, too, and must present a Jesus "corresponding entirely with the demands of National Socialism." And it must no longer present an "exaggerated emphasis on the crucified Christ." This tenet was defeatist and

depressing, which was to say Jewish. Germany needed hope and victory! Krause also mocked "the theology of the Rabbi Paul with its scapegoats and inferiority complex," and then he mocked the symbol of the cross, "a ridiculous, debilitating remnant of Judaism, unacceptable to National Socialists!" Furthermore, he demanded that every German pastor must take an oath of personal allegiance to Hitler! And the Aryan Paragraph that demanded the expulsion of every church member of Jewish descent must be heartily accepted by every German church![45]

The response to Krause's speech was outrage and shock. He had clearly overplayed his hand and the vast majority of Christians who learned of his remarks were repulsed, leading to the demise of the group known as "German Christians." Thus, "The Nazis used the German Christians while it was convenient, giving them a chance to do what was likely impossible. It simply hadn't worked out."[46] Those professing Christians who continued to support Hitler and his murderous plans had to leap across a massive, anti-Christian chasm in order to do so.

Then, in 1938, after Hitler annexed Austria in a brazen act of military expansionism, some "Christian" leaders were giddy with excitement, making fresh commitments to the Führer. As Metaxas notes,

> Bishop Sasse of Thuringia was first in line, aching to say 'thank you' to his Führer, and doing so by demanding that all of the pastors under him take a personal "oath of loyalty" to Hitler. His telegram to Hitler has been preserved: "My Führer, I report: in a great historic hour all the pastors of the Thuringian Evangelical Church, obeying an inner command, have with joyful hearts taken an oath of loyalty to Führer and Reich. . . . One God—one obedience in the faith. Hail, my Führer!"[47]

As horrific as this was, Dr. Friedrich Werner, who headed up the official Nazi-recognized church, went one step further, "demanding that every single pastor in Germany take an oath of obedience to Adolf Hitler." And this was the oath:

> In the recognition that only those may hold office in the church who

are unswervingly loyal to the Führer, the people and the Reich, it is hereby decreed: Anyone who is called to a spiritual office is to affirm his loyal duty with the following oath: "I swear that I will be faithful and obedient to Adolf Hitler, the Führer of the German Reich and people, that I will conscientiously observe the laws and carry out the duties of my office, so help me God." . . . Anyone who refuses to take the oath of allegiance is to be dismissed.[48]

That is what church allegiance to Hitler looked like, and there is not even a hint of comparison to evangelicals who support Trump.[49] To insinuate as much is to be guilty of egregious error, if not willful misrepresentation. (I'm not accusing the IBS of doing this overtly. I would, however, like to hear them state clearly that they are making no such comparison.) To a person, I believe evangelical leaders who support Trump would instantly flee from him should he be associated in any way, shape, size or form with the sentiments espoused by Krause. Not only so, but his evangelical voting base would disappear just as quickly. We have a hard enough time supporting him with his cruelty towards others, with his pettiness, his contrariness, his divisiveness, and his outbursts. If he truly became Hitlerian, refusing to hear our warnings and rebukes, we would leave him overnight, sounding the alarm loudly and clearly as we went on our way.

ELEVEN

The Shot Heard Around the Evangelical World

According to the *Christianity Today* website and with reference to Billy Graham, "Over sixty years ago, the beloved evangelist felt the urgent need for balanced reporting, biblical commentary, and a loving posture on the social cultural, and theological trends, issues and opportunities facing Christians.

"From that need came a unique vision that has helped shape the minds and hearts of tens of millions of Christian leaders ever since."[1]

That vision led to the founding of *Christianity Today*, which has been considered the flagship evangelical publication for decades. And even though it has leaned leftward in some respects in recent years, it is quite conservative compared to far-left evangelical publications like Jim Wallis' *Sojourners*. So, it represented a serious moment when Mark Galli, the outgoing editor in chief of *Christianity Today* (henceforth *CT*), wrote an editorial calling for the removal of President Trump.[2] The shock was felt around the world, including outside of evangelical circles, and the repercussions continue until this day.

The editorial was published on December 19, 2019, and it generated so many responses that Prof. James Beverley published an entire book containing those responses, amounting to almost 70,000 words – and it could have been much longer had every response been published in full.[3] In fact, Galli informed Beverley that the editorial generated more response than any editorial in the history of the magazine.[4] And overwhelmingly, the evangelical response to Galli's editorial, published in an almost endless stream of online articles, has been negative – meaning, standing with Trump and against Galli. What can we learn from this major episode?

In his editorial, Galli recalled Billy Graham's vision in founding *CT*, namely, that the magazine "will help evangelical Christians interpret the news in a manner that reflects their faith." And while *CT* normally did not focus on political issues, recognizing the diversity within evangelicalism, it "welcomes Christians from across the political spectrum, and reminds everyone that politics is not the end and purpose of our being." Nonetheless, said Galli, the impeachment of the president called for comment, and so Galli would share his thoughts with conviction and love.

After affirming *CT's* love and prayers for President Trump, Galli acknowledged how the Democrats have "had it out for [Trump] from day one," recognizing the partisan, even unfair nature of the impeachment hearings. Nonetheless, he wrote, "the facts in this instance are unambiguous: The president of the United States attempted to use his political power to coerce a foreign leader to harass and discredit one of the president's political opponents. That is not only a violation of the Constitution; more importantly, it is profoundly immoral."

Why is it, then, that many evangelicals are not shocked by this? It is because, Galli says, "this president has dumbed down the idea of morality in his administration." Not only so, but "[h]is Twitter feed alone—with its habitual string of mischaracterizations, lies, and slanders —is a near perfect example of a human being who is morally lost and confused."

On this basis, Galli argued, Trump should be removed, and no amount of good that he has done could justify his continuing in office with our support. Rather, "The impeachment hearings have illuminated the president's moral deficiencies for all to see. This damages the institution of the presidency, damages the reputation of our country, and damages both the spirit and the future of our people. None of the president's positives can balance the moral and political danger we face under a leader of such grossly immoral character."

Back in 1998, *CT* said of then-impeached President Clinton,

"Unsavory dealings and immoral acts by the President and those close to him have rendered this administration morally unable to lead." Consistency, Galli argued, calls for them to say the same thing today about President Trump.

And then he offered this impassioned plea:

> To the many evangelicals who continue to support Mr. Trump in spite of his blackened moral record, we might say this: Remember who you are and whom you serve. Consider how your justification of Mr. Trump influences your witness to your Lord and Savior. Consider what an unbelieving world will say if you continue to brush off Mr. Trump's immoral words and behavior in the cause of political expediency. If we don't reverse course now, will anyone take anything we say about justice and righteousness with any seriousness for decades to come? Can we say with a straight face that abortion is a great evil that cannot be tolerated and, with the same straight face, say that the bent and broken character of our nation's leader doesn't really matter in the end?

How should we respond?

What Galli Got Right and What Galli Got Wrong

First, I'm glad that Galli spoke his mind as an evangelical leader on behalf of *CT*. Surely, he echoed the sentiments of many others, and the Church and world need to hear this perspective too. It's true, of course, that this also speaks of disunity within our ranks. But where it is written that we must have political unity to be one in Christ? Where does the Bible say we must have the same view of the president to stand together for the larger cause of the gospel? As I've said many times before, when we stand before God on that day, He will ask us what we have done with Jesus, not what we have done with Trump.

I'm certainly aware of how the secular media has spun this, and Galli's editorial has been used to deepen the divide between us. It has also been used to make rejection of Trump a litmus test for true evangelical Christianity. (Ironically, in other circles, it is support of Trump that serves as a litmus test of one's true faith. See Chapter Two.) And it has been used to discourage evangelicals from voting for Trump, if not to shame them from voting for him. But again, because a substantial minority of evangelicals concur with Galli's words, they needed to be spoken.[5]

Second, there are many evangelicals who did not believe the Democratic charges against Trump and who saw the impeachment as a witch hunt and a sham.[6] In their minds, the charges were hardly "unambiguous." Quite the contrary. If, then, the president did not abuse his power as president, would Galli still believe that Trump should have been removed from office because of his offensive tweets and comments?

It is one thing to urge evangelicals to say, "Let's put forward an alternate candidate during the Republican primaries who will more closely mirror our values." It is another thing to say the president should be removed from office. For what crimes, based on the Constitution?

Third, I share Galli's concern that we evangelicals sometimes seem more closely aligned with the president than with the Lord, a subject I have written and spoken about time and again.[7] Have we sold our integrity and our ethics in support of a strong-willed president who fights for our sacred causes and gets in the trenches on our behalf?

At the same time, we are fooling ourselves if we think that the world will suddenly listen to us if we called for Trump's removal. Not a chance. Mark Galli might have been the talk of leftwing media for a short time (which, I do not believe was his goal in writing). But soon enough, they will view him as just another bigoted, hateful, homophobic, misogynist who opposes women's rights and believes in an antiquated book.

Galli wondered if anyone will "take anything we say about justice and righteousness with any seriousness for decades to come" if we don't seek to remove Trump. The answer is that it depends on how we conduct ourselves.

As I will argue throughout this book, we can support the president for the very real good he does do, much of it on behalf of causes that are of great importance to evangelicals. Religious liberty really does matter. Protecting babies in the womb really does matter. Helping the poor get better jobs really does matter. These, too, are issues of justice and righteousness. We simply need to be consistent when it comes to our ethics, meaning, we call balls and strikes with fairness and impartiality, and we call for ethical behavior as loudly as we call for righteous legislation. Why can't we do both?

I agree with Galli that, under the current administration, there has been a dumbing down of the idea of morality. And it's true that many evangelicals now wink at things that once grieved them, thankful to have a man like Trump who will stand up and fight (many would say, "Finally!"). But that doesn't mean we remove him for his alleged dumbing down of morality. It means we are careful not to lose our own morality in the process.

Fourth, I believe those on Galli's side need to listen to Trump-supporting evangelicals who feel that, despite his evident shortcomings, the man has been a God-send. During a recent trip to California, a pastor spoke to me about the very real threat to religious liberties Christians were facing there, among other, major problems. He was convinced that, with Hillary Clinton as president, irreparable damage would have been done and that Trump has served as a strong anti-Hillary leader. "Like a wedge in the door," I suggested to him, and he agreed.

But he also agreed that the wedge can only do so much. Only the Church, through the gospel and with God's empowerment, can open the door and turn the tide. That is where we must put our emphasis: living as Jesus would have us live, with politics an important and yet much more distant priority for most of us.[8]

My proposal today for my fellow-evangelicals is this. Let us each humble ourselves before God and pray, "Father, what is Your heart in all this? And what would you have me do? Show me my blind spots, and strengthen my convictions when they reflect yours. I only want Your will." Then, let's have honest conversations with our brothers and sisters who differ with us, starting with this: "Please share your perspective with me. I want to understand where you're coming from." Then, when they're done and you've heard their heart, ask if you can share yours. Finally, go back to prayer and meditation on the Word. The stakes are very high, and our nation is dangerously divided. Let us be sure that, as God's people, we do not follow suit.

A Further Response from Christianity Today

In a follow-up to Galli's editorial *CT* president Timothy Dalrymple noted that, "We are also a global ministry" and "partly on behalf of that global body, we can no longer stay silent." He wrote,

> Out of love for Jesus and his church, not for political partisanship or intellectual elitism, *this* is why we feel compelled to say that the alliance of American evangelicalism with this presidency has wrought enormous damage to Christian witness. It has alienated many of our children and grandchildren. It has harmed African American, Hispanic American, and Asian American brothers and sisters. And it has undercut the efforts of countless missionaries who labor in the far fields of the Lord. While the Trump administration may be well regarded in some countries, in many more the perception of wholesale evangelical support for the administration has made toxic the reputation of the Bride of Christ.[9]

When it comes to America, I have no doubt that, *to some extent*, this is true. I've experienced it myself.[10] On the other hand, for every person I've interacted with who finds my vote for Trump objectionable, I've interacted with 10 (or, more likely, 50 or 100) who find my biblical values objectionable. In particular, this applies to my opposition to LGBT activism and, less so, to pro-life views. That's why, when different venues in the UK cancelled scheduled events with Rev. Franklin Graham, they cited his views on LGBT issues, not his support for President Trump.[11] So, while some people may not listen to our witness because we voted for Trump, even more people will not listen to us because of our moral convictions. That's an obstacle we have to overcome.

What about the claim that evangelical support for Trump in America "has undercut the efforts of countless missionaries who labor in the far fields of the Lord"? Is this as pervasive as *CT* claims? Is their sampling wide-ranging and representative?

I personally interact with a good number of international Christian leaders, and most of them view Trump in a positive light, overall. I also help lead an organization that helps support and oversee scores of missionaries working around the world.[12] I do not believe that most of them would concur with the assessment of *CT*.

I also asked this question on Facebook (where we have almost 600K followers, about half of them from outside the USA), as well as on Twitter (where we have 37K followers). On Facebook, where only two polling choices can be given, I asked, "If you are a Christian living outside America or a missionary working overseas, would you say that evangelical support of Trump has hurt your witness?"[13] The results were overwhelming, with 83 percent saying No and only 17 percent saying Yes.

On Twitter, where I could offer four choices, the answers were (in descending order): Not at all (44 percent); Not sure (22 percent); Not an issue (19 percent); and Definitely (16 percent).[14] So, while the Twitter response was more nuanced, the overall results were similar. In both polls, the *overwhelming majority* disagreed with *CT*'s statement that evangelical support for Trump has undercut the efforts of countless missionaries who labor in the far fields of the Lord."

On Facebook, RJ wrote from Australia, "A Christian voting for the party of sexual immorality, infanticide and Christophobia is a far worse witness!"

Lloyd wrote, "I am a full time missionary to Mozambique, Africa. I have not had any issue of my witness being scrutinized for my support of our President. Being a missionary also allows me to be in the lives of people from all over the world and Trump has been a frequent topic. For the most part, people feel he has been treated unfairly and his policies are liked. I have spoken with people from India, Romania, Australia, France, the Caribbean, South Africa and Brazil. God bless Dr. Brown."

Muroslav opined, "Absolutely not, many Canadians support President Trump and would love to have [a] Man like TRUMP running things in Canada!"

From rural Nigeria, Joanne opined, "International politics is not on the minds of most of the people I interact with."

CA added, "Missionary in West/Central Africa... NOPE. Like 0%. People don't really talk to me about it but I do know some people here who support Trump."

And Yvonne posted, "Although I'm not a missionary I have many friends in various countries that I know through our orphan ministry & our support of native ministers (not American missionaries) Some are Christians some are not- but all like Trump!"

According to Diane, "I live in New Zealand and I am proud of the evangelical support. I wish even more would give support."

Nzinga said, "Like in UK. I voted no. I follow politics through a Christian lens and can relate to the stumbling block Trump's presidency presents for us. For me, provided a sound, logically coherent and biblically consistent argument is put out, I'm all ears. I'm not closed to reason. However, don't get me wrong, I waver occasionally, but the political polarisation is so stark, that the alternative to a Conservative President is unthinkable."

Jonathan (formerly from Australia, now living in the US but part of an international ministry) wrote, "Why is it not a far worse witness to vote for Democrats who: Make the State their god, violating the first commandment. Love abortion, thus violating the commandment against murder. Love confiscatory taxation and wealth redistribution, thus violating the commandment against theft. Foster envy by their attacks on the 'rich' (as long as they are not rich leftists), thus violating the commandment against covetousness. It's also a poor witness to enable them by self-righteously refusing to vote for the only realistic alternative."

And even here in America, there were comments like these, from Richie: "I run an inner-city ministry in the US and we saw 100s come to the Lord in 2019! Hasn't affected us at all."

Others, of course, dissented. Izuchukwu (from somewhere in Europe) said, "Many missionaries outside the US grapple with this problem. You would be shocked."

He added in a separate post,

It is a very pertinent question. I attend an American church in the heart of a European capital. Every sermon every Sunday is as though there was a need for the clergy, all who are American by the way, to thoroughly distance themselves from the image of Christianity emerging from home. That there is even a thought of a concept of an American brand of Christianity is a incredulous by itself. With respect, if you do not venture outside the US very often, it might be difficult to completely understand this problem. And yes, it is a problem. A problem to witness to people who have no idea why a Christian in the US is as protective of their guns as they are of their bibles, or why virtually no one can have a different opinion to that of the president and not be labeled a communist, socialist or traitor. Or how, there is no open exhortation of restraint from the evangelical community when the president 'lashes out' on any TV celeb who draws his ire, giving graphic descriptions of how they have or have not had cosmetic surgery or how ugly they look.

David wrote, "I'm a missionary in Mexico. I feel like since Trump was elected there is more animosity for America and Americans. I've been there 9 years and it changed after the 2016 election. Of course, all of the news reporting in left wing, anti-Trump." (In this case, one wonders if the issue is evangelical support of Trump or Trump's battle with Mexico about building a wall, among other things.)

What, then, are we to make of this? Let me repeat that I believe the bigger challenge we face is the branding of our moral values as hateful and antiquated and bigoted. That's part of our ongoing gospel challenge. I also realize that much of the world media (in particular, in Europe) is quite hostile to Trump and will present him in the most negative way possible, thereby discrediting his supporters as well. And we can never discount international opposition to our witness in some circles because we stand with Israel against her mortal enemies. Ultimately, though, we cannot adjust our morality or our political convictions to accommodate others. As for the specific claims of *CT*'s regarding our international witness, I have to question their assessment.

Either way, however, whether accurate or inaccurate, we must declare our allegiance to Jesus infinitely louder than we declare our allegiance to Trump. And by no means should we defend the president's failings. This certainly does hurt our witness. But again, as I've said time and again, our message must be that "Jesus died for my sins and in return gets my life. The president gets my vote." That is what we must emphasize: Donald Trump is our president, not our Savior, not our role model, not our Lord.

It's up to us, then, to change the narrative and get our message out to the world rather than letting the world or our critics or the media disseminate our message for us. When people want to argue with us about Trump, we must find a way to turn the conversation in the right direction. Trump is not our message. Jesus is.

The Great Evangelical Divide

Having said all this, I have no desire to minimize the growing divide that exists between pro-Trump and anti-Trump evangelicals. Still, I want to do my best to improve the communication, since, for the most part, we are likes ships passing each other in the night, reacting to each other more than responding to each other. Worse still, the dispute over the Galli editorial was played out before a watching world, and it made for a nasty, Christmas-season news cycle.

On Christmas Eve, the Drudge Report, which is read by multiplied tens of millions, featured headlines such as: "Christian mag raises issue of 'unconditional loyalty'";[15] and, "Editor Quits Amid Evangelical Civil War";[16] and, "PAPER: God did not elect Trump, people did . . ."[17] Then, relating more broadly to the Trump era as a whole, there was, "In the age of Trump, it's OK to be (deeply) conflicted."[18]

It's one thing to have an in-house dispute behind closed doors. All families do that. It's another thing to air our dirty laundry for outsiders to see. Yet, both sides believe it's important to make our statements openly and publicly, feeling that if we do not, our integrity is at stake.

Of course, we will always have our differences. And sometimes it's even necessary to divide and separate. Yet in the current evangelical war over Trump, there seems to be little effort for either side to understand the other.

Like it or not, there are fine, genuine Christians on each side of the debate, yet we seem quicker to condemn each other than to communicate with each other. The polarization is growing by the minute, especially as things trickle down on the popular level to the world of social media.

The op-ed pieces by *CT* editor-in-chief Mark Galli and the *CT* president Timothy Dalrymple have triggered a flood of individual and even corporate replies,[19] with each side feeling deeply insulted or misunderstood by the other. The deepening divide between brothers and sisters in Jesus is appalling. In fact, things are now so bad that some on each side are even questioning the salvation of those on the other side, as if, to say it again, your stance on Trump, rather than your stance on Jesus, determined your standing with God.

Unfortunately, previous statements by Galli did not endear him to evangelical Trump supporters, as Dr. Richard Land, senior editor of the *Christian Post*, was quick to point out. Land quoted Galli's remarks shortly after Trump was elected:

> I know hardly anyone, let alone any evangelical Christian who voted for Trump. I describe evangelicals like me as 'elite' evangelicals … and this class of evangelicals has discovered that we have family members so different they seem like aliens in our midst. These other evangelicals often haven't finished college, and if they have jobs (and apparently a lot of them don't), they are blue-collar jobs or entry-level work. They don't write books or give speeches; they don't attend conferences of evangelicals for social justice or evangelicals for immigration reform. They are deeply suspicious of mainstream media. A lot of them voted for Donald Trump.[20]

Land pulled no punches in his response:

> These words are chillingly similar to former President Barack Obama's description of rural voters who "cling to their guns and Bibles," former Secretary of State Hillary Clinton's characterization of Trump supporters as "deplorables," and most recently, Beto O'Rourke's smug threats against biblically orthodox churches and citizens who own a certain type of rifle. These are the words of elitists who look down upon opponents as inferior human beings who need to be controlled, not debated.[21]

So, it was now a battle between the evangelical elites and the evangelical deplorables. The divide deepened yet again.

President Trump also responded to Galli's article, referring to *CT* as "far left,"[22] which is certainly an exaggeration. But then Galli, who describes himself as "center-right,"[23] referred to Trump-supporting evangelicals during a CNN interview as "far right."[24] This is also an exaggeration.

But all this is downright polite when compared to the mudslinging on the ground, where post after post accuses either Trump-proponents or Trump-opponents of being unsaved or unchristian or unspiritual or of the devil. People are lashing out rather than listening, not even attempting to understand each other's concerns. Even my attempts at mediation have been met with derision by many, as if I'm calling for moral compromise or lacking in conviction.

This conflict feels like a battle between the evangelical elites and the evangelical deplorables, with each side claiming the higher moral and spiritual ground. May I at least attempt to mediate some of the dispute by pointing out blind spots on each side?

When evangelical Trump proponents hear criticism of the president from his evangelical opponents, let alone calls for his removal, their immediate response is, "So, you would have preferred Hillary Clinton? Or you would prefer one of the current crop of Democratic candidates? You'd rather have abortion and socialism and LGBT activism?"

But I don't know a single evangelical opponent of the president who wants any of these things. Rather, they're saying, "We can find a better Republican candidate, a better conservative. We can find someone who shares our values without embarrassing us and degrading us as a nation." That distinction is rarely heard by the Trump proponents. But there's a reason for that, and this is what the opponents normally miss.

The proponents do not believe there is another candidate who can defeat the Democrats or, if elected, would have the backbone that Trump has. In their minds, it's either Trump or a radical Democrat, and they cannot fathom how any God-fearing Christian would want the latter. That distinction is rarely heard by the Trump opponents.

When it comes to character issues, the supporters hear the critics saying, "We think Donald Trump is a terrible person who is destroying the nation with his nasty tweets and mean behavior. And to the extent evangelicals support him, we are destroying our witness." In response, the supporters say, "How can you be so shortsighted? We are fighting an existential battle for the soul of our nation, standing at the precipice of freedom or bondage, hope or destruction, for the generations to come. And you're getting upset about a few tweets? Trump is sacrificially helping America on so many fronts, and he's one of the first presidents we've had who keeps his word. In my view, that's real character. The other things are superficial and not worthy of our attention."

But what the supporters fail to hear from the critics is that: 1) We evangelicals have been famous for shouting, "Character counts!" Just look at what some of our top leaders said during the Bill Clinton campaigns. Our mantra was, "We will not and cannot cast our vote for an immoral, ungodly candidate!" Yet now, it seems, we have cast our lot with a man with many, glaring moral deficiencies. Do we not see how hypocritical this makes us look in the eyes of the nation? (See further Chapter Four).

2) The critics are not so upset that the supporters voted for Trump. Rather, the critics are disturbed by the proponents' wholesale support of him and their defense at him at any cost. 3) The critics believe that whatever ground we have gained through Trump's many fine appointees to the courts and other legislative acts, we have lost even more ground through turning hearts against the gospel and allowing our nation as a whole to degenerate into crassness and rudeness and cruelty.

Conversely, what the critics fail to understand is that the supporters are looking at a bigger picture as well, akin to a general fighting off an invading army that was poised to kill our men, rape our women, and sell our children into slavery. (I'm painting a graphic picture to make a point. I'm not saying the Democrats want to do all this.)

Yes, it would be great if that general was a kind man, married once, who was careful in his speech. But we'd rather have a cussing, mean-spirited, nasty general who could defeat the invading army than a really nice general who had lost his fighting skill. And when that cussing, mean-spirited, nasty general keep his promises to us and saves our nation from extermination, we feel a sense of loyalty to him. Which general should have our support?

So, the critics have their reasons for saying, "The man is so immoral!" But the supporters have their reasons for saying, "He's moral where it counts!"

When it comes to the question of whether God put Trump in office – meaning, in an unusual display of divine sovereignty – here too there is a gap in understanding. When the critics hear talk of Trump being appointed by God, what they hear is, "The man now has carte blanche to do whatever he desires. And if you speak against him, you are speaking against God's anointed."

Not only do they see that as a very dangerous concept (unchecked, political power can be very treacherous), but they are absolutely shocked that their evangelical friends and co-workers can view such a godless man to be God's anointed servant who stands above all criticism. In their view, he has a very checkered, misogynist, narcissistic past, and they view him today as an unstable liar who could lead us into an international conflict. "That is the man you call anointed and appointed by God? What has become of you?"

In reality, what the proponents often mean when they speak of God appointing Trump is that: 1) His election seemed so farfetched, from the primaries to the general elections, that this must have been the Lord's sovereign plan. 2) He is such an unlikely candidate and the last one many evangelicals would have supported that we see parallels in the Bible where the Lord used non-believing, pagan kings to do good for God's people. It's a parallel more than a prophecy, and it doesn't mean the president is above criticism.[25]

Unfortunately, as things stand today, there is often more heat than light, especially on the popular level. That's why I appeal once again for evangelical believers on each side of the divide to have some respectful, gracious interaction.

Perhaps we could first ask each other, "So, who is Jesus to you?" And, "What do you believe about the importance of God's Word?" And, "Do you have a burden to reach the world with the gospel?" And, "Do you believe we should be known for our good works and our integrity and our helping the poor and the needy?" In more cases than not, you'll find yourselves in harmony. Next, you can ask, "Are you pro-life? Pro-family?" Again, you'll probably be in essential harmony. Then, "What's your view of President Trump?"

Some sparks might fly. But hopefully, having humanized each other and recognized each other as fellow-children of God and members of the same eternal family, you can at least understand each other if not respect each other. How about we give it a try?

TWELVE

When the Left Demonizes the Right

Can I ask you an honest question? Why is it fine for Christians on the left to be involved politically but not Christians on the right? Why are the "progressive" Christians who mix politics with religion doing something noble while the conservative Christians who do the same are trying to establish a theocracy? Why are the leftwing Christians who supported Obama or Hillary viewed as altruistic and selfless while the rightwing Christians who support Trump are viewed as power hungry white nationalists? Why the double standard? And why the extreme judgmentalism?

Tom Gilson is a colleague and friend, a level-headed, gracious evangelical thinker who spent years working on college campuses. He is quick to see the other side of an argument and is sympathetic to those who differ with him. Yet even Tom could not help but find Katherine Stewart's 2020 book *The Power Worshippers: Inside the Dangerous Rise of Religious Nationalism* to be highly judgmental and unfair.[1] As he wrote on The Stream on May 7, 2020,

> Although the term "Christian nationalism" means very different things to different folks, to Stewart it means Christianity like what you see here on The Stream. It's a book about you and me, not some fringe hothead group. You may not have a theocratic bone in your body, but

if you agree with anything we write here, you're a "Christian nationalist anyway." Your church is "Christian nationalist" if it distributes voter guides, or if there's any teaching on marriage or morality and public policy.[2]

To be sure, the sword always cuts both ways, and in the case of this book, Stewart does document some unhealthy and even dangerous tendencies and goals among some evangelical supporters of Trump. But it is her broader perception of conservative evangelicals that is so disturbing. Yet this perception is typical of the left.

Some of the blurbs posted on the Amazon page[3] for Stewart's book paint a succinct and disturbing picture. This is a small sampling:

- "We are faced with a religious movement that is fundamentally opposed to pluralism and has long-term plans to transform America into a Christian nation. An adept, highly readable and important work." - *Julie Ingersoll, author of BUILDING GOD'S KINGDOM*
- "Katherine Stewart knows from years of investigative reporting why the Trumpvangelicals who use faith to whitewash corruption are a preeminent threat to American democracy. Read *The Power Worshippers* and you will understand why nothing is more important to the health of our common life than challenging the false moral narrative of religious nationalism." - *William J. Barber, II, President of Repairers of the Breach & Co-Chair of the Poor People's Campaign: A National Call for Moral Revival*
- "Stewart provides a comprehensive, chilling look at America's Christian nationalist movement, which she convincingly portrays as a highly organized political coalition that has 'already transformed the political landscape and shaken the foundations upon which lay our democratic norms and institutions.' . . . Her insightful investigation places the power of Christian nationalism into full context." - Publishers Weekly

And what of the radical, leftist agenda of some of those praising the book, such as Rev. William J. Barber, II, a man whom, while accusing Trump of playing the race card, equated "white evangelicalism" with "slaveholder religion"?[4] That's different. That's good. That's to improve America. They're not like these nefarious, power-hungry rightwingers. Do you see my point?

Rob Boston of Americans United for Separation of Church and State said this about Stewart's book: "Employing a sharp investigative eye, Stewart connects the dots between radical theocratic groups that want to create an officially 'Christian nation' and extreme free-market libertarians who despise social programs for the poor, taxes and public institutions. After reading this book, you should be prepared to fight back like nothing less our democracy is at stake – because it is."[5]

Did you catch that? Boston says that "our democracy is at stake" and that "you should be prepared to fight back." But when *we* say something like that, we are fear-mongering power-worshipers. Again, the double standard is glaring. Why is it always the conservative evangelical side that is duplicitous and power hungry? Why are we the bad guys?

When a liberal Democratic candidate preaches in a liberal church, almost no one raises an eyebrow. But when a conservative Republican candidate preaches in a conservative church, there's a cry of, "That's not right! What about separation of church and state?"

When Jesse Jackson ran for president in 1988, he was known as "The Reverend Jesse Jackson," with "reverend" being used as a title of honor and esteem. Yet in that same year, 1988, when Pat Robertson ran for president, he turned in his ordination as reverend, dropping that description from before his name. It would have been used against him as a title of opprobrium and shame. And what was the difference between Jackson and Robertson, other than the color of their skin? Jackson was a liberal; Robertson was a conservative. Enough said.

When a lesbian clergywoman, Bible in hand, calls on parishioners to get out and vote for LGBT causes, she is hailed as a true woman of God representing the best qualities of America. But when a straight clergyman, Bible in hand, calls on parishioners to get out and vote for biblical values, he is bashed as a dangerous fundamentalist representing the worst qualities of America. And again, very few accuse the lesbian clergywoman of violating the separation of church and state while, in contrast, a large chorus of media pundits and political leaders rebuke straight clergyman for crossing the line. To repeat: why the double standard?

Millions of Trump voters genuinely believe that the Democratic Party is lurching so far left that its policies could be a threat to the very fabric of our nation, that socialists like Bernie Sanders and Alexandria Ocasio Cortez have a very different vision for America than our Founders did. Yet when we express this conviction with our votes, that makes us power hungry (white) nationalists who have become intoxicated with our connection to the White House.

And what of the millions of professing Christians who voted for Barack Obama or Hillary Clinton? Were they equally intoxicated, equally biased, equally power hungry? And what of the liberal ministers who had access to President Obama? Were they noble, spiritually minded men and women without ulterior motive, while the conservative ministers who have access to Trump are unspiritual power worshipers who want to impose their religion on America, even by force? Why does a seat at the able only intoxicate the conservatives? Why are only the Bible-believers deemed to be worshipers of power? To quote Gilson again, in the eyes of Stewart,

> the evangelical church is about power. Political power. Stewart sees a young Christian woman at a Trump rally and says, "It's as if I can see the lines of power traced in her eyes." I don't know how one sees that kind of thing, but apparently Stewart does. She sees political power-grabbing everywhere in the evangelical community. Worship for God? Nah. Only power. Political power.
>
> This is the perception: Christianity isn't about life in Christ, it's about packing the Supreme Court and establishing theocracy in America.[6]

He continues:

> Don't think I'm exaggerating. Yes, it's light-years distant from the reality you and I see in our churches. You must realize, I'm very closely involved with the political side of Christian action. (Obviously. I work with *The Stream*.) So if anyone was positioned to see politics usurping

true Christian belief on the scale Stewart supposes, I'd be one of them. I don't see it at all.

Of course we have our social beliefs. For many of us they translate into public policy opinions. They're real beliefs and opinions — but they're secondary. Our primary belief, the main thing, is the centrality of Jesus Christ, the value and urgent necessity of life in him, the beauty of following his way, and the goodness of living in a land that chooses to follow rather than rebel against their heavenly King.

But this isn't about reality, it's about perception. Stewart approvingly quotes former evangelical youth pastor Bradley Onishi, who tells her,

"For the evangelical church right now, membership is not based on color. It is also not really based in religion anymore, either. Your litmus test for religious belonging comes via your political beliefs."[7]

All I can say to Onishi's quote is "wow."

To be sure, in this very book, I decry the increasing politicization of the church. But it is hardly the norm in evangelical circles, and the world Onishi describes is a world I barely know. As Gilson wrote, Stewart "discounts every hint of true worship, every trace of love for God, every Great Commission ministry, everything your church does except seek power." The left, apparently, knows us better than we know ourselves. All our acts of devotion, of worshiping and praying, of sharing our faith and serving our communities, are suspect. They are convenient cloaks for who we really are: power-worshiping nationalists.

As summed up in the blurb for the book:

For too long the Religious Right has masqueraded as a social movement preoccupied with a number of cultural issues, such as abortion and same-sex marriage. But in her deeply reported investigation, Katherine Stewart reveals a disturbing truth: America's Religious Right has evolved into a Christian nationalist movement. It seeks to gain political power and to impose its vision on all of society. It isn't fighting a culture war, it is waging a political war on the norms and institutions of American democracy.[8]

There you have it. Our social concerns are a masquerade. Our spiritual language is a sham. This is about power, period. This is a political war. So says the left.

Ironically, this dangerous judgmentalism often comes in the name of the Lord, since it is the "progressive" Christians who see clearly while the conservative Christians are blind. That's why not a few of the staunchest critics of Trump are liberal clergy. In fact, when evangelical ministers prayed over President Trump in public, Rev. William Barber claimed that it was "a form of theological malpractice that borders on heresy."[9]

Once Again, the New York Times Misunderstands and Mocks Evangelical Christians

Before Katherine Stewart published her book in April 2020, she wrote a series of articles making similar claims. In a year-end op-ed piece for the *New York Times*, she alleged that, "The Christian nationalist movement today is authoritarian, paranoid and patriarchal at its core. They aren't fighting a culture war. They're making a direct attack on democracy itself."[10]

According to Stewart, when evangelicals like Lance Wallnau compare Trump to King Cyrus in the Bible, they are actually wanting Trump to be a king. Indeed, she claimed that "in Mr. Trump, they have found a man who does not merely serve their cause, but also satisfies their craving for a certain kind of political leadership."

Evangelicals, whom she consistently characterized as "Christian nationalists," want a king, not a president. They want someone to impose their views on the nation. They are theocratic, not democratic. That's why Trump is their man.

She wrote,

> I have attended dozens of Christian nationalist conferences and events over the past two years. And while I have heard plenty of comments casting doubt on the more questionable aspects of Mr. Trump's character, the gist of the proceedings almost always comes down to the belief that he is a miracle sent straight from heaven to bring the nation back to the Lord. I have also learned that resistance to Mr. Trump is tantamount to resistance to God.

Let's analyze these claims one at a time, as factually and as dispassionately as possible.

First, as we have previously seen with regard to the Cyrus comparison,[11] those using the analogy did not do so with reference to Trump ruling over the nation like a king. To the contrary, as evangelical Americans, we trace our roots back to those who overthrew British rule. We reject a king over America just as much as we reject any attempt to set up a theocracy where religious leaders rule the land by fiat and force.[12] The Cyrus analogy had to do with the unlikelihood of someone like Trump being raised up by God, just as it was unlikely that God would raise up someone like Cyrus (an idol-worshiping, non-Israelite), to restore the Jewish exiles from Babylon. We recognized that the Lord was raising up Donald Trump, apparently a non-evangelical, non-Christian, to help America and, in particular, to help the Christian cause. It had nothing to do with him reigning as a king.

Second, we evangelicals are not paranoid. We are fighting a very real battle for our liberties. We are standing up for the rights of our children. Even *Time Magazine* published an article on June 29, 2016 titled, "Regular Christians Are No Longer Welcome in American Culture."[13] And already in 2003, David Limbaugh could write his well-documented book, *Persecution: How Liberals Are Waging War Against Christians*.[14] There's a reason that, for many years now, I have been urging fellow-evangelicals to rise up and speak up.[15] (For a fair, academic evaluation of the present situation in America, see George Yancey and David A. Williamson, *So Many Christians, So Few Lions: Is There Christianophobia in the United States?*)[16]

Third, we evangelicals *are* fighting a culture war. We are *not* fighting "democracy itself." To the contrary, we believe the democratic principles of our country are being undermined by radical ideologues who have a very different vision for America. We see a rise in mobocracy, not democracy. We see a push towards socialism, which will destroy the democracy.[17] We see an anti-Constitutional, even anti-American vision from the radical left that is destructive, and we see Trump opposing that.

For good reason Tom Gilson started 2020 writing about, "Leftist Totalitarianism: Your 'Freedom of Conscience' Under State Control."[18] For good reason, Dennis Prager has warned about where the left wants to bring us in 2019.[19] It is the radical left that is attacking Democracy. Evangelicals are trying to protect it.

Fourth, it is downright disingenuous to speak of American evangelicals as "Christian nationalists," with all the ugly connotations such a term stirs up. I don't know a single evangelical leader who would use such a term, nor do I know any who would prefer being labeled as such. (I can only speak of those I know, but I know quite a few.) The truth be told, Stewart could just as well label liberal and "progressive" Christians as "Christian nationalists," since they too speak about what is right for America, they too believe that their candidates would do the best job for America, and they too claim to be following the principles of Jesus.

Fifth, these evangelical leaders are not standing up for a primitive and harmful patriarchy. They are resisting radical feminism,[20] which ultimately hurts women more than anyone. They are pushing back against the "Shout Your Abortion" movement, against the war on the unborn.[21] They are pro-woman and pro-family.

Sixth, virtually all evangelical leaders I know wish that Trump would not call people dogs, that he would not be so nasty and demeaning in his tweets. They like the fact that he fights back. They like the fact that he takes on the media. But they often groan over the way he does it, and I can say with confidence that quite a few evangelical leaders have urged him to reconsider some of his methodology, even if their words fall on deaf ears. But, as one black evangelical said during the primaries (this was quoted to me by a colleague), "I'm not voting for his morality or his spirituality. I'm voting for his constitutionality." Or, as expressed in a tweet from an evangelical Trump supporter: "I support the job President Trump has done as president, but I cringe over 90% of the time when he speaks or tweets."[22]

Seventh, Stewart forgets that most of us voted for Trump because we were voting against Hillary. He was not the first choice for most of us. And yes, given the circumstances, we do believe he was elected with God's help.[23] But since he has been elected, the Hillary-type forces (by which I mean the liberal media, the Democratic Party, and the leftist agenda) have only become more extreme. More anti-Christian. More anti-democracy. More anti-freedom.

Should we now hope that Trump is removed so that these forces come to power? And would the resistance to Mike Pence be any less intense?[24] In reality, Stewart has things upside down, since it can easily be argued that it is really the radical left that wants to take over the nation and rob us of our liberties. And evangelicals see Trump, with all his massive flaws and blemishes, as fighting against this hostile takeover. And for that we are glad. What's so unchristian about that?

Are (White) Evangelicals Responsible for the Spread of COVID-19 in America?

But Stewart had more to say about these dangerous evangelicals (in particular, white evangelicals), actually blaming them (us!) for the spread of the coronavirus in America.[25] But this is not the first time that a national tragedy occurred and Christians were scapegoated and blamed. Remember Nero blaming the Christians for the burning of Rome? On March 27, 2020, it was Stewart with an op-ed column in the *New York Times* blaming evangelicals for the spread of a deadly disease. As proclaimed in the bold, provocative, and utterly irresponsible *Times* headline: "The Road to Coronavirus Hell Was Paved by Evangelicals." Yes, "Trump's response to the pandemic has been haunted by the science denialism of his ultraconservative religious allies."

According to Stewart, "Donald Trump rose to power with the determined assistance of a movement that denies science, bashes government and prioritized loyalty over professional expertise. In the current crisis, we are all reaping what that movement has sown." At least she makes herself clear.

She quotes prominent evangelical leaders (one of whom is Hispanic, for the record) who downplayed the danger of holding public gatherings to the point of ridiculing pastors who chose to follow the government's guidelines. (My own stance, especially in March and April, was quite the opposite, encouraging pastors to comply out of love for their neighbors as well as out of wisdom.)[26]

Stewart also noted that some evangelical leaders in high places in the government had scorned the danger of the virus, meaning in general, outside of church settings. But where was her evidence that these pastors and leaders influenced Trump's policy decisions? What proof did she have? To be generous, we could call it specious. To be precise, we could say she had none. A court of law would not even find her reasoning worthy of being called circumstantial.

Specifically, Stewart argued that Trump commonly differed with the experts during his press briefings on the virus. But where was her proof that this was because of outside religious influences rather than Trump simply following his gut? (She acknowledged that he does, in fact, trust his gut.) She also failed to consider that, for the moment, these were just words, while his policy decisions closely followed the respected medical leaders.

She argued that Trump spoke of his hope that churches would be full again on Easter. But how does this prove that he was listening to evangelical voices in terms of science-based decisions? How was this different from his talk about getting businesses back open around that time as well? Why wasn't this simply Trump seeking to instill hope? (And, in retrospect, we can see that he did not, in fact, counsel churches to gather on Easter Sunday.) Stewart also failed to name the many leading evangelical pastors who are close to Trump and who have fully complied with his guidelines. Is that because this didn't fit her narrative?

As for Trump's actions, it is true that, in the earliest days, he seemed to downplay the danger of the virus when speaking publicly. At the same time, he was combating the hysteria of the media, which would have us believe that 15 millions Americans could die of the disease. Plus, many media outlets and liberal politicians also downplayed the potential danger of the virus.[27]

But what of his actions? He enacted the China travel ban in January, to the jeers of some of the left, with former Vice President Biden calling it "xenophobia." As Tom Pappert pointed out on the *National File* on March 12, "While Democrats in March attack President Donald Trump for not doing enough to end the coronavirus epidemic, the same Democrats were bashing the president's decision to ban travel from China in January.

"In January, President Trump banned all foreign nationals who were in China during the time of the coronavirus outbreak from entering the United States. Many pundits and health experts have since credited this decision with helping to slow the coronavirus pandemic on American shores." To quote Biden directly, "This is no time for Donald Trump's record of hysteria and xenophobia, hysterical xenophobia, to uh, and fear mongering."[28] Yet according to Dr. Anthony Fauci, this ban made a real difference in saving lives.[29] Does Stewart mention that? Of course, she does not. That would contradict her narrative.

It is true that a recent Pew Research poll found that, "Most white evangelicals don't think COVID-19 poses a major threat to Americans' health."[30] But again, what does that have to do with life and death policy decisions that the president is making? Where were the evangelical ministers standing with him at his daily press briefings on the virus? They were not there because they do not establish policy on the virus.

And what of the large number of leading scientists who themselves are conservative Christians, like Katherine Hayhoe? According to the *Washington Post*, she is "both an evangelical Christian and a climate scientist" – in fact, a "top climate scientist."[31] And she is just one among countless top scientists who are committed Christians, and some of them are close to the president.

The bottom line is that there is virtually no factual support for the misleading and even dangerous *Times* headline. And Stewart has no support whatsoever that science-denying evangelicals are influencing the president's decisions. To the contrary, wherever his gut and his optimism might lead, it appears that he is following scientific guidelines in order to save as many lives as possible.

If Stewart had focused her article on the cavalier attitudes on a handful of Christian leaders, I would have added my hearty "Amen," having written and spoken similar things as well. But her article painted a very false picture, recklessly scapegoating evangelical Christians in the process. And what she did in her article, she does in her book, demonizing evangelical supporters of Trump.

Ironically, with critics of Trump warning us that evangelical leaders are now engaging in fear-based politics, as we warn our constituents of the imminent demise of America if we do not stand up for what is right and vote accordingly, the left is doing exactly the same thing. The main difference, according to Stewart, is that *we*, meaning conservative evangelicals, are the danger, all the more now as we allegedly seek to take over the nation and install Trump as king.

In light of this fear-mongering on the left, along with accusations of fear-mongering on the right, I'd like to make a proposal. How about we take one another at our word? How about we address the issues rather than demonize each other? How about we state clearly what our objectives and goals are, without prejudging each other's motives? There's enough that divides us that there's no need for us to exaggerate those differences. The chasm already is gaping, long, and wide. There's no reason to make it any deeper by publishing falsehoods about each other and claiming nefarious secret goals. The differences between the Democratic and Republican platforms are more than sufficient to get each other's blood boiling. So, to repeat: Let's make the issues the issues. The judgmentalism (on both sides) must stop.

THIRTEEN

What If Hillary Had Been Elected?

On December 22, 2019, I tweeted,

> A two-word answer to all those who still ask, How could you as a
> Christian vote for Trump?
> Hillary Clinton.[1]

That, in short, is why many evangelicals voted for Donald Trump:
we were voting against Hillary Clinton, truly believing that her presidency would spell disaster for the nation. But were our concerns valid?
Perhaps we were like Chicken Little, warning America that the sky was
falling when it really wasn't at all. If so, this would not be the first time
this has happened in our history.

In his book, *Why Liberals Win the Culture Wars (Even When They
Lose Elections): The Battles That Define America from Jefferson's Heresies to
Gay Marriage*, American history professor Stephen Prothero traces back
America's culture wars to the early days of our republic in the late
1790s,[2] claiming that,

> American politics has always been a staging ground for moral and
> religious conflicts. The culture wars did not begin in the 1960s or
> 1970s, when most books on this topic open. They did not begin in the

1920s, as some dissenters claim. They began in the birth pangs of the republic itself. More than two centuries before Barack Obama was accused of being a covert Muslim, Thomas Jefferson was said to be a secret "believer in the alcoran [Quran]."[3]

To be sure, accusations flared in both directions as John Adams and Thomas Jefferson fought for the presidency. As Prothero noted, "The Federalist *Gazette of the United States* called Jeffersonians 'the very *refuse* and *filth* of society' while the Democratic-Republican *Philadelphia Aurora* judged Adams 'blind, bald, crippled, toothless.'"[4] But it was Jefferson's conservative Christian opposers who issued dire warnings of what would happen if a rank infidel like Jefferson was elected president.[5] And the warnings were applied to Jefferson's entire political party, the Democratic-Republicans.

Two years after Adams was elected president in 1796, "Rev. Timothy Dwight, Yale's president and a staunch Federalist, was still preaching a politics of fear and anxiety. Should the 'enemies of Christ' (the Democratic-Republicans) ever come to power, he prophesied, America could well see the end of both religion and family."[6] These were his exact words:

> We may see the Bible cast into a bonfire, . . . our children, either wheedled or terrified, uniting in the mob, chanting mockeries against God . . . our wives and daughters the victims of legal prostitution; soberly dishonoured; speciously polluted; the outcasts of delicacy and virtue, and the lothing of God and man.[7]

One publication, *The Connecticut Courant* (August 18, 1800), questioned "whether Mr. Jefferson believes in the heathen mythology or, in the alcoran [Quran]; whether he is a Jew or a Christian; whether he believes in one God, or in many; or in none at all."[8] Could America survive with such a man in the White House? Indeed, "Some New England ministers also saw a conspiracy afoot between Jeffersonians and the Order of Illuminati, a secret society of freethinkers that had supposedly masterminded the French Revolution and was now dedicated to creating a post-Christian 'New World Order.'"[9] Does this sound familiar?

Some evangelical leaders are sounding similar warnings today – including warnings against an insidious New World Order (for more on this, see Chapter Fourteen). But once again, I ask: Are these warnings accurate? Or are we crying wolf yet again, except that in our case, every time we cry wolf, we believe it to be true?

Prothero writes:

"Should the infidel Jefferson be elected to the Presidency," wrote an alarmist in *The Hudson Bee*, "the *seal of death* is that moment set on our holy religion, our churches will be prostrated, and some infamous prostitute, under the title of the Goddess of Reason, will preside in the Sanctuaries now devoted to the worship of the Most High." Outside the churches, "murder, robbery, rape, adultery, and incest will all be openly taught and practiced," prophesied *The Connecticut Courant*. The American people, a "Christian Federalist" from Delaware added, would become "more ferocious than savages, more bloody than tygers, more impious than demons."[10]

And what actually happened after Jefferson was elected in a tightly fought battle? He was reelected in a landslide and died an American hero. There was no "seal of death" on the Christian faith and the "Goddess of Reason" did not displace "the worship of the Most High." To the contrary, during Jefferson's first term in office the Second Great Awakening erupted, to the point that, in many ways, America was *more Christian* after Jefferson's terms in office than before.

And what of the dire warnings of Yale president Timothy Dwight, cited above? According to Christianity.com,

Yale University experienced a revival of Biblical Christianity under President Timothy Dwight, Jonathan Edwards' grandson. Christianity was almost nonexistent then at Yale, the campus church almost extinct. For four years Dwight preached a series of weekly sermons on Christian belief; when he finished the series, he started over again. Finally, in 1801, after seven years of preaching, revival came to Yale. At least half of the student body was converted to Christianity under Dwight's Presidency. One college tutor wrote home to his mom, "Yale College is a little temple; prayer and praise seem to be the delight of the greater part of the students while those who are still unfeeling are awed with respectful silence."[11]

Perhaps it would be the same today? Perhaps, rather than a Hillary Clinton (or, Bernie Sanders, or Elizabeth Warren, or Pete Buttigieg, or Joe Biden) presidency destroying America it would actually spark revival and awakening? Perhaps we are getting all worked up over nothing? Worst still, perhaps we are fighting a losing battle?

According to Prothero, "The 'big idea' behind modern conservatism is this: a form of culture is passing away and it is worth fighting to revive it. What activates this idea, transforming it into action, is a feeling. This feeling is akin to nostalgia, but it runs deeper and is more fierce."[12] But, "in the end the arc of our culture wars bends toward more liberty, not less. As each of our cultural battles comes to an end, we are left with a more inclusive country, with an understanding of 'we the people' that reflects more of 'us.'"[13]

Without a doubt, we can exaggerate the significance of an election, as if the fate of the nation was being determined every four years. And how many times have we heard in recent years, "This is the most important election of our lifetime," only to hear that same mantra again, four years later? One of my evangelical colleagues actually said to me recently, "I believe that this will be true for every election until Jesus returns. Each one will be more important than the last."

Learning from the Lessons of the Past

But is this true? Is there nothing we can learn from the lessons of the past? And isn't Prothero right in terms of the consistent direction of America, namely, *away* from conservative, Christian narrowness and *towards* a more "inclusive" society? Prothero points out how Catholics and Mormons and Jews were once looked at with suspicion as outsiders, if not excluded from certain functions in our society, but now they serve in our government, with some in the Senate or Supreme Court. It's the same with gays and lesbians and others. To cite Prothero again,

as sociologist Nathan Glazer put it, "We are all multiculturalists now." Most high school students remain religiously and culturally illiterate, and today's college students look very much like the young people Allan Bloom described roughly three decades ago in *The Closing of the American Mind*. Pop culture, especially, has gone over to the liberal side. Movies today make the sort of entertainment decried by the Moral Majority look like *It's a Wonderful Life*. *Modern Family*, a sitcom featuring a gay couple and celebrating the diversity of American families, won five straight Emmy awards for best comedy series. The HBO hit *Girls* is clothing optional. And transgender stars now grace the cover of *Entertainment Weekly*. Reagan may have been a tax revolutionary, but when it comes to cultural politics the Reagan Revolution is a misnomer. "The Left . . . was never in danger of losing the so-called culture wars," writes historian James Livingston. "At the end of the twentieth century . . . the United States was much less conservative than it had been in 1975." And American culture is much less conservative now than it was in 1999.[14]

Ironically, however, Prothero has just underscored the very arguments *for* opposing leftist candidates. They *are* undermining the moral foundations of our nation. They *are* eroding Christian, family values. They *are* doing serious, lasting damage to our country. And so we are *not* like Chicken Little crying out "the sky is falling" when it is not. The sky *is* falling. We are not like the boy crying wolf when no wolf is around. The wolves are everywhere, spiritually and morally speaking, and their vision for America is very different than ours. We either wake up and speak up and stand up, or we apologize to our children and our grandchildren.

Today is not like the days when Thomas Jefferson was running for president. There was no such thing as the sexual revolution in his day. There were no radical feminists. There was no "shout your abortion" movement. Twelve-year-old children were not exchanging naked images of themselves. The idea of "gay marriage" would have been inconceivable, let alone the idea of a homosexual man and his "husband" potentially serving as President and First Gentleman.

Back in 1800, the population of America was a little over five million.[15] Yet, for every single person living in America in 1800, we have slaughtered *thirteen* unborn babies since 1973 – a total of sixty-five million and counting. You better believe our dire warnings have basis.

Jefferson's generation didn't have to deal with the American Library Association recommending Drag Queens reading to toddlers. Or fifteen-year-old boys sharing school locker rooms with fifteen-year-old girls. Or nineteen-year-old kids getting sex-change surgery. Or business owners being prosecuted and fined for declining to participate in gay "wedding" ceremonies. Or teachers being forbidden to mention God in their classrooms. Or pastors being disciplined for refusing to affirm homosexuality. Or states banning counselors from helping someone with unwanted same-sex attractions.

Perhaps Prothero is right in stating that America is heading in one direction – a less conservative one. But if he is right, woe be to our nation. The left is lurching more ominously left by the day, to the point that even former President Barack Obama recently issued a warning to his party. Speaking to a group of wealthy Democratic donors in November, 2019, he said, "Even as we push the envelope and we are bold in our vision we also have to be rooted in reality. The average American doesn't think we have to completely tear down the system and remake it."[16] And he argued that the country is "less revolutionary than it is interested in improvement."[17]

What, then, if one of these "revolutionary" Democrats becomes president? What if he or she pushes the envelope even further? What if radical socialism cripples our economy, resulting in great hardship for millions? What if abortion becomes even more entrenched? What if the family unit becomes even more distorted? What if the attack on our religious freedoms becomes even more pronounced? What then?

It is certainly possible that America's collapse will lead to America's recovery, and that it is only by hitting rock bottom that we will fall to our knees in repentance, leading to revival and awakening. But, as I suggested earlier, to be complicit with this intentionally is akin to allowing the cancer to spread in your body unchecked so your healing will be more miraculous. Not only so, but with our moral standards and our family values so deeply eroded, who will set examples for the children raised in broken homes? For the kids for whom porn is the norm? For little ones who have been raised without clear gender roles or distinctions? How easy will it be to rebuild?

To be perfectly clear, I am not throwing my hands up in despair, nor am I putting my trust in the government to restrain evil. As I have written and preached for decades, the key to America's health is the state of the church. To quote from my 1993 book *It's Time to Rock the Boat*, "The Church of America must come to a difficult conclusion. We must face the cold, hard facts. *It's too late for our nation!* It's too late for moral reform; too late for a social transformation; too late for a return to the 'good old days'—unless masses of sinners get saved. Otherwise there is no hope."[18]

Indeed,

For years we put our trust in the government. We hoped that the President would hold the line, that the right appointees to the Supreme Court would help stem the flood of unrighteousness, that a politically active church would turn our nation back. But we have been misled! *We have put our confidence in the flesh.* In our fight for religious rights we have subtly confessed, "In man do we trust." But government cannot save! Only Jesus can save. And He must be our message.[19]

But, I also added, we do not disengage from the political system entirely.

Oh yes, we *should* exercise our rights and vote. We *should* meet with our children's educators and write to our elected officials. We *should* pray for mercy on our nation, although the best we can pray now is the prayer of Habakkuk 3:2: "In wrath remember mercy."

How can we *not* do these things? How can we *not* speak out against the aggressive homosexual agenda? How can we *not* vote for candidates who will fight for the truth? If it's right to *pray* for the salvation of elected officials once they are in office why not *vote* for godly candidates to get into office? (See 1 Timothy 2:1-4.) We are not called to roll over and die. We must stand firm for what is right.

But here is where so many of us have missed it. We cannot expect radical feminists, militant pro-abortionists, hate-filled racists, committed secular humanists, or degraded sexual perverts to respond to our call for morality. . . . It will never happen. Our only hope, and the only hope of our nation, is for these ungodly sinners to become born anew. They need a change of heart. Their minds are foregone and depraved.[20]

So, it is a matter of both-and, as long we keep our priorities right: first, getting our own house in order and being the people God has called us to be; second, voting and getting involved in the political process. The stakes are very high. Still, there is reason for hope in the midst of the moral decline: there is a pushback taking place.

Prothero had written that "the most important reason [liberals] win is because their opponents attach themselves to lost causes. In culture wars from 1800 to today, conservatives picked fights they were already losing."[21] But is this is always true? More importantly, *must* this always be true?

When it comes to the fight against slavery, it was strong Bible believers who led the battle.[22] So, even though these committed, abolitionist Christians were fighting other, committed Christians, many of whom saw slavery as justifiable in God's sight, it was Bible-based conviction that turned the tide, ultimately turning the hearts of many Americans. And even though this battle was clearly not one of "conservative vs. liberal" in the more traditional sense of the words, it was a culture war in the deepest sense, and in the end, biblical convictions prevailed.

Someone might protest, "Yes, that's true, but slavery was here from the start, and the abolitionist movement changed the status quo. When was a major societal change implemented, only to be reversed? And just look at what happens when conservatives try to legislate their views, as in the Prohibition era. It backfires terribly."

Learning from the Pro-life Movement

There is certainly some truth to these observations, but again, none of this is fixed and inevitable. Consider the pro-life movement in America. Writing for the *National Review* on January 18, 2019, two days before the annual March for Life, Prof. Michael J. New observed that, while the pro-life cause in America might not be making all the progress we desired, pro-lifers have made very important progress in other ways. One key metric of pro-life progress is the declining abortion rate. The U.S. abortion rate has been falling consistently since 1980. It has fallen during both Republican and Democratic presidential administrations. It has also fallen during both times of recession and times of economic prosperity. Data from the Guttmacher Institute show that the U.S. abortion rate fell by more than 50 percent between 1980 and 2014. Furthermore, the most recent data indicate the abortion rate is currently lower than what it was in 1973 — the year Roe v. Wade was decided.

The long-term decline in the U.S. abortion rate is certainly an important trend that deserves more attention. However, I would argue that an even more important metric of pro-life progress is the significant and durable increase in the percentage of unintended pregnancies carried to term. In 1981, 54 percent of unintended pregnancies resulted in an abortion. By 2011 that figure had fallen to 42 percent. Additionally, preliminary analysis of more recent data indicates that percentage has continued to fall during the past several years.

It is true that declining birth rates in America also contribute to lower abortion rates, as do women terminating their pregnancies at home via abortion pills.[23] Nonetheless, as New pointed out,

As pro-lifers gather in Washington, D.C., on Friday for this year's March for Life, we should take heart. Forty-six years of praying, marching, and engaging in other efforts to build a culture of life have borne fruit. We have made progress politically and legislatively. We have succeeded in changing hearts and minds. Most important, unborn lives continue to be saved because of our efforts. It is true that progress has not come as fast as many of us had hoped. However, it is indisputable that progress is being made. And we should have every confidence that if we stay the course, victory will someday be ours.[24]

Good friends of mine are involved in the pro-life movement in North Carolina and beyond, and the results they are getting are wonderful. Many lives have been saved and many families have been preserved![25] And this is all through hands-on, compassion-based, prayerful activism. On the legislative side, on May 7, 2019, Elle.com reported with concern, "Across the country, restrictive abortion bills continue to be introduced at the state level, all while President Trump is spouting anti-abortion rhetoric and nominating conservative, anti-choice judges. One type of bill in particular, the 'fetal heartbeat' bill, comes back in the news time and again as various legislatures try their hand at passing the law."[26]

This is just one legislative effort among many, leading to the biggest question of all: What happens if Roe v. Wade is overturned? We can't predict the future, but CNN analyst Jeffrey Toobin has predicted that it will, in fact, be overturned, becoming more certain from 2018 to 2019.

Looking back at his predictions about the overturning of Roe v. Wade first spoken in June, 2018, he said this to Anderson Cooper in May, 2019, with specific reference to pro-life laws in Alabama:

I -- for better or worse, I think I was right. I mean, look, Donald Trump said in the third debate with Hillary Clinton, if I get two or more appointments to the Supreme Court, automatically, that's the word he used, automatically Roe v. Wade will be overturned, and I think the president was exactly right.

Roe v. Wade is gone and every woman in Alabama who gets pregnant is going to be forced to give birth soon, and that's going to be true in Alabama. It's going to be true in Missouri. It's going to be true probably in Georgia, and that's what the law is because that's what the presidential election was about in part last time.[27]

Even if Roe v. Wade is not overturned and legalized abortion is not eradicated (I pray both *will* take place), it's clear that there has been a major pushback against this baby-killing spirit in America, and it has been led by conservative Christians. Just as importantly, countless thousands of lives have been saved. This is nothing to snivel at.

There are even signs that LGBTQ+ activists have overplayed their hand, with the acronym ever growing with no end in sight. For example, a June 24, 2019 headline in *USA Today* announced, "The young are regarded as the most tolerant generation. That's why results of this

LGBTQ survey are 'alarming'."[28] The article, by Susan Harris, noted that,

> Young people are growing less tolerant of LGBTQ individuals, a jarring turn for a generation traditionally considered embracing and open, a survey released Monday shows.
>
> The number of Americans 18 to 34 who are comfortable interacting with LGBTQ people slipped from 53% in 2017 to 45% in 2018 – the only age group to show a decline, according to the annual Accelerating Acceptance report. And that is down from 63% in 2016.
>
> Driving the dilution of acceptance are young women whose overall comfort levels plunged from 64% in 2017 to 52% in 2018, says the survey conducted by The Harris Poll on behalf of LGBTQ advocacy group GLAAD.[29]

How many cultural pundits saw this coming?[30]

Not only so, but some states are pushing back against the growing trend of drag queens reading to toddlers,[31] other states are pushing back against biological male students who identify as female competing against biological females,[32] still other states are pushing back against minors having sex-change surgery,[33] and still other states are pushing back against bans on counseling individuals with unwanted same-sex attractions or gender identity struggles. Shall I also mention the surge in national prayer gatherings and repentance gatherings? And shall I cite some of the major, Supreme Court rulings that have gone in our favor?

Let's not forget that Trump, at least for now, has pushed back against the onerous Johnson Amendment.[34] He has also declared that there's nothing stopping organized public prayer in schools.[35] In keeping with this, Secretary of Education Betsy DeVos wrote on January 20, 2020:

> There's a reason why the First Amendment comes first. Our country was founded upon the "first freedoms" it protects. The freedom to express ourselves — through speech, through the press, through assembly, through petition and through faith — defines what it means to be American.
>
> And no American forfeits these freedoms — including the right to

pray — to anyone or in any place, especially in public schools. The notion of "separation of church and state" is not an invitation for government to separate people from their faith.

Yet, too many students and too many teachers are separated from their faith while they are in school.[36]

She then outlined the challenges faced by students of faith today, declaring,

Thanks to President Donald Trump's leadership, we are adhering to the Constitution, which protects the people's right to pray in their houses of worship, in their homes and everywhere else — including in public schools. The Elementary and Secondary Education Act was amended in 2002 to ensure that taxpayer-supported schools are following the law when it comes to constitutionally protected prayer in public schools. Under the law, the Department of Education is to issue guidance every two years for states and local communities concerning every student's and every teacher's right to pray in public schools.[37]

Obviously, none of us know for sure what would have happened had Hillary Clinton been elected, but we can be almost certain that: 1) she would have nominated pro-abortion, pro-LGBT liberals to the Supreme Court and other federal courts; 2) she would have kept in place President Obama's aggressive LGBT-activist policies in our children's schools; 3) she would have strengthened Planned Parenthood; 4) her Justice Department and Attorney General would not have sided with conservative Christians in legal disputes.

In short, America today is very different than it was in the days of Thomas Jefferson, and while some of the change is very positive (no slavery; much less racism; the improved status of women and minorities, among other things), much of it is very negative. That means that there *is* substance to our warnings and concerns, and the vote for Trump in 2016 *was* very important. It also means that the 2020 elections will be just as important, if not even more so.

Ultimately, whether we win this round of the culture wars or not, our only choice is to hold our ground as followers of Jesus. To capitulate is to surrender and to seal America's moral, spiritual, and cultural collapse for a generation or more.

God forbid that the salt of the earth and the light of the world – you and me – would even contemplate such a scenario. God forbid that we who are overcomers and more than conquerors in Jesus would ever embrace defeat. And while we understand that the ultimate battle is fought in the prayer closet far more than in the voting booth, we will continue to push back with our votes as well as with our prayers.

FOURTEEN

Trump, the 'New World Order,' and Israel

I have to admit it. I've always been a little skeptical when I've heard people talk about the coming "new world order." In my view, it was something to be parodied, as when a number of professional wrestlers, led by Hulk Hogan, dubbed themselves the nWo (New World Order).[1] A 2013 article in the *New York Magazine* explains it like this:

> The New World Order is not so much a single plot as a way of reading history. At its most basic level: A cabal, working in secret as well as through official-seeming, aboveground means, seeks to establish an all-powerful, possibly Luciferian, one-world government. Suspicions surrounding a shadow Establishment date back at least to the 1700s, with the birth of the Freemasons and the Illuminati. But it was the past century's global wars, political realignments, and media innovations that gave new purchase to this age-old paranoia. In the modern version, the New World Order hides in plain sight, a Mad Libs–style metastory about how the free people of the West have begun to willingly, blindly surrender ourselves to our coming totalitarian overlords. What they want to do to us is never exactly clear —the anxiety tends to be more about the "new" part than the "order" part.[2]

It's the Illuminati. Or the Masons. Or the Jews. (More specifically, the Rothschilds.)[3] They are secretly conspiring to take over the world.

Others, however, have used the term in a more circumspect way, including President George H. W. Bush. As summarized on Wikipedia:

The term "new world order" has been used to refer to any new period of history evidencing a dramatic change in world political thought and the balance of power. Despite various interpretations of this term, it is primarily associated with the ideological notion of world governance only in the sense of new collective efforts to identify, understand, or address worldwide problems that go beyond the capacity of individual nation-states to solve.

So, in this sense, it is not so Luciferian and threatening – at least at first glance. Wikipedia continues:

The phrase "new world order" or similar language was used in the period toward the end of the First World War in relation to Woodrow Wilson's vision for international peace; Wilson called for a League of Nations to prevent aggression and conflict. The phrase was used sparingly at the end of World War II when describing the plans for the United Nations and the Bretton Woods system partly because of its negative associations with the failed League of Nations. However, many commentators have applied the term retroactively to the order put in place by the World War II victors as a "new world order."

The most widely discussed application of the phrase of recent times came at the end of the Cold War. Presidents Mikhail Gorbachev and George H. W. Bush used the term to try to define the nature of the post-Cold War era and the spirit of great power cooperation that they hoped might materialize. Gorbachev's initial formulation was wide-ranging and idealistic, but his ability to press for it was severely limited by the internal crisis of the Soviet system. In comparison, Bush's vision was not less circumscribed: "A hundred generations have searched for this elusive path to peace, while a thousand wars raged across the span of human endeavor. Today that new world is struggling to be born, a world quite different from the one we've known". However, given the new unipolar status of the United States,

Bush's vision was realistic in saying that "there is no substitute for American leadership". The Gulf War of 1991 was regarded as the first test of the new world order: "Now, we can see a new world coming into view. A world in which there is the very real prospect of a new world order. [...] The Gulf war put this new world to its first test".[4]

Bush's speech actually became known as his "New World Order Speech."[5] Perhaps there is something to this after all?

Trump vs. the "New World Order"

Writing on Facebook on March 14, 2016, pastor and revivalist Rodney Howard-Browne explained why he was endorsing Donald Trump for president. (Note that Howard-Browne and his wife Adonica were born and raised in South Africa before moving to America decades ago.) He wrote:

> Coming from outside America (and having become citizens of the USA) we see things a little differently - we see it from a global perspective - from what is happening globally. We know that the Bible tells us that the devil's end-time plan is a one-world religion, one-world money system, and one-world government - a "new world order" (NWO). This is a plan that threatens every freedom we have and hold dear.
> Christianity and the Bible is a threat to this global plan. So is anyone who thinks for themselves. The American Constitution - the document that made America the great nation it is - stands in the way of this global agenda. This is why it has been under attack - from our own president, and others, on down. We realize that it is the New World Order's Agenda to destroy the United States.

And why support Donald Trump? For Howard-Browne, none of the Democratic candidates were viable and, in his view, all the Republican candidates, other than Trump, had major political weaknesses. As for Trump, Howard-Browne claimed,

A mark of a person's standing is who backs them and who attacks them. The New World Order and the establishment are spending tens of millions to take him down. When the Pope attacks him, plus two former Mexican Presidents and other world leaders - then that tells me he is a threat to the New World Order and the One World Government. When the world's financial elite met in Davos, Switzerland, and said they are afraid of Trump - I said that's good enough for me.

Trump is bad news to the New World Order and the One World Government, spoken about by George Bush (Snr) in his "1000 points of light" speech.

Trump is good news to American Sovereignty.[6]

In keeping with this mindset, a video posted by The Jim Bakker Show on July 4, 2019 was titled, "We Are In A Last Minute Reprieve - Rodney Howard Browne on The Jim Bakker Show."[7] In the video, Bakker points out that "Glenn Beck says that if Trump doesn't win [meaning, in 2020], we are officially at the end of this country as we know it."[8] Howard-Browne says this in response: "When I saw the [2016] candidates lined up and I saw [Trump], the Lord said, 'My hand is on him. I'm going to use him like a wrecking ball, and he's going to win.' And everybody said I was crazy."[9]

He continued, "We are in the final hour now - the final grains of sand are slipping through the hour glass. We stand on the brink of a one-world government, one-world religion, one-world money system, and the rise of the antichrist.

"I will say that a Trump presidency will give us a stay of execution, only."[10]

To be candid, given my skepticism about the New World Order, I wasn't sure what to make of this back in 2016. (This was also a time when I was strongly opposed to Trump being the Republican candidate.) Still, I wondered how much of it could be true, even if claims of a one-world government were exaggerated. Now, writing in 2020, it is hard to deny that there was something to Howard-Browne's claim.[11]

A May 19, 2019 article in *PCMD News* noted that, "German chancellor Angela Merkel has admitted that the New World Order is 'under threat' due to the rise of President Trump and the trend of Trump-supporting populist leaders winning elections around the world in the past year." Yes, "The German leader slammed the rejection of open borders and globalism, and poured scorn on the patriotic movement currently sweeping across Europe, the U.S, Brazil, Australia and other parts of the world."[12]

But this is not only the opinion of Angela Merkel. On December 27, 2018, *Foreign Policy* posted a special Year in Review article titled, "Trump's War on the World Order." According to Colum Lynch, who introduced the article, "From his earliest days on the campaign trail, U.S. President Donald Trump made clear his disdain for the international organizations that have regulated trade, promoted human rights, and advanced international peace since the end of World War II."

Lynch continued, "Some of the people Trump surrounded himself with after the election pushed back on his isolationist tendencies, including Defense Secretary James Mattis, Secretary of State Rex Tillerson, and National Security Advisor H.R. McMaster. But those officials are all gone or on their way out now, replaced by people who share the president's skepticism for these organizations . . . ."[13]

Lynch then listed the five most relevant *Foreign Policy* articles from 2018:

1. Stewart Patrick, "The World Order Is Starting to Crack" (July 25)
2. James Kirchick, "Trump Wants to Destroy the World Order. So What?
3. (July 26)
4. James Traub, "RIP the Trans-Atlantic Alliance, 1945-2018" (May 11)
5. Quinn Slobodian, "You Live in Robert Lighthizer's World Now" (August 6)
6. Robbie Graner and Colum Lynch, "Trump Stealthily Seeks to Choke Off Funding to U.N. Programs" (October 2)

Now, *Foreign Policy* is a respected, left-leaning publication (it endorsed Hillary Clinton for president in 2016) rather than an extremist, conspiratorial rag. Yet it freely speaks of the "World Order" in terms that are not that far from Howard-Browne's "New World Order." Similarly, but coming from a staunchly conservative perspective, Patrick Buchanan asked on March 13, 2020, "Will the Coronavirus Kill the New World Order?" Specifically, he noted, "It may one day be said that the coronavirus delivered the deathblow to the New World Order, to a half-century of globalization, and to the era of interdependence of the world's great nations."[14] How interesting!

But my purpose here is not to focus on the reality of the "New World Order," and I have no desire to indulge in conspiracy theories about it. (As I noted at the outset of this chapter, I am quite skeptical of such theories.) My purpose, instead, is to give a broader perspective as to why many evangelical Christians support Trump despite his very unchristian ways. It is because they believe there is a dangerous globalism afoot and that Donald Trump is the best man to fight it.[15]

For Such a Time As This?

Put in that context – the context of Trump combating a dangerous, worldwide trend – should we be as concerned about his juvenile tweets? Or his insulting comments at campaign rallies? Or his exaggerations and misrepresentations? After all, if he is successfully fighting a global, ideological war, doesn't that greatly outweigh his other faults? This is not to minimize his faults or the negative fruit of his faults. It is simply to put Trump's strengths and weaknesses into a larger global context.

Since Patrick Buchanan mentioned the coronavirus, let me use that as an example. Let's say that, God forbid, the virus became so severe that it threatened the lives of 50 million Americans. And let's say that our government had to decide between two famous specialists who would lead the war against this deadly disease. One of the specialists was famed for his personal kindness, his strong marriage, and the respect with which he treated his peers. Yet, when it came to effectively treating a virus of this kind, he had a very poor track record. The other specialist was married four times and was infamous for his nasty tongue and prideful comments. Yet he had an incredible track record of saving millions of lives when confronting similar epidemics in other countries. Who would we hire for the job?

As an American whose own family was being threatened with terrible loss, what specialist would you want at the helm? Would you want the nice, family guy who had a poor track record in combatting similar plagues? Or would you want the nasty-tongued, prideful, oft-married man who was known for stopping these diseases in their tracks?

More specifically, *from a Christian perspective*, who would be the better choice? In a case like this, would God be more concerned with the person being nice yet inept, resulting in the deaths of tens of millions of Americans? Or would He be more concerned with the saving of all these lives, despite the man's carnality?

We could go on with hundreds of similar examples. If your family was trapped in a burning building, would you want the best firefighter to rescue you (even if he used profanity and his kids hated him)? Or would you want the nicest, yet worst, firefighter? What about a doctor performing heart surgery on your infant? Or a general leading your son into battle against terrorists? Or even the local dog catcher, tasked with rounding up Rottweilers with rabies?

In each case, our criteria would *not* be: How is his marriage? Or, do his kids respect him? Or, is he into pornography? Or, does he use a lot of profanity? Instead, our primary question would be: How well does he do his job?

We think like this all the time, in everyday life. Your friend asks you to recommend an exterminator. You reply, "Well, there's a guy we use who is terrific. He is very thorough and has eliminated virtually all the bugs from our house. But to be honest, I don't know a lot about his marriage. And I've heard him use profanity at times. So, I'm not sure I can recommend him."

Your friend would probably reply, "Honestly, with the problem we have with roaches and termites, I'm not really concerned about his marriage. And I can keep the kids away from him if he has a bad mouth. I just need someone to get rid of these pests!"

It would be the same with a more serious recommendation, such as with a heart surgeon. Did you ever think of asking, "What's his (or, her) marriage like? And how does he (or, she) treat the staff?" Instead, you want to hear, "I can tell you firsthand that this is the number one heart surgeon in our city. I wouldn't trust anyone else to come near me (or my family) with a scalpel."

To be sure, when it comes to our choice of president, morality does play an important role, just as, say, sobriety would play an important role with a heart surgeon. If you knew the surgeon was an alcoholic, would you still trust his or her track record? In the same way, when it comes to the president, we don't want a hothead who could needlessly start World War III. We don't want a liar who can't be trusted. We don't want someone who is so divisive and mean-spirited that he tears the nation in two. As I stated in Chapter Four, character does count and morality does matter.

It's just that character and morality are multifaceted, and for many of us, a president who will fight for the life of the unborn demonstrates good character. The same with a president who will combat Islamic terrorism. Or stand for religious liberties. Or push back against a dangerous globalism (aka, New World Order). Or stand up to the repressive regime of China. And while we regret many of the president's words and actions, in balance, we think he's the best man (among possible current candidates) for the job.

In the measured but strong words of Christian journalist Steven Strang, "This is the very reason Trump's reelection is so important. He is a historic political reformer who has totally changed the geopolitical narrative to the real issue of our time: nationalism versus globalism. The global establishment has seen, in two years, its one-hundred-year plan for a total consolidation of its financial, political, and institutional power into a world government implode before its very eyes."[16]

It's the same when it comes to Israel and the Middle East. Many evangelicals believe that God cares about our relationship with Israel and that He truly blesses those who bless Israel.[17] They also believe that our alliance with Israel is important for world security and Middle East stability, and they feel it is very significant that it was Donald Trump, not Bill Clinton or George W. Bush or Barack Obama who moved our embassy to Jerusalem. And, while we do care about justice and equity for the Palestinians, we believe that we cannot throw Israel under the bus for the sake of a Palestinian state (or to appease Muslims worldwide).

Here, too, we find Trump's consistent, strong, pro-Israel stance much more important than his shortcomings. In fact, we find it hard to compare the courage that it took for him to move our embassy to Jerusalem with his narcissism in a press conference. While we do not like the latter, we are willing to tolerate it for the former.

Early in 2020, I was picked up at an airport in Australia by a Chinese driver. He was born in China but came to Australia to study twenty years ago, ultimately moving there and becoming a citizen. He had also become a Christian.

I asked him how he felt about the direction of China under President Xi Jinping. He expressed his deep concern about Xi's leadership, feeling it was oppressive and dangerous, potentially following in the murderous footsteps of Mao. I then asked him how he felt about President Trump. "He's a hero," he replied.

Yes, for this Chinese Christian, now a citizen of Australia but with his parents still living in Communist China, Trump was a global hero, a man with the guts to stand up to China, a man with the guts to stand with the protestors in Hong Kong.[18] Do you think he cares if Trump talks about himself too much or if Trump can be cruel to his political foes? Not in the least. For this man, Trump was doing the right thing where it mattered most, and that's what mattered to him.

Evangelical author Bert Farias wrote that,

> **For more than two centuries the United States of America has been one of the most prosperous and powerful nations of the world. Its military power and its economic superiority actually holds the world together. If the U.S. crumbled or imploded, China would take over the whole of the Far East. Pakistan and India would more than likely break out in war, as both possess nuclear weapons. Iran would cause unlimited chaos and madness in the Middle East. These are just a few examples of what could happen.[19]**

According to Farias, who shares the sentiments of many evangelical Trump supporters, "God foresaw that this hot-blooded and temperamental man would have the backbone and character to stand up against the hordes of demonic forces that were intent on destroying our nation."[20] Obviously, from this perspective, the stakes are very high.

As for the alternatives to Donald Trump, Farias opines, "I must honestly say: I cannot imagine how any true Christian or Messianic Jew could be a Democrat today. It is quickly morphing into a Marxist socialist, violently atheistic party with great greed for power. One cannot read his Bible and be a leftist liberal democrat. You have to feed on humanistic ideologies and go to humanistic schools to be one."[21]

Again, I don't write these things (or, really, anything in this book) with the goal of minimizing Donald Trump's failings. Rather, I write this (in keeping with the theme of this book) to explain why so many God-fearing, morality-loving, Bible-believing Christians can vote for Trump. The picture is much bigger than the man himself.

FIFTEEN

Trump Is Trump

When I was in high school, I heard a joke about an Indian guru and his students. This was at a time when Eastern religious practices were becoming more popular, including Transcendental Meditation (TM), and a number of my friends had tried TM for themselves, seeking to empty themselves of themselves. (Yes, it was quite a concept.)

In the joke the guru sat on the floor in the lotus position surrounded by his adoring students. He then said to them, "We are now going to take the next five minutes and completely empty ourselves of any self-consciousness. We will lose all sense of 'self' and become absorbed in a heightened spiritual awareness. Let us close our eyes and begin, remaining totally silent."

The guru closed his eyes, as did all students, and they sat in total silence for the next five minutes. Then, one by one, they began to open their eyes and look around, smiling and nodding their heads. It worked! What an amazing experience! How wonderful to be totally emptied of self!

The guru then said to his students, "Wasn't that a great idea of mine?" It appears the guru still had some "self" left after all.

What does this have to do with Donald Trump? It is simply this. Barring dramatic divine intervention in the coming months or years, Trump is going to be Trump. His world will always revolve around him.

International events will revolve around him. America will revolve around him. He will praise himself and defend himself as if he, not the wellbeing of the nation, was the major focus of the hour. And, to repeat, he may never change, even to his dying day.

During Trump's daily news briefings during the coronavirus crisis, he referenced the popularity of the briefings, noting how many people were watching every day. As reported by *Business Insider* on April 10, 2020, "President Donald Trump has taken to Twitter three days in a row this week to boast about TV ratings for the daily coronavirus press briefings.

"Meanwhile, nearly 17 million Americans have filed for unemployment in the past few weeks, and the death toll from the coronavirus pandemic in the US surpassed 18,000 as of Friday afternoon."[1]

In Trump's own words,

> The Radical Left Democrats have gone absolutely crazy that I am doing daily Presidential News Conferences. They actually want me to STOP! They used to complain that I am not doing enough of them, now they complain that I "shouldn't be allowed to do them." They tried to shame the Fake News Media into not covering them, but that effort failed because the ratings are through the roof according to, of all sources, the Failing New York Times, "Monday Night Football, Bachelor Finale" type numbers (& sadly, they get it $FREE). Trump Derangement Syndrome![2]

So, thousands of Americans are dying and millions have lost their jobs, yet the president is comparing his TV ratings to Monday Night Football and the Bachelor's finale episode. He is also using the briefings to attack his political opponents and critics. This even irked TV host Piers Morgan, considered to be a good friend of Trump. Morgan said during an interview on CNN on April 19, 2020, "He's turning these briefings into a self-aggrandizing, self-justifying, overly defensive politically partisan, almost like a rally to him." And he urged the president, "Please drop your angry, petty, disingenuous, blame-gaming, self-aggrandising daily briefing antics & start being a proper wartime president."[3]

There Is More to Donald Trump

But here's what many are missing. Trump's world may revolve around himself. He may be narcissistic and self-centered. He may even be petty and unforgiving. Yet that doesn't mean that he doesn't care about others. Or that he will not work tirelessly for the good of America. Or that he is not willing to make major, personal sacrifices to improve the lifestyle of millions of others. To the contrary, it appears that he really does care for people and that he really does want to help America. So, the packaging may be offensive, but the contents, overall, are healthy.

I have the privilege of knowing a number of people who have spent time face to face with the president or who have a fairly close relationship with the president. One, in particular, can call Trump on his personal cell phone and has spent hours together with him. And these friends of mine, people of high personal integrity, tell me the same thing: Donald Trump cares about America. He is willing to take the hatred and abuse that comes with the office (some of it, to be sure, has been self-inflicted) because his greatest concern is the wellbeing of our nation.

To a person, they tell me that he is grieved with the plight of the poor in our inner-cities. That he genuinely wants to help the average American worker. That he is upset with the attacks on our freedoms, especially our religious freedoms. At the same time he is who he is, and he sits firmly entrenched in the center of his universe.

Pastor Jim Garlow, a highly respected national evangelical leader who served on the Trump Faith Advisory Board in 2016, is often asked, "What is Donald Trump really like?" He responds: "I always answer the same way."

According to Pastor Garlow (this is just an excerpt from his list):

1. **He is a man of his word.** In all my years of following government and political life (which I have done since age nine), I have never seen a nationally elected official so committed to honoring his word. This indicates character.
2. **He really wants to do what is right.** That bears repeating, so I will re-state it: He really wants to do what is right. He is sincere.

3. [He is] a man of the common person.
4. **He listens to people**. . . . I have shared something with him directly on a couple of occasions. He is a superb and intent listener.
5. **He is a quick study.**
6. **He is flawed.** We all are. I have never known of a person who does not have flaws. Governor Mike Huckabee, who highly respects our President has said (in effect) – in humor, tongue in cheek – in an interview, "Most people try to be nice in public and are not always quite so nice in private. The President is the opposite. He is always nice in private, but not always in public." (Reminder, this was said in humor.)[4]

Garlow also added, "He has kept an open door to Bible-believing believers, unlike any modern president. . . . Trump is unique. He opens the door to Scripturally solid faith leaders. It is stunning."[5] So, there are many excellent qualities about President Trump, along with his very evident shortcomings. For the most part, the liberal media focuses almost entirely on the latter.

Picture it like this. Your father, now in his 70s, is facing delicate, open-heart surgery. Very few doctors are willing to perform the surgery, and even fewer are considered specialists. It so happens that the world top's specialist bases his practice in the very city in which you and your father and family live. And to your great relief, he is willing to operate on your dad.

At the consultation, though, you are a little put off. All the man does is talk about himself, pointing to all the awards hanging on his walls and telling you how lucky you are that he was able to schedule you in. After all, his most recent surgery was for a member of the Saudi royal family (they flew all the way here for the operation), and before that, the doctor operated on a member of the British royal family. "This guy is really full of himself," you think to yourself.

But before you leave the office, he looks your father in the eye and says, "You've got nothing to worry about. I've done this 500 times. You're going to come out fine. You could not be in better hands."

Sure enough, the surgery is a total success, and your dad's life is wonderfully saved, thanks to this egotistic heart specialist. And when you see him afterwards to thank him, he says, "I told you your dad was in good hands. No one does it better than me. In fact, I'm going to be the subject of a special documentary next month. You'll probably want to watch. As for your dad, he's going to do great. The prognosis is excellent."

So, this is who the man is. He is into himself. He likes to boast about himself. But he is the best in his class when it comes to heart surgery. More importantly, when he is operating, he has one thing on his mind: Save this patient's life. Don't lose your focus. People are trusting you to get this right.

Is it possible this doctor went into the medical profession to make a name for himself? Perhaps. Is it possible that, even as he's operating, he's saying to himself, "Am I good or what?"? Maybe so. At the same time, he's doing what he's doing because he wants to save people's lives. He's making (and has made) many personal sacrifices to put his patients first. He may be narcissistic, but when the rubber meets the road, his focus is not on his reputation but on the wellbeing of the person on the operating table. He may boast about his exploits after he's done (like the self-congratulatory guru in the joke), but he got the job done. He may even cause offense in your family, fracturing some relationships, which is inexcusable. But he saved your dad's life.

The parallels with Trump are obvious, even if my story here was presented in exaggerated terms. I trust you get the point.

The Packaging vs. the Contents

But there's a twofold reason I share all this. First, when it comes to the best interests of the country, you have to look beyond the packaging of President Trump, which is often quite offensive. As you know by reading the pages of this book, I have no desire to downplay or excuse that offensiveness in the least. It is what it is, and I don't like it. And some of that offensiveness has to do with him making something like the COVID-19 crisis into a platform to talk about himself.

I'm aware, of course, that his enemies in Washington and his detractors in the media attacked him over the crisis from day one. He's not doing enough, they say. He has blood on his hands. He's a terrible leader. He has failed the test. He should be impeached over his mishandling of the pandemic. And on and on it goes, and so it's only natural for him to push back against these attacks, using his main platforms during the crisis, namely, the news conferences and his Twitter account, to blast back.

But when you're talking about tens of thousands of people dying and tens of millions out of work it's important for the president *not* to make this about himself, *not* to boast about how well he has handled things, and *not* to savage his political opponents and lash out at the media while speaking to the nation about the crisis. As Piers Morgan noted,

> You will win the election in November if you get this right. If you stop making it about yourself and make it about the American people and show that you care about them over yourself, you will win. And, conversely, you will lose the election in November if you continue to make it about yourself, you continue playing silly politics, continue targeting Democrat governors because that suits you for your electoral purposes.[6]

I believe Morgan is right. Yet, to repeat, this doesn't mean Trump doesn't care deeply about those who have died, or about the families of the bereaved, or about those fighting for their lives, or about the millions who have suffered financially. Even if he wants his name on the stimulus checks, that doesn't mean that he is not genuinely interested in Americans to get those checks.

It's the same with bringing our troops home from overseas. According to numerous accounts, Trump has been deeply affected by the deaths of our military, and his reason for wanting to bring our troops home is more about them than about his legacy.

On February 11, 2020, NPR news reported,

> President Trump cut short a raucous New Hampshire campaign rally on Monday to make a last-minute flight to Dover, where America's fallen service members are brought to be prepared for transport to their final destination. There, he met up with Vice President Mike Pence, who had also spoken at the rally. It was the first time since

transfers were opened to the press more than a decade ago that both a president and vice president attended together.

"These were fallen heroes and we were close by and the president wrapped his rally early so he could come and see these families," Trump's national security adviser Robert O'Brien told the pool of reporters traveling on Air Force One. "It's tough for the president, but he thinks it's important."[7]

That is also who the man is.

So, to repeat, I share all this to say: Look beyond the packaging. Look beyond the ego. Look at the good that is being done. Look beyond the outward appearance and the sometimes offensive speech.

The second reason I share that "Trump is Trump" is because I've given up on the idea of him becoming a radically different person while in the White House. Of course, I'd love to see that happen, as would tens of millions of others. And I pray for God's very best for his life. It's just that I've reconciled myself to the fact that this is who the man is. The good is mixed with the bad, the praiseworthy with the offensive. The same man who so tirelessly and courageously fights for our causes sometimes hits below the belt.

On July 7, 2017, I attended a meeting at the White House with about twenty other national Christian leaders. As of this writing, this was my one and only time there, and we did not meet with the president, although he was made aware of the meeting and we were assured that our comments in the meeting would be passed on to him. After we were briefed on a number of developments important to our communities, we were asked if we would like to make any comments or raise any questions.

I took the opportunity to speak, raising what I felt was an important issue in the culture wars relevant to our faith community. I then asked if there was any way for him to moderate some of his tweets, since, I explained, they often make it hard for us to gain support for him among our fellow evangelicals. One of his closest advisers, who was conducting the meeting, said with a smile, "It's not likely for a seventy-year-old man to change."

That was 2017, yet still, in my mind, anyone can change. That's the power of the gospel. That's the nature of conversion. That's what God can do in the life of anyone who truly cries out to Him with a sincere heart. And, in that sense, I still have hope. Donald Trump could one day be known for his Christlike character. But I'm not waiting for it or expecting it. I'm not holding my breath with the hope that, before the year is out, the whole world will see the changes in his life.

Again, it would be absolutely awesome if he was dramatically transformed, if he could be just as strong and immovable when it comes to doing what is right without at the same time being so self-centered and, at times, harsh and even cruel. And it would be wonderful if the Donald Trump my friends have met in private, described as humble, attentive, welcoming prayer, God fearing, and a terrific listener, would be the man that people see in public. But I'm not holding my breath. It is what it is and he is who he is.

Do I find it ironic that a man who surrounds himself with committed Christians can at times act in such unchristian ways? Absolutely. Yet I do not find him insincere in surrounding himself with these people, nor do I see it as a protracted political ploy. To the contrary, he sees the quality of their lives and he is attracted to them. He believes in the power of prayer and asks for it regularly. And he genuinely cares about pro-life issues and religious freedoms. This is not a show.

The good news is that what you see is what you get. The bad news is that what you see is often not good. The better news is that, when it comes to tangible results, just like the heart surgeon in my illustration, he's getting a lot of very good and important things done, and that's why he has my vote.

In sum, I regret the fact that Trump is Trump but he has my vote because Trump is Trump.

SIXTEEN

The Bottom Line Is Simple

There are quite a few, well-researched, full-length books which paint a very disturbing picture of the presidency of Donald Trump. There is Bob Woodward's *Fear: Trump in the White House*, which was a #1 New York Times Bestseller.[1] There is Philip Rucker and Carol Leonnig's *A Very Stable Genius: Donald J. Trump's Testing of America*, which was also a #1 New York Times Bestseller.[2] There is Michael Wolf's *Fire and Fury: Inside the Trump White House*, which was a #1 New York Times Bestseller as well.[3] There is Joshua Green's *Devil's Bargain: Steve Bannon, Donald Trump, and the Nationalist Uprising*, with an emphasis on the alleged alt-right connection, and yes, this too was a #1 New York Times Bestseller.[4] There is David Frum's *Trumpocracy: The Corruption of the American Republic*, which was a New York Times Bestseller, although not #1.[5] There is even *The Dangerous Case of Donald Trump: 37 Psychiatrists and Mental Health Experts Assess a President*, yet another New York Times Bestseller.[6]

On and on the list goes, with one bestselling title after another, and with some of the charges against Trump being quite serious.[7] For example, according to Jeffrey D. Sachs, Ph.D., in the foreword to the second edition of *The Dangerous Case of Donald Trump*, "Donald Trump is a profound danger to Americans and to the rest of the world. He will remain a profound danger until he is no longer president, since the dangers clearly result from Trump's serious mental impairments that are untreated and are most likely impervious to treatment."[8]

Some would ask, "How, then, can you vote for someone like that? How could you still support Trump?"

To be sure, there were quite a few bestselling books that brought very serious charges against President Obama.[9] And I'm sure there were similar books bashing President Bush before that and President Clinton before that. There will always be those who bring harsh criticism. Sometimes it is truthful. Other times it is not.

But either way, the bottom line for me is simple. I have the privilege of casting a vote for a presidential candidate every four years, so I evaluate who will best represent the issues that are important to me. And so, even if some of the content of these anti-Trump books was true, I would still rather see Trump in the White House than Hillary Clinton or Bernie Sanders or Joe Biden or Mario Cuomo or any of the other major Democratic candidates.[10] It's possible that I couldn't vote for either candidate, in good conscience, but weighing the pros and cons, at this point in time (as I write in mid-2020), I would vote for Trump. (Of course, if I agreed with Dr. Sachs, I would not vote for Trump. Obviously, I do not concur with Sachs's assessment.)

It's really not that complicated. And it's only a vote. That's it. I am not selling my soul. I am not making a deal with the devil (or any other spiritual entity). I am not pledging my life to a party. I am not putting all my eggs in a political basket. I'm simply casting a vote.

If the person I vote for loses, so be it. Life goes on. Ministry goes on. Loving God and loving my neighbor goes on. I will continue to pray and study the Scriptures. I will continue to care for my wife and family. I will continue to write books and articles. I will continue to travel and preach and teach and do radio broadcasts and debates and take a stand for what I believe is right. I will continue to speak up and speak out – at least, as long I have the freedom to do so.

And when it's time for the next election, I will cast my vote again, unless I cannot in good conscience vote for either major candidate. In that case, I would either sit out the election or vote for a third party candidate, just to make a statement.

In the 2016 elections, some evangelicals felt they could not vote for Trump or Hillary, so they either sat things out or cast their vote for a protest candidate. If they did that out of conscience before God, I respect that. We give ultimate account to Him, not to one another.

Some voters may choose to do that in 2020, and if that is their choice before God, especially if they gave the matter serious thought, that's their business. It's not for me to lay a guilt trip on them or tell them that they must vote for a particular candidate or remind them that they owe it to God and country to vote or that, by failing to vote, they fail to live up to their responsibilities as citizens of our democratic republic.

Of course, simply having the ability to vote is something very special, a privilege not enjoyed by most human beings through history. And, to this day, voting is a privilege not enjoyed in many countries worldwide, where despotic rulers or monarchic systems make voting impossible. So, I appreciate how important our votes can be, and we have no right bemoaning the outcome of an election if we choose not to vote ourselves. Let us use our system as best we can, let us advocate for the best candidates, and let us vote wisely. After all, America is about "we the people."

But, at the end of the day, a vote is a vote. And, whether you cast your vote with enthusiasm (as many of us did when voting for Ronald Reagan), or whether you cast your vote with some hesitation (as many of us did when voting for Trump), it still counts as one vote. Even then, when all is said and done, you have no idea if your candidate will live up to his or her promises. And even with the best intentions, you have no idea if your candidate will be able to keep those promises because of our whole political system. Then, even if your candidate succeeds in keeping every single promise made, that doesn't mean that the court system might not interfere or that the educational system won't get in the way or that society will ultimately change for the better. And even then, the president must be the president of the entire nation, which means looking out for the best interests of everyone, not just the best interests of one particular group. So a vote is just a vote, and politics is just one of method among many of helping to improve the nation.

Why, then, do we make voting into such a life and death issue? Why do we let our emotions get so wrought up in every election cycle? Why do we elevate a vote for or against Trump (or another candidate) into a vote for or against the kingdom of God? I get caught up in this too, and we really need to be cured of our election fever if we are to fulfill our greater calling and mandate.

It Came Down to Trump vs. Hillary in 2016

As I have often stated, I preferred other Republican candidates to Trump in 2016, but since it came down to Trump vs. Hillary, I voted for Trump. Why? Above all, it was a vote against Hillary Clinton, since I felt some of her key policies would be terrible for the nation. As for Trump, I hoped he would keep his campaign promises and: 1) fight for the life of the unborn; 2) support our religious liberties; 3) appoint conservative justices to the courts; 4) stand with Israel and move our embassy to Jerusalem; 5) push back against LGBT extremism; and 6) strongly oppose radical Islamic terrorism. I also hoped he would be a good economic leader, but that was not as high on my list. Immigration issues were even less important to me, as were a host of other issues that mattered to other voters. The items on my list were what mattered most to me when voting, especially the first five.

How has Trump performed? For the most part, on these key issues, he has done above and beyond what I hoped for or expected. He has been a man of his word. He has kept his campaign promises. I give him very high marks.[11]

As for my hesitation in casting my vote for Trump in 2016, it was for two reasons. First, I wondered if he would let down his evangelical supporters, as past presidents had done, using us to vote him in and then abandoning us afterwards. Thankfully, in that regard, he has not disappointed, and I honestly don't see him changing if reelected. Well done, Mr. President. In the words of John Zmirak, "He has appointed better judges, by pro-life and pro-family standards, than any recent president. Including Reagan. Not one of the dire predictions hurled by GOP insiders in the build up to the 2016 vote has come to pass. Not one."[12]

Second, I was concerned about Donald Trump the man, concerned about the potential damage he might do if elected. In that regard, there is no denying the collateral damage done to our nation, as I have admitted freely in this book. It is true, to quote Zmirak again, that "Trump hasn't acted lawlessly, groped any passing women, or shot people on Fifth Avenue to see if he could get away with it."[13] But there is no question in my eyes that his behavior and method of governing have had a negative, moral impact on the country.

One of my evangelical friends who lives in California is passionately opposed to Trump. He wrote to me privately, "You quote people who hold him up as good news for Conservatives. Not where I live! He is chaos personified. And I don't have to prove it. The evidence is mountainous."

He continued, "All the criticisms [of Trump] you list are true and disastrous. Calamitous. Destructive to the soul and future of America. When the pastor of a large church is fired for consorting with prostitutes or for child molestation, how long does it take for the church to truly recover? How long will it take for America to recover from this walking disaster? It won't be a couple of years. It may be decades. And it may be never."[14]

Needless to say, Trump supporters would have a strong response to these criticisms, arguing with certainty that he has done far more good than bad and that the lasting effects of his presidency will be far more positive than negative. The debate will continue for a long time to come, and it will only intensify in the days leading up to the next election, especially as we make our choice between the candidates who will be available.

Yet that's what happens when we vote. We are voting for imperfect people in an imperfect system, and they are governing an imperfect nation. Every politician is flawed and each party is flawed, which means that each and every vote is, at best, a vote to elect a flawed person to lead a flawed party in the midst of a flawed system. Yet we act as if casting a vote was equivalent to getting married or, more extreme still, praying the prayer of salvation. Why?

It's true that some Christians make political leaders into idols, identifying so deeply with their candidate that people know them more for their political convictions than for their devotion to the Lord. They talk about their man (or woman) more than they talk about Jesus. They are much quicker to defend him (or her) than to defend their faith. And while they are quite hesitant to give out a gospel booklet or tract, they are more than happy to wear a campaign hat and tee-shirt, to erect a big sign on their front yard, and to put a bumper sticker on their car. I would say that such Christians have their priorities out of whack, although I certainly recognize that some are called to political involvement more than others.

But what about the millions of others who do *not* have their priorities skewed? What about those for whom voting is just one of many ways to impact the nation? Why is their vote for a flawed candidate, among other flawed candidates, such a big deal? Why the outrage when a Christian votes for Trump?

Again, it's one thing if that Christian defends the indefensible or puts country before God or venerates Trump in a cult-like way. It's another thing if, given the available choices, they choose to vote for Trump.

Let's Not Forget About the Courts

I have not said a lot about the importance of judicial appointments, but conservative radio host Mark Levin drew national attention to this issue in his blockbuster book *Men in Black: How the Supreme Court Is Destroying America*.[15] Writing in July 2016, law professor and radio host Hugh Hewitt added this perspective:

> If Hillary Clinton wins, the Left gavels in a solid, lasting, almost certainly permanent majority on the Supreme Court. Every political issue has a theoretical path to SCOTUS, and only self-imposed judicial restraint has checked the Supreme Court's appetite and reach for two centuries.
>
> That restraint will be gone when Hillary Rodham Clinton's first appointee is sworn in. Finished. This is not hyperbole. I have the advantage of having taught Conservative Law for 20 years, of having argued before very liberal appellate judges like Judge Stephen Reinhardt of the very liberal Ninth Circuit, of practicing with the best litigators in the land. I know what a very liberal Supreme Court means: Conservatism is done. It cannot survive a strong-willed liberal majority on the Supreme Court. Every issue—EVERY issue—will end up there, and the legislature's judgments will matter not a bit.[16]

But Levin and Hewitt would readily acknowledge that, since more than 99 percent of major cases never make it to the Supreme Court, the federal courts also play an extremely important role. And each term, the president has the ability to appoint scores and scores of judges to the courts, judges who will serve for life. The potential impact on the nation is massive.

That's why the *New York Times* declared in a March 16, 2020 headline, "A Conservative Agenda Unleashed on the Federal Courts." Yes, "President Trump's imprint on the nation's appeals courts has been swift and historic." Specifically, "The lifetime appointees — who make up more than a quarter of the entire appellate bench — were more openly engaged in causes important to Republicans, such as opposition to gay marriage and to government funding for abortion."[17]

A PBS headline announced on October 25, 2019, "Trump's conservative picks will impact courts for decades" – and that means impacting the nation for decades, especially since Trump's judicial appointees, on average, are younger that judges appointed by other presidents.[18] In keeping with this, a January 4, 2020 headline on Real Clear Politics stated that, "Trump Is Remaking the Federal Judiciary at a Historic Rate"[19] while a January 6, 2020 headline on The Hill spoke of "The Trumpification of the federal courts."[20]

As explained on Vox.com on February 4, 2020, "Trump hasn't simply given lots of lifetime appointments to lots of lawyers. He's filled the bench with some of the smartest, and some of the most ideologically reliable, men and women to be found in the conservative movement. Long after Trump leaves office, these judges will shape American law — pushing it further and further to the right even if the voters soundly reject Trumpism in 2020."[21] That's what you call a lasting legacy.

"But," someone will protest, "we need to change people's hearts. Changing laws won't do the trick."

Actually, I agree, but stated slightly differently: changing laws *alone* will not change the nation, and we must always prioritize changing hearts and minds. But we cannot ignore the importance of judicial decisions that are made every day across our nation. And so, once again, the bottom line for me is simple: *if another candidate was elected with a very different agenda, our courts would look very different and our laws would look very different, and, in the end, our lives would look very different.*

Whoever we elect as president is going to appoint many new judges (as of this writing, Trump had appointed nearly 200), and so, when casting our vote, it makes sense to support the person who will appoint the best available judges, judges who will make America better, not worse. This is common, voting sense.

Looking, then, at the big picture, when I weigh in the balance the negative impact Trump has had on our nation vs. the positive impact he has had in terms of judicial appointments alone, I say the impact is more positive than negative. I don't minimize the damage he has done and I do my best to separate myself from the aspects of Trump's behavior that are destructive or divisive. He's my president, not my role model, and he got my vote, not my soul.

Is There a Better Strategy?

Of course, a larger philosophical argument could be raised, namely, that we should simply concentrate on reaching people with the gospel, doing good works, and being a godly presence in the society, leaving politics and the culture wars to others. And even if we do not drop out of politics and the culture wars entirely, our emphasis must change radically. In support of this concept is sociologist James Davison Hunter who claimed that it is "not an exaggeration to say that the dominant public witness of the Christian churches in America since the early 1980s has been a political witness."[22]

As explained by Professor John Fea,

> In grasping for political power, Hunter says, evangelicals have made it more difficult to spread the gospel, promote justice for the poor and oppressed, and pursue human flourishing in the places where God has called and placed them. In one of the more telling and prophetic passages of the book, he writes: "The proclivity toward domination and toward the politicization of everything leads Christianity today to bizarre turns, turns that . . . transform much of the Christian public witness into the very opposite of the witness Christianity is supposed to offer." Christians were never meant to change this world; instead, they are called to "honor the creator of all goodness, beauty, and truth, a manifestation of our loving obedience to God, and a fulfillment of

God's command to love our neighbor." Hunter urges evangelical Christians to stop fighting the culture wars and pursue a course of "faithful presence" in their local communities and neighborhoods.[23]

How should we respond to this? Again, I agree that we (meaning evangelical Christians) have become far too politicized in America. And I agree that our greatest role as believers is the role we play in our local communities as living Christian witnesses and servants. At the same time I differ with Professor Hunter's assessment that it is "not an exaggeration to say that the dominant public witness of the Christian churches in America since the early 1980s has been a political witness." This is simply not true.

Watch Christian TV and listen to Christian radio for an entire week, 24/7. How much of the content is political in nature? Very little.[24] Review the top 1,000 evangelical books published in the last five years. How much of *that* content is political in nature? Again, very little.[25] Then, interview people in your community who have firsthand experience with the local gospel preaching churches, and ask them how much of the preaching and teaching is political in nature. Once again, the answer is very little.

Why, then, does someone as astute as Hunter make such a comment? And why is that many others will nod their heads in agreement with him? It's because, for the last five decades, we have had prominent, national evangelical voices with strong political messages, such as Jerry Falwell, Sr., James Dobson, Franklin Graham, and Robert Jeffress. And it is these men whose faces are seen on major TV networks and who are quoted in well-read publications.

But they are hardly the voice of your average evangelical congregation (and I do not disparage these men in saying this). In other words, the local community know its local churches, and the people in that community know the members of that local church. And that is how most of our witness is spread and most of our work is done, face to face, one on one, in the communities where we live.

I realize, of course, that the voice of even one evangelical leader on national TV carries a lot of weight, deeply affecting public perception. Along with this, the leftist media will highlight every pro-Trump comment made by one of our conservative Christian leaders, shouting it even more loudly for the nation to hear. That's why it's important that we nuance our statements and watch our words, not to please people but to honor the Lord and to remember the importance of our larger Christian witness. But frankly, nothing less than the complete renunciation of President Trump will satisfy our critics, and so, it's a losing game even to try.

Let's also not forget that, if Mike Pence were president, despite his personality being the opposite of Trump's in many respects, the leftist media, along with Democratic politicians, would warn us day and night that he and his team were seeking to establish a theocracy. I addressed this in a September 12, 2018 article titled, "The Left's Hatred of Mike Pence Undermines Its Hatred of Donald Trump,"[26] noting that we've been told time and again why Trump is so hated. We've been told that he is out of control. That he is mentally unfit. We've been told he's a threat to national security. That he has damaged our international standing. That he is unstable. That he is volatile. That he's in totally over his head. That no one can work for him.

Yet many loathe Vice President Pence even more than they loathe Trump, pledging to get rid of him once they get rid of Trump, despite the fact that Mike Pence is an experienced politician, having served in the House of Representatives from 2001-2013 and as governor of Indiana from 2013-2017. And Mike Pence is not unstable or volatile, nor does he have a history of alienating those who work for him, nor has he been accused of being an autocratic narcissist. He is clearly in control of his words and actions, he has not insulted or maligned his opponents, and he has done nothing to disgrace the office of the Vice President. Yet he too must go. He too is a threat. He too must be removed.

To quote Maxine Waters, who passionately called for the impeachment of Trump, and with reference to his expected demise, "You knock one down, and then we'll be ready for Pence. We'll get him, too."[27] Yes, Mike Pence must also go. Away with this man too! And for what reason would *he* be impeached? What did Pence do?

Waters' words drew a sharp rebuke from Trump supporter Philip Schuyler, who tweeted, "When Maxine Waters says, 'We'll impeach Trump,' she's fantasizing, since he didn't do anything wrong. But when she says re Pence, 'We'll get him too,' isn't she admitting that her party is closer to a vengeful mob than to a lawful org?"[28]

But it's not just Maxine Waters who said something like this. The anti-Pence rhetoric has been building for many months. Omarosa Manigault Newman also echoed these sentiments in 2018. As reported on Yahoo News, "Ms Manigault Newman, who is busy promoting her book, *Unhinged: An Insider's Account of the Trump White House*, was asked by TMZ which of the top White House executives was worse - the president or the vice president? 'Pence,' she shouted, before being driven away in a black SUV."[29] Yes, Pence is worse than Trump!

In July, 2018, *New York Times* op-ed writer Frank Bruni penned a piece titled, "Mike Pence, Holy Terror. Are you sure you want to get rid of Donald Trump?"[30] His article opens with these chilling words: "There are problems with impeaching Donald Trump. A big one is the holy terror waiting in the wings.

"That would be Mike Pence, who mirrors the boss more than you realize. He's also self-infatuated. Also a bigot. Also a liar. Also cruel."[31]

Mike Pence is a monster! The man would bring a reign of terror!

But there's something even worse, and it lies at the heart of Bruni's concerns: Pence "adds two ingredients that Trump doesn't genuinely possess: the conviction that he's on a mission from God and a determination to mold the entire nation in the shape of his own faith, a regressive, repressive version of Christianity. Trade Trump for Pence and you go from kleptocracy to theocracy."[32]

Yes, Mike Pence wants to turn America into a Christian theocracy, with himself the earthly tyrant ruling in God's stead. Oh, the horror!

The Tylt website conducted a poll (apparently late in 2017), asking the question: "Who should liberals fear more: President Trump or a potential President Pence?"[33] By a vote of 51.9 to 48.1 percent, the answer was that a Pence presidency would be more dangerous. In support of this claim, Tylt cited a *New Yorker* article by Jane Mayer dated October 23, 2017. According to Mayer, "Pence has the political experience, the connections, the discipline, and the ideological mooring that Trump lacks. He also has a close relationship with the conservative billionaire donors who have captured the Republican Party's agenda in recent years."

But that is not the worrying part. Rather, "Even as [Governor]

Pence argued for less government interference in business, he pushed for policies that intruded on people's private lives. In the early nineties, he joined the board of the Indiana Family Institute, a far-right group that supported the criminalization of abortion and campaigned against equal rights for homosexuals. . . ." [34]

In short, Pence is an evangelical Christian, a biblically-based conservative. As such, he could be a worse threat to the left than Donald Trump. (Really now, if the left could turn President George Bush into a religious fanatic who allegedly waged war based on Bible prophecies, what will it do to Mike Pence?)[35]

So, while anti-Trumpers might harp on his bad behavior and his presidential flaws, most of the concerns raised by the left are merely a convenient ruse for the real issue: They hate the fact that their own agenda is being thwarted. They despise the fact that some of their strongholds are being demolished. And they will do whatever they can to remove anyone who dares to get in their way, be it Donald Trump or Mike Pence.

The more conservative the leader, the more they will oppose him (or her). The more Christian and conservative that leader is, the more intense their opposition will be. And this means that, unless we drop out of politics completely, there will be hatred and opposition toward our views, and that hatred then will trickle down toward us as Bible believing Christians.

Why Not Drop Out Entirely from Politics and the Culture Wars?

When Franklin Graham was stopped from holding major rallies in several UK venues, the protesters said it was because of his "anti-LGBTQ" views.[36] The same was true when Samaritan's Purse encountered opposition while serving COVID-19 victims in New York City. They were opposed because of their Christian values, specifically their statement of faith affirming marriage as the union of a man and a woman. And, of course, some liberals had a problem with Franklin Graham, the head of Samaritan's Purse, who was blasted as a bigoted homophobe.[37] But note carefully: the focus was not on his vocal support for Trump or even his comments about Muslims. Instead, the primary attack was on his Christian beliefs about sexuality and marriage and family.

Someone might say, "Well, that proves the point. Christians need to drop out of politics and the culture wars. Otherwise, our witness will be tainted, and that's the biggest issue. Let us be known as being *for* Jesus instead of being against all these other things."

For argument's sake, let's say we embrace that line of thinking, not talking about the elections, not endorsing candidates, not writing letters to the editor in our local newspaper about divisive issues, not rocking the cultural boat. Instead, we just shared the gospel with people and gave ourselves to works of service.

But what happens when your pastor is preaching through the Bible and he gets to passages that forbid homosexual practice? Does he skip them or give some watered-down explanation? If so, he is sinning against God and the flock. If not, he and the church will be branded bigots and haters, and that is simply for preaching the Word.

And what happens when your local library announces the next drag queen reading hour for toddlers, and your little one wants to know why she can't go? Or when your five-year-old boy comes home from kindergarten confused about the picture book with two boys kissing? Or when your ten-year-old son is confused about his gender identity, but it is illegal in your state for him to receive professional counseling? Or when your fifteen-year-old daughter comes home crying after having to share the locker room with a teenage male who is now on her softball team? Or when that same daughter, now twenty, gets kicked out of her college program because she could not, in good conscience, support the class's gay pride agenda?[38]

Do you say, "Well, we don't get involved in the culture wars?" Or do you do what is right for your children, which means speaking up and speaking out and taking action. And what happens when you learn that, in your district, the big problem is an ultra-liberal school board, led by two, anti-Christian, lesbian activists? Along with praying for them and even reaching out to them, do you consider voting for school board members the next time around? Or perhaps you will even feel prompted to run for a seat on the board? And would there be anything fundamentally unchristian about any of this involvement? If it was all done in a right spirit, certainly not. In fact, in many ways, it would be quite Christian.

You see, if we don't stand up for what is right today, then our culture will deteriorate even more rapidly tomorrow, and with that, our free- doms will quickly deteriorate – and even evaporate – as well. And the day will soon come when, as a pastor, you will be required to perform a gay "wedding" under penalty of the law. And as a conservative Christ- ian, you will not be able to get a teaching position at a major, secular university. And as a medical doctor, you will lose your job for telling the truth about unsafe sexual practices. In fact, some of this happened already, and what has not already happened is right at the door.[39]

And what will we tell our kids and grandkids, the ones who will feel the brunt of the cultural collapse? How will we explain to them that this happened on our watch because we didn't want to rock the boat and be controversial? Can you imagine telling them, "Well, we didn't want to hurt our public witness," when, in doing so, we made it much harder for them to be public witnesses?

Not only so, but doesn't our public witness include preaching against sin? When was that ever popular? Even today, when we are sharing our faith and someone asks us our views on abortion or homo- sexuality, do we tell them the truth? Or do we avoid the issue or, worse still, change what the Bible says, not wanting to offend them, thereby offending the Lord?

And what happens when we realize that one of the reasons our society is in moral decline is because of bad laws and bad legal prece- dents and bad government policies? Do we still drop out of politics and quit fighting the culture wars, or do we engage constructively, with our biblical priorities intact?

To be perfectly honest, I have often wondered if the church would do better with a president who was hostile to our values and a society that more deeply opposed us. Would that wake us up more acutely? Would we live more fully in the light of eternity? Would our prayers become more fervent? Would our sacrifices be more enduring? Those are important questions, and we may find answers to them in the years ahead. But I for one would hate to see the nation turn against the church, even viciously so, because we abdicated our responsibilities.

Why can't we be fervent, committed, and fully Christian even with a president who stands with us?

For me, then, the bottom line is simple. Since I have the opportunity to vote, I use it judiciously, and since I have the opportunity for make a positive difference in the world in which I live, I get involved as the Lord leads and as the needs arise. As long as I put first things first and major on the majors, it's the biblical thing to do. And that brings us to the closing chapter of the book where I lay out ten essential steps for our effective forward progress. If we are to pass the Trump test, it is crucial we get this right.

SEVENTEEN

Ten Essential Keys for Passing the Trump Test

There can be little doubt that Donald Trump has been a wrecking ball, especially when it comes to political correctness. But the problem with a wrecking ball is that it swings forward and backward, knocking down everything in its path. That means that, while a wrecking ball might be great for demolition, it is not so great for renovation. It leaves quite a mess in its path. In the case of President Trump, not only has his presidency been a wrecking ball to political correctness, it has also wreaked havoc on religious hypocrisy.

It is true that through the Trump presidency, the corruption of the Washington system (what Senator Ted Cruz calls "the Washington cartel") has been exposed.[1] The existence of the Deep State (or, whatever term you want to use to describe it) has been revealed.[2] The extreme, shameless, and at times childish bias of the liberal media (along with the degree to which some rightwing media pundits are willing to go to cover their man) has been laid bare. The radical nature of the Democratic party has been unmasked, as it has lurched dangerously left. The deepest divisions in the nation have been brought to the surface. Because of Trump, simply by him being himself, for better or worse, we are seeing people and parties and movements for who and what they truly are. The spectacle is unvarnished. And it is often ugly.

At the same time, through the person of Trump, some real

hypocrisy and shallowness in parts of the Church has been exposed. Speaking especially of some of our evangelical circles (again, I say *some*, not *all*), the Trump presidency has helped to reveal: our double standards, emphasizing character and morality when rejecting Bill Clinton but downplaying character and morality when embracing Trump; our willingness to ignore Trump's shortcomings for a seat at the table of political influence; our dividing over a man rather than uniting around Jesus; our equating patriotism with the kingdom of God (or, even exalting patriotism above the kingdom of God); our putting our hope in a human being to the point of giving him almost cult-like veneration; and our emulating the behavior and speech of the president even when it is diametrically opposed to the teachings of Scripture.

In these ways, among others, as evangelical followers of Jesus, some of us have failed the Trump test. But we do not have to fail again. In fact, there's no reason why we can't pass the next exam with flying colors. We can keep our testimony sound, we can be Jesus-centered people, and we can still vote for Trump (if we feel that is the right thing to do). Here are some keys for passing the test.[3]

1. We must clearly and emphatically put the cross before the flag.

Throughout much of Church history, this has been easily done, since the countries in which we have lived have often been overtly hostile to our faith. In the first centuries of the Church, as Christians were persecuted by Rome, I don't believe that "making Rome great" or "keeping Rome great" was high on their list. Rather, while seeking to remain obedient citizens of the empire, as much as was possible, their focus was simple and clear: We must preach the gospel. We must win the lost. We must make disciples. We must extend the kingdom of God.

And so, as Nero was slaughtering Christians, they were not thinking to themselves, "May Rome be great again!" They were thinking, "May the people of the Roman Empire come to know Jesus! May Nero repent and be saved! May the kingdom of God replace the kingdom of Rome!"

Many of these early Christians were also familiar with the prophecy in Daniel 2:40-45, where a little stone, representing the kingdom of God, would smash the great kingdoms of the world. Rome would certainly be at the top of the list. As expressed some centuries later by

Theodoret of Cyr (c. 393–466 AD), "The stone that was cut without hands and grew into a great mountain and fills the whole earth is the second advent, and it will strike against the feet of the vessel . . . and all kingdoms will be destroyed and delivered up to oblivion, and the kingdom without end will be established."[4] Or, with reference to the transforming effect of the gospel on the kingdoms of the world, Augustine (354-430 AD) wrote, "We know that the stone cut from the mountain without hands is Christ, who came from the kingdom of the Jews without human father: the stone that shattered all the kingdoms of the earth, all the tyrannies of idols and devils; the stone that grew and became a great mountain and filled the whole world."[5]

There is, then, a great difference between praying, "Your kingdom come, Lord" and praying, "God bless America." The former asks for God to visit our nation and bring about change; the second can mean, "Make us bigger and better and stronger, Lord!" – without a stitch of repentance on our part.

It is true that America has been a blessed nation and that our country has done much good for the world. And it's true that we have some deep and beautiful Christian roots that have positively impacted our history. But we are hardly the proverbial "city set on a hill" for the world to see (see Matthew 5:16).[6] We lead the world in the production and exportation of pornography.[7] We lead the world in single-parent homes.[8] Our national debt is over 25 trillion dollars and rising.[9] We have been ranked one of the worst countries in the world for human trafficking.[10] We have the world's largest prison population and the highest reported rate of incarceration per capita.[11] And we have not fully overcome our history of slavery and segregation.[12] Accordingly, a 2011 article in *Business Insider* listed "20 Shameful Categories In Which America Leads The World."[13] To this day, we still lead in many of these shameful categories.

Again, there are many great qualities about America, and it is fine to be patriotic. But it is not fine to confuse our loyalties since our ultimate citizenship is in heaven (Philippians 3:20). Jesus, not Caesar, not Trump, not any man, is our Lord. This earth is not our eternal home, and our prayer is for the full manifestation of God's kingdom, not the exaltation of America. Our focus, then, is clear: the cross comes before the flag, overwhelmingly so.

In that respect, America is not so much divided between right and left, conservative and liberal, Republican and Democrat, but between saved and lost, either of God or of "the world." And "the world," according to Scripture, lies under the power of the evil one (1 John 5:19; 2 Corinthians 4:4). In that respect, we are more connected to the worldwide Body of Christ, our spiritual family, then we are to fellow Americans, despite our deep ties.

And so, our greatest dream is not MAGA ("Make America Great Again") as much as it is MAG ("Make America Godly"). Keeping this central – which means keeping our focus on the gospel more than politics – we will keep our bearings. Keeping this central, we will be the greatest possible blessing to our nation.

In his classic work *Screwtape Letters*, C. S. Lewis records the counsel of a senior demon, named Screwtape, to a less experienced demon in training, maned Wormwood. As the discussion turns to how to distract a Christian from his or her highest priorities, the question is raised as to whether patriotism or pacifism would be the better distraction. The senior demons explains,

Let him begin by treating the Patriotism or the Pacifism as part of his religion. Then let him, under the influence of partisan spirit, come to regard it as the most important. Then quietly and gradually nurse him on to the state at which the religion becomes merely a part of the "cause," in which Christianity is valued chiefly because of the excellent arguments it can produce. . . . Once [he's] made the world an end, and faith a means, you have almost won your man, and it makes very little difference what kind of worldly end he is pursuing.[14]

Enough said.

2. We must proclaim that Donald Trump is our president, not our Savior.

As I write these words, I'm wearing a flag-colored t-shirt given to me by a friend, carrying these words: **Jesus Is My Savior. Trump Is My President**. That is in keeping with the title of my 2018 book, *Donald Trump Is Not My Savior: An Evangelical Leader Speaks His Mind About the Man He Supports as President.*[15]

This, of course, is self-evident to any devoted Christian. We owe our souls to the Savior, not the president. Yet this is a message we need to make clear to the world, preaching Jesus and exalting Jesus and focusing on Jesus rather than preaching Trump and exalting Trump and focusing on Trump.

We can have our political discussions. And we will certainly have our political disagreements, some of them sharp. But at the end of the day, let's make it a point to say to those we differ with, "Hey, we can have our passionate debates about the president, but there's something much more important. How are *you* doing? How is your relationship with God? And who is Jesus to you? He is everything to me."

Let Him be our theme. Let His name be mentioned through the day. Let Him be the one who drives our passion. And let's be sure to help everyone know, without any doubt, that we identify with Jesus, our totally perfect Redeemer, infinitely more than we identify with Trump, our very imperfect president.

It's also crucial that our *attitudes* reflect this reality, that our hope for the nation is in the Lord, not in a man, that our expectations are tied in with the name of Jesus, not the name of Trump. And let's remember that, on that final great day, the entire universe will bow down and confess Jesus as Lord, willingly or unwillingly. At that moment, not only will the name of Trump be forgotten, along with all of our names, but no one will notice him among the billions bowing the knee with awe and wonder. Only Jesus is Lord. Only Jesus saves. Donald Trump is just one of many billions created by the Son and for the whom the Son died. Let us not lose our perspective.

3. We must put greater emphasis on spiritual activity than on political activity.

On May 12, 2020, I tweeted, "If only we were as passionate about prayer as we are about politics! The nation would be rocked almost overnight and our own lives would be transformed."[16] There was no hyperbole in this tweet, and many agreed with the comment. But this is easier said than done.

Our emotions get so stirred. Families become divided. Passions rise at the name of Trump, both for him and against him. And with every election cycle, we are told, "This is the most election of our lifetime! The stakes are incredibly high! We need to get out the vote!"

Then there are the endless newscasts and talk shows and sensational headlines, to the point that we do not have an election focus every four years or even every two years. Instead, we have it around the clock almost every day of the week. The election cycle never ceases. Nor do the campaign speeches or the email appeals or the fundraising. And the monetary numbers involved are staggering.

As the *Washington Post* reported on April 14, 2017,

> The final price tag for the 2016 election is in: $6.5 billion for the presidential and congressional elections combined, according to campaign finance watchdog OpenSecrets.org.
>
> The presidential contest — primaries and all — accounts for $2.4 billion of that total. The other $4 billion or so went to congressional races. The tally includes spending by campaigns, party committees and outside sources. It's actually down, slightly, in inflation-adjusted terms from 2012 and 2008.
>
> $6.5 billion is a staggering sum. With that much money you could fund the Corporation for Public Broadcasting for 15 years, fix the Flint, Mich., lead pipe problem 30 times over or give every public school teacher a $2,000 raise.
>
> Instead, Americans used that money to fuel a 596-day political contest that most of us were 'disgusted' by well before it was over.[17]

And here's the worst part of all. The spending could be reduced by 90 percent with the same results overall, meaning, if Candidate A did not spend as much money attacking Candidate B, then Candidate B wouldn't have to spend as much money counterattacking Candidate A. Yet the spending battle continues apace, and a good part of that money comes from committed Christians.

If only we had spent that money on local evangelism (let alone on world evangelism). Or on caring for the needy in our communities. Or in helping advance the cause of justice in our cities. I would hope that true Christians on all sides of the political divide would agree with me on this.

But it's not just a matter of money. It's a matter of emphasis and heart and focus. Have we forgotten what Paul wrote in Ephesians 6? There he said, "For we are not fighting against flesh-and-blood enemies, but against evil rulers and authorities of the unseen world, against mighty powers in this dark world, and against evil spirits in the heavenly places" (Ephesians 6:12, NLT). Elsewhere he wrote, "For though we walk in the flesh, we do not wage war according to the flesh. 4 For the weapons of our warfare are not fleshly but powerful through God for the tearing down of strongholds. We are tearing down false arguments 5 and every high-minded thing that exalts itself against the knowledge of God. We are taking every thought captive to the obedience of Messiah" (2 Corinthians 10:3-5, TLV).

Shortly before Jesus ascended to heaven, His disciples asked Him a perfectly valid question: "Lord, are you at this time going to restore the kingdom to Israel?" He did not rebuke them but answered, "It is not for you to know the times or dates the Father has set by his own authority. But you will receive power when the Holy Spirit comes on you; and you will be my witnesses in Jerusalem, and in all Judea and Samaria, and to the ends of the earth" (Acts 1:6–8).

That's where our emphasis must be as well, and this must be our greatest activity: being Spirit-empowered witnesses of the Lord, beginning right where we live. Our battle is with Satan more than anyone else, and we win the battle with prayer, with fasting, with the truth of the Word, with the power of the Spirit, with holiness, with compassion. Who or what can stand in the way of *that*?

4. We must not get caught up with election fever.

I just referenced how, these days, the election cycle seems continuous, with enormous amounts of money spent each campaign season. And it seems that election polling is non-stop as well, with pollsters telling us how people are feeling more than eighteen months before a single vote will be cast. Does this information help at all? And do we really need to know it?

But, just like a compelling sports event, we get caught up in the drama of the moment. We get angry with the talking heads on TV. We get outraged over the latest headline ("Fake news!"). We get embroiled in social media battles. We get in the flesh. (Please don't tell me that all your emotions reflect a holy and righteous indignation and that you are always "in the Spirit" when it comes to politics. Forgive me if I'm a bit skeptical.)

And again, nowadays, this is not just something that happens once every four years. It is a continual cycle, and it is a cycle in which we cannot afford to get caught. We must step higher.

In keeping with my last point, may I suggest that we spend more time worshiping the Lord than watching the news? That we spend more time reading the Word (and edifying Christian literature) than reading about politics? That we meditate on the sovereignty of God until we are convinced that, having cast our vote and done our part in influencing the elections, we acknowledge the Lord as King, no matter who wins?

I can address these issues pointedly because I have so often failed to live them out, not in terms of my overall faith, but in terms of my emotions. And the fact that I'm a radio host and a columnist and author doesn't change the facts at all: there is no reason for me (or any of us) to get caught up in election fever.

It would be more understandable if we were directly involved in a campaign, working tirelessly to get our candidate elected. But for the vast majority of us, that is not the case. Let us step up and worship the Lord of the universe, focusing on His eternal virtues and His worldwide kingdom. It will change our perspective a lot. And it will bring us a lot more joy and peace along the way.

5. We must not justify carnality and unchristian behavior.

Have you ever heard an off-color joke and tried not to laugh? The joke itself was very funny, but the humor was inappropriate, hence the attempt not to show approval, despite the evident humor. It's the same thing with many a Trump tweet or comment. He can be very funny with his insults. His barbs can be enormously clever. And some of them are unforgettable, helping to sink an opponent's candidacy. But is it right for us to laugh along with them or, worse still, to defend them?

It's one thing when he stands up to his adversaries, be they in the media or politics or Hollywood, but it's the way that he does it that is often carnal and destructive. As I said earlier in the book, I'm all for fighting and taking a stand, as long as it is done rightly. But, when it comes to our president, I fear that we have gotten caught up in the carnality, that we have been sullied by the mudslinging, that we have lost our sensitivity out of solidarity with "our man."

For many years now, I have worked with fine Christian leaders in India, and sometimes they want an update on what is happening in America, from an evangelical perspective. In December, 2019, I sought to explain the challenges faced by evangelicals when it came to President Trump, as laid out throughout this book. Despite the language and cultural barriers (everything is translated into Telugu as I speak, sometimes into Telugu and Hindi), I tried to paint a picture of the bombastic side of Trump, using his "Rocket Man" designation for the leader of North Korea. (Yes, I had to explain the song too. It wasn't easy.)

The pastors were laughing over this, as was I when I told the story. It's hard not to laugh, and this was Trump at his best and worst simultaneously. But this is only the tip of the iceberg. There is often downright nastiness and immature, self-centered behavior. Why on earth would we want to defend it?

Not surprisingly, the *New York Times* railed on the president for his words during one particular day in May 2020 (Thursday, the 14th) in the midst of the ongoing COVID-19 crisis. A team of journalists wrote:

> Far from a one-day onslaught, it was a climactic moment in a weeklong lurch by Mr. Trump back to the darkest tactics that defined his rise to political power. Even those who have grown used to Mr. Trump's conduct in office may have found themselves newly alarmed by the grim spectacle of a sitting president deliberately stoking the country's divisions and pursuing personal vendettas in the midst of a crisis that has Americans fearing for their lives and livelihoods.[18]

And their points are well-taken, even if I would beg to differ with some of the specifics of the article. Just think of how much better things would be in the American psyche had the president not focused on himself during such difficult times and stepped higher in his dealings with the press.

Unfortunately, the press has been unrelenting, vicious, unfair, and very personal, making it very difficult for a fighter like Trump *to* step higher. For our part, it's too easy for us to fall into this vicious cycle, which basically looks like this: 1) In the beginning, many of us were not fond of Trump, not so much voting for him but rather voting against Hillary. 2) To our pleasant surprise, he stayed true to his campaign promises, also surrounding himself with solid evangelicals. 3) The media (and his opponents in the political world and the world of entertainment) attacked him unceasingly, claiming he was mentally unstable, claiming he colluded with Russia, calling for his impeachment, posting memes of his murder, and more. 4) Trump, unlike some of his predecessors, decided to fight back, and we, in turn, stood up for him. 5) Then we crossed a line, feeling it our sacred duty to defend him no matter what.

We must step back from that dangerous line, supporting our president for the good that he does, calling out unfair attacks against him, but never defending his mean-spirited, ugly, and carnal behavior. Let us remember that the world is watching.

6. We must regain our prophetic voice.

On June 11, 1967, Martin Luther King, Jr., spoke these piercing and prescient words:

> The church must be reminded that it is not the master or the servant of the state, but rather the conscience of the state. It must be the guide and the critic of the state, and never its tool. If the church does not recapture its prophetic zeal, it will become an irrelevant social club without moral or spiritual authority. If the church does not participate actively in the struggle for peace and for economic and racial justice, it will forfeit the loyalty of millions and cause men everywhere to say that it has atrophied its will. But if the church will free itself from the shackles of a deadening status quo, and, recovering its great historic mission, will speak and act fearlessly and insistently in terms of justice and peace, it will enkindle the imagination of mankind and fire the souls of men, imbuing them with a glowing and ardent love for truth, justice, and peace. Men far and near will know the church as a great fellowship of love that provides light and bread for lonely travelers at midnight.[19]

What an incredible message, and what a relevant warning: "If the church does not recapture its prophetic zeal, it will become an irrelevant social club without moral or spiritual authority." Isn't this what has largely happened in America for the last generation? We are either associated with a self-centered prosperity message or with a partisan political message. We are not largely associated with bringing a prophetic message from the heart of God to a confused and lost society. But this is a role we must recover. We have no choice.

It's true that there were prophetic "yes men" in the Bible, but they were the false prophets, not the true prophets. They spoke by means of a lying spirit, not the Holy Spirit (see 1 Kings 22). They were people pleasers rather than God pleasers. But the Spirit of God has no political ties, no concern with public opinion, no fear of human repercussions. Prophets spoke (and speak) the truth, as moved and stirred and even compelled by God. That is why they are often hated, even to the point of being killed (Matthew 5:10-12; 23:29-31; Acts 7:51-53). It will be the same for us today, even as we walk in humility, even as we walk in love, even as we beseech and appeal.

In the end, we will be "equal opportunity offenders," challenging the religious and societal status quo, challenging the complacent and the compromised, calling for change, however costly. That makes us popular with God and unpopular with man. So be it! We give account to Him.

According to T. Austin Sparks, prophetic ministry "is the interpretation of everything from a spiritual standpoint; the bringing of the spiritual implications of things, past, present and future, before the people of God, and giving them to understand the significance of things in their spiritual value and meaning. That was and is the essence of prophetic ministry."

And, writing in 1948, he said this:

> I am quite sure that those who have any knowledge whatever of the times, spiritually, will agree with me when I say that the crying need of our time is for a prophetic ministry. There never was a time when there existed so extensively the need for a voice of interpretation, when conditions needed more the ministry of explanation. One does not want to make extravagant statements or to be extreme in one's

utterances, but I do not think it would be either extravagant or extreme to say that the world today is well-nigh bankrupt of real prophetic ministry in this sense - a voice that interprets the mind of God to people. It may exist in some small degree here and there, but in no very large way is that ministry being fulfilled. So often our hearts groan and cry out, Oh, that the mind of God about the present situation could be brought through, in the first place to the recognition of His people, and then through His people to others beyond! There is a great and terrible need for a prophetic ministry in our time.[20]

If this was true in 1948, how much truer is it today? Proverbs 29:18a says it all: "Where there is no prophetic revelation, people cast off restraint" (my translation). We urgently need that prophetic word today.

7. We must be holistic Christians, truly pursuing justice and righteousness for all.

Some years ago, I took an online political survey, responding to questions about where I stood on certain social and political issues. To my surprise, when the survey was completed, it informed me that 100 percent of my views were in harmony with the Republican platform at that time and zero percent of my views were in harmony the Democratic platform. To be sure, I knew that was the case with my views on issues relating to abortion and marriage and family. Yet I seriously doubt that, if I went through every item of both party platforms at that time, I would have found myself agreeing with every single item of the one while rejecting every single item of the other.

Even with something as important as the appointing of conservative justices, which I strongly support and which factors largely into my voting, there is another side to the story, namely, the concern that these same justices tend to pass harsher sentences on African Americans. Is this a fair accusation in particular? Writing in the *Washington Post*, September 18, 2018, Radley Balko noted that,

A couple years ago, Sen. Tim Scott (R-S.C.) gave a powerful speech on the floor of the U.S. Senate. Scott talked about how he had been repeatedly pulled over by police officers who seemed to be suspicious of a black man driving a nice car. He added that a black senior-level staffer had experienced the same thing and had even downgraded his car in the hope of avoiding the problem. Given that Scott otherwise has pretty conservative politics, there was little objection or protest from the right. No one rose up to say that he was lying about getting pulled over.

The thing is, most people of color have a similar story or know someone who does. Yet, there's a deep skepticism on the right of any assertion that the criminal-justice system is racially biased. In early August, National Review editor and syndicated columnist Rich Lowry wrote a column disputing the notion that our system is racist. Andrew Sullivan wrote something similar in New York magazine. (Interestingly, both Lowry and Sullivan cite criminologist John Pfaff to support their positions. Pfaff has since protested on Twitter that both misinterpreted what he wrote.) And attempting to refute the notion that the system is racist has become a pretty regular beat for conservative crime pundit Heather Mac Donald.

What of Balko's view? He wrote, that "after more than a decade covering these issues, it's pretty clear to me that the evidence of racial bias in our criminal-justice system isn't just convincing — it's overwhelming."[21] And he devotes the rest of his lengthy, detailed article to presenting this "overwhelming" evidence.

I'm sure that there are conservative counter-arguments to these points, even as Balko begins his article by linking to some of them. But his arguments must be taken seriously as well, especially if we truly have God's heart for justice for all. Righteousness is bigger than either party, and both parties express care for hurting and needy Americans, for those who are unfairly treated, for those who are objects of discrimination.

An African American pastor in New York City once said to me, "You want to get prayer back into the schools. I want to get education back into the schools!" Our perspectives, both valid, were very different, but from his vantage point as an inner-city pastor, I would say his concern was the more relevant. I've also spoken with solid, committed,

Jesus-honoring, African American evangelicals who do not vote Republican, and when they explain their reasoning, even though I differ with them, I do see their points.

Some tell me they hate abortion and oppose homosexual "marriage," but they don't see these issues being solved politically, so they vote for the other issues that concern them, issues they feel political leaders can address. Then they work to change hearts and minds on these other issues. Again, I do not agree with their voting decisions, but I understand their heart, and they often bring to my attention issues of systemic unfairness in our society that we, as followers of Jesus, must address.[22] Even as we oppose many of the goals of LGBTQ activism, may we demonstrate true Christian love for them as individuals created in God's image. Let us be holistic in our concerns and burdens.

8. We must walk in love towards those who vilify us and oppose us.

I addressed this at length in Chapter Three, but allow me to cite (and repeat) some important verses here. May we live this out for the glory of the Lord!

- "You have heard that it was said, 'Love your neighbor and hate your enemy.' But I tell you, love your enemies and pray for those who persecute you, that you may be children of your Father in heaven. He causes his sun to rise on the evil and the good, and sends rain on the righteous and the unrighteous. If you love those who love you, what reward will you get? Are not even the tax collectors doing that? And if you greet only your own people, what are you doing more than others? Do not even pagans do that? Be perfect, therefore, as your heavenly Father is perfect." (Matthew 5:43–48)
- "Bless those who persecute you; bless and do not curse. . . . Do not repay anyone evil for evil. Be careful to do what is right in the eyes of everyone. If it is possible, as far as it depends on you, live at peace with everyone. Do not take revenge, my dear friends, but leave room for God's wrath,

for it is written: "It is mine to avenge; I will repay," says the Lord. On the contrary: "If your enemy is hungry, feed him; if he is thirsty, give him something to drink. In doing this, you will heap burning coals on his head." Do not be overcome by evil, but overcome evil with good." (Romans 12:14, 17-21)

- "To this you were called, because Christ suffered for you, leaving you an example, that you should follow in his steps. 'He committed no sin, and no deceit was found in his mouth.' When they hurled their insults at him, he did not retaliate; when he suffered, he made no threats. Instead, he entrusted himself to him who judges justly." (1 Peter 2:21–23)

- "Remind the people to be subject to rulers and authorities, to be obedient, to be ready to do whatever is good, to slander no one, to be peaceable and considerate, and always to be gentle toward everyone. At one time we too were foolish, disobedient, deceived and enslaved by all kinds of passions and pleasures. We lived in malice and envy, being hated and hating one another. But when the kindness and love of God our Savior appeared, he saved us, not because of righteous things we had done, but because of his mercy. He saved us through the washing of rebirth and renewal by the Holy Spirit, whom he poured out on us generously through Jesus Christ our Savior, so that, having been justified by his grace, we might become heirs having the hope of eternal life." (Titus 3:1–7)

Then, this last reminder as to how we are to treat one another as brothers and sisters in Jesus: "A new command I give you: Love one another. As I have loved you, so you must love one another. By this everyone will know that you are my disciples, if you love one another." (John 13:34–35)

9. We must unite around Jesus rather than divide over Trump.

According to Jon Meacham, as Billy Graham got older, he got less involved in political issues (although, to be sure, he actively opposed redefining marriage in 2012.[23] Meacham writes, "For Graham, then, politics became 'hot-button issues' to be avoided. 'At my age,' he said when he was eighty-seven, 'I have one message': the Gospel."[24] Ultimately, that must be our message as well, the thing we are most known for, the thing that comes to mind when people think about us. We are gospel people. We are Jesus people. He is our theme, our song, our message, our life.

I touched on this above, in the first two points, but I emphasize it again here because this is also the key to our unity, since, when push comes to shove, despite our political differences, in Jesus, we are one. The world hates us. Satan opposes us. Jesus redeemed us. And we will be with Him – and each other – forever in the world to come.

We can have our disagreements, even our passionate ones. That's what families do. In fact, we sometimes have even more intense disagreements within the family then outside the family. But that's because we're family. We can talk to each other a certain way. We can use strong words. But our unity is strong. Blood *is* thicker than water.

It is urgent that we recover that unity today, recognizing that our differences over Trump are a tiny molehill when compared to the mountain of common ground that we share in the Lord. We know what it means to have our sins forgiven. We know what it means to encounter God. We know what it means to be "saved" and to be in right relationship with our Maker. We know what it means to tremble at His feet, to worship Him with joy, to walk in His Spirit, to revere His Word.

The non-believing world knows none of this, looking at us as if we're crazy, labeling us as if we've lost our minds, often mocking our precious beliefs and scorning our sacred dogmas. In the words of John, "You, dear children, are from God and have overcome them, because the one who is in you is greater than the one who is in the world. They are from the world and therefore speak from the viewpoint of the world, and the world listens to them. We are from God, and whoever knows God listens to us; but whoever is not from God does not listen to us. This is how we recognize the Spirit of truth and the spirit of false-hood." (1 John 4:4–6)

I do understand that the moment the name "Trump" comes up there is controversy and division and tension and passion. But if we start with Jesus? What if we exalt Him first? What if we ask one another, "How has He changed your life?" Then, as believers, rejoicing in our mutual faith, we ask, "So, explain to me why you support (or, don't support Trump)." And then, once we're done explaining our perspectives, rather than debate them and then divide, we pray for him, we pray for America, we pray for each other, and we go back to praising the Lord. Can you imagine what this would do our nation, let alone for the Church?

And let's never forget that preserving our testimony as followers of Jesus is far more important than who is in the White House. We can survive a bad president, as costly as that might be, but we cannot survive the loss of our testimony.[25]

10. We must lead the nation in repentance, knowing that repentance prepares the way of the Lord, opening a path for revival, visitation, and awakening.

We all agree that elections play an important role in our society, other-wise you would not be reading this book and I would not have written it. But let's be candid. If every president for the next fifty years was an equal to George Washington or Abraham Lincoln, that would not solve our country's deepest problems. If every Supreme Court justice adjudi-cated righteously, that would not heal our wounds. Only a massive, sweeping revival in the Church, leading to a glorious awakening in the society, can turn the tide. Otherwise, we will continue sliding down the slope of immorality, injustice, carnality, hatred, division, murder, addic-tion, and so much more.

Of course, America will never be a fully "Christian" nation in this age. No nation will. And a theocracy is *not* the answer. (Who among us would want clergy of any background ruling over the nation, by alleged divine command, and making authoritative judgments to be obeyed by all, enforced under penalty of law?) I'm simply talking about turning things in a more positive direction, about undoing some of the damage caused by the sexual revolution and radical feminism and homosexual activism, all of it aided and abetted by a compromised, self-exalting message from our pulpits.

We can debate the meaning of "Make America Great Again," especially from the vantage point of a Native American or African American. When was America "great" for them? What point in time are we seeking to recover? Still, it's hard to deny that, not that long ago, our society was more innocent, families were more intact, there was more fear of God, and churches were more committed to the Word. We were not as addicted or as distracted or as in debt. The idea of homosexual "marriage" was unthinkable, as was the idea of middle school children exchanging naked photos. And who would have imagined, when the first Playboy centerfold came out in 1953, featuring Marilyn Monroe, that today, on average, children would be exposed to pornography at the age of eleven?[26] And what of the ongoing racial divisions in America? Or the plague of human trafficking? Or a host of other, deep-seated problems which no president or congress of court can solve?

Our only hope is a national revival, and that revival must begin with us, the church, the people of God. The very mention of the word "revival" presupposes that, as Charles Finney (1792-1875) so clearly observed, explaining that, "It presupposes that the church is sunk down in a backslidden state, and a revival consists in the return of the Church from her backslidings and the conversion of sinners."[27] And what, exactly would this look like? Finney offered this vivid description, emphasizing that revival starts with us, the people of God, which also means that repentance starts with us, the people of God. From there, it sweeps over to the world. He wrote:

> **1. The foundations of sin need to be broken up.** A revival always includes conviction of sin on the part of the church. Backslidden professors [meaning, backslidden Christians, here called "professors" as in "professors of faith"] cannot wake up and begin right away in the service of God without deep searchings of heart. The fountains of sin need to be broken up. In a true revival, Christians are always brought under such conviction; they see their sins in such a light that often they find it impossible to maintain a hope of their acceptance with God. It does not always go to that extent, but there are always, in a

genuine revival, deep convictions of sin, and often cases of abandoning all hope.

2. Revival is a new beginning of obedience with God. Just as in the case of a converted sinner, the first step is a deep repentance, a breaking down of heart, a getting down into the dust before God, with humility, and a forsaking of sin.

3. Christians will have their faith renewed. While they are in their Backslidden state they are blind to the state of sinners. Their hearts are hard as marble. The truths of the Bible appear like a dream. They admit it to be all true; their conscience and their judgment assent to it; but their faith does not see it standing out in bold relief, in all the burning realities of eternity. But when they enter into a revival, they no longer see "men as trees, walking," but they see things in that strong light which will renew the love of God in their hearts. This will lead them to labor zealously to bring others to Him. They will feel grieved that others do not love God, when they love Him so much. And they will set themselves feelingly to persuade their neighbors to give Him their hearts. So their love to men will be renewed. They will be filled with a tender and burning love for souls. They will have a longing desire for the salvation of the whole world. They will be in an agony for individuals whom they want to have saved--their friends, relations, enemies. They will not only be urging them to give their hearts to God, but they will carry them to God in the arms of faith, and with strong crying and tears beseech God to have mercy on them, and save their souls from endless burnings.

4. A revival breaks the power of the world and of sin over Christians. It brings them to such vantage ground that they get a fresh impulse towards heaven; they have a new foretaste of heaven, and new desires after union with God; thus the charm of the world is broken, and the power of sin overcome.

5. When the Churches are thus awakened and reformed, the reformation and salvation of sinners will follow. Their hearts will be broken down and changed. Very often the most abandoned profligates are among the subjects. Harlots, and drunkards, and infidels, and all sorts of abandoned characters, are awakened and converted. The worst of human beings are softened and reclaimed, and made to appear as lovely specimens of the beauty of holiness.[28]

While there may be debate about some of Finney's theology and methods, I find his words here to be deeply sobering and thoroughly scriptural. As for when a true revival could be expected, Finney said this: "A revival may be expected when Christians have a spirit of prayer for a revival. That is, when they pray as if their hearts were set upon it. When Christians have the spirit of prayer for a revival. When they go about groaning out their hearts desire. When they have real travail of soul."[29] In other words, we can expect a true revival when our hearts long for God with a holy desperation, when our burden for the lost brings us to the point of "travail," when our cries become a mighty crescendo reaching the throne of our heavenly Father.

Then the answer will come, as surely as God is God. As He said through the prophet Isaiah, "For this is what the high and exalted One says— he who lives forever, whose name is holy: 'I live in a high and holy place, but also with the one who is contrite and lowly in spirit, to revive the spirit of the lowly and to revive the heart of the contrite.'" (Isaiah 57:15)

Let us, then, lead the nation in private and public repentance, in confession of sin and wrongdoing, of turning to righteousness, of turning to God. That is the great hope of America, not four more years of Donald Trump, or any political candidate, but a heaven-sent revival and awakening.

Until that time comes, we pray, we reach out, we serve, we speak, we love, and we get involved in the political process, but with our focus in the right place and our hopes firmly rooted in the Lord and the Lord alone. If we do this, we will pass the Trump test with flying colors. And who knows? Perhaps he too will be mightily touched by God and help lead the nation into deeper repentance and awakening. What is impossible with people is possible with God.

Notes

1. The Enigma of Donald Trump and the Quandary of Evangelicals

1. Email correspondence, September 20, 2019.
2. I'm quoting author and apologist Frank Turek, who shared this with me directly.
3. "White Evangelicals See Trump as Fighting for Their Beliefs, Though Many Have Mixed Feelings About His Personal Conduct," Pew Research Center, March 12, 2020, https://www.pewforum.org/2020/03/12/white-evangelicals-see-trump-as-fighting-for-their-beliefs-though-many-have-mixed-feelings-about-his-personal-conduct/.
4. Wayne Grudem, "Trump Should Not Be Removed From Office: A Response to Mark Galli and *Christianity Today*," The Stream, January 1, 2020, https://stream.org/trump-should-not-be-removed-from-office-a-response-to-mark-galli-and-christianity-today/. Dr. Grudem had misnumbered these in his article, accidentally skipping #16, and then mislabeling #16-19 as 17-20.
5. Marc A. Thiessen "The 10 best things Trump did in 2019," *The Washington Post*, Dec. 26, 2019, https://www.washingtonpost.com/opinions/2019/12/26/best-things-trump-has-done/.
6. The Times Editorial Board, "Trump's presidency is a train wreck. Let us count the ways," *Los Angeles Times*, October 20, 2019, https://www.latimes.com/opinion/story/2019-10-20/trump-failures-outrages.
7. Peter Wehner "Trump is Not Well," *The Atlantic*, September 9, 2019, https://www.theatlantic.com/ideas/archive/2019/09/donald-trump-not-well/597640/.
8. Both of these comments were posted on November 16, 2019.
9. Stephen E. Strang, *God, Trump, and the 2020 Election: Why He Must Win and What's at Stake for Christians if He Loses* (Lake Mary, FL: Frontline, 2020).
10. Veronica Stracqualursi, "Ex-Christian publication editor who quit says he had 'no other choice' after pro-Trump editorial," CNN, December 26, 2019, https://www.cnn.com/2019/12/26/politics/napp-nazworth-christian-editor-trump-cnntv/index.html.
11. See The Christian Post Editors, "Donald Trump Is a Scam. Evangelical Voters Should Back Away," *The Christian Post*, February 29, 2016, https://www.christianpost.com/news/donald-trump-scam-evangelical-voters-back-away-cp-editorial.html.
12. Ibid. Emphasis in the original.
13. John Grano and Richard Land, "Christianity Today and the problem with 'Christian elitism'," *The Christian Post*, December 23, 2019, https://www.christianpost.com/news/christianity-today-and-the-problem-with-christian-elitism.html.
14. Victor David Hanson, *The Case for Trump* (New York: Basic Books, 2019).
15. Brandy X. Lee, ed., *The Dangerous Case of Donald Trump: 37 Psychiatrists and Mental Health Experts Assess a President* (updated and expanded edition; New York: Saint Martin's Press, 2019).
16. Eric Jensen, "Jon Voight attacks 'radical left,' hails Trump as 'the greatest president

of this century'," *USA Today*, August 20, 2019, https://www.usatoday.com/story/entertainment/celebrities/2019/08/20/jon-voight-trump-the-greatest-president-century/2059215001/.

17. Kathy Frankovic, "Trump better than Lincoln? Republicans think so," YouGov, December 2, 2019, https://today.yougov.com/topics/politics/articles-reports/2019/12/02/greatest-republican-president.

18. Pam Key, "Schumer: 'No Person Has Done More to Destroy the Honor and Values of America Than Donald Trump'," Breitbart News, January 13, 2020, https://www.breitbart.com/clips/2020/01/14/schumer-no-person-has-done-more-to-destroy-the-honor-and-values-of-america-than-donald-trump/.

19. Pam Key, "James Carville: Trump 'Greatest Threat' America Has Faced Since Fall of Communism," Breitbart News, January 14, 2019, https://www.breitbart.com/clips/2020/01/14/james-carville-trump-greatest-threat-america-has-faced-since-fall-of-communism/.

20. Michael Brown, "Equivocating or Evolving, President Obama is Wrong Either Way," Townhall, May 12, 2012, https://townhall.com/columnists/michaelbrown/2012/05/12/equivocating-or-evolving-president-obama-is-wrong-either-way-n823824.

21. Shane Claiborne, Twitter Post, February 1, 2020, https://twitter.com/ShaneClaiborne/status/1223488570691915781.

22. Shane Claiborne, Twitter Post, January 28, 2020, https://twitter.com/ShaneClaiborne/status/1222037524354420736.

23. At the time he made these statements, I took strong but respectful issue with him. See Michael Brown, "An Open Letter to Pastor Robert Jeffress," Charisma News, March 7, 2016, https://www.charismanews.com/opinion/in-the-line-of-fire/55653-an-open-letter-to-pastor-robert-jeffress; for his original quotes, see Leonardo Blair, "Robert Jeffress: Christians Not Voting for Donald Trump If He's the Nominee Are Foolish, Prideful," *The Christian Post Reporter*, March 2, 2016, https://www.christianpost.com/news/robert-jeffress-christians-not-voting-donald-trump-foolish-prideful-158881/. Since 2016, Jeffress has become one of Trump's most vocal evangelical supporters.

24. To be sure, there are aspects of Shane's Christianity which are absolutely heterodox, including his willingness to affirm (and even celebrate) long-term, monogamous same-sex "marriages." For my interview with Shane, recorded May 14, 2020, see https://youtu.be/ZOOUR-X-DEs.

2. Since When Was Loyalty to Trump the Dividing Line for Christians?

1. Ed Mazza, "Jim Bakker To Christians: You Must Love Trump To Prove You're 'Saved'," *Huffington Post*, January 7, 2020, https://www.huffpost.com/entry/jim-bakker-trump-saved_n_5e1401f8e4b0b2520d26d35e

2. Ibid. From the opposite perspective, cf. the remarks of Southern Baptist leader Russell Moore, who wrote in 2015, "To back Mr. Trump, these voters [evangelicals] must repudiate everything they believe." See idem, "Have Evangelicals Who Support Trump Lost Their Values?," *The New York Times*, September 17, 2015, https://www.nytimes.com/2015/09/17/opinion/have-evangelicals-who-support-trump-lost-their-values.html.

3. *The Immoral Majority*, 42.

4. Ibid., 40.

5. Ibid., 44-45.

6. Howe, *The Immoral Majority*, 69.

3. Have We Failed the Love Test?

1. Most recently, see *Jezebel's War with America: The Plot to Destroy Our Country and What We Can Do to Turn the Tide* (Lake Mary, FL: Frontline, 2019), especially 180-196.

2. Michael Cruse, "If He's Not in a Fight, He Looks for One," *Politico Magazine*, September, 23, 2019, https://www.politico.com/magazine/story/2019/09/23/trump-ukraine-scandal-enemy-228152.

3. Posted here and elsewhere: Evan Sayet, "He Fights," The Stream, November 15, 2018, https://stream.org/he-fights/.

4. The previous sentences were, "You are deceived if you think that a Christian can live without persecution. He suffers the greatest who lives under none." See Alban Butler, *Lives of the Saints*, 1866, Bartleby.com, https://www.bartleby.com/210/9/301.html.

5. As cited in Michael Cruse, "The 199 Most Donald Trump Things Donald Trump Has Ever Said," *Political Magazine*, August 14, 2015, https://www.politico.com/magazine/story/2015/08/the-absolute-trumpest-121328.

6. From his book *How to Get Rich*, cited in ibid.

7. Sarah Pulliam Bailey, "'God has given Trump authority to take out Kim Jong Un,' evangelical adviser says," *The Washington Post*, August 9, 2017, https://www.washingtonpost.com/news/acts-of-faith/wp/2017/08/08/god-has-given-trump-authority-to-take-out-kim-jong-un-evangelical-adviser-says/?utm_term=.ad2d29ac2f9d.

8. "First Baptist's Robert Jeffress: 'God has given Trump authority to take out Kim Jong Un'," *The Dallas Morning News*, August 8, 2017, https://www.dallasnews.com/news/faith/2017/08/09/first-baptist-s-robert-jeffress-god-has-given-trump-authority-to-take-out-kim-jong-un/.

9. It has been my habit for some years now to remind readers that "James" was really "Jacob," as written in the Greek. See Michael Brown, "Recovering the Lost Letter of Jacob," Charisma News, March 11, 2013, https://www.charismanews.com/opinion/38591-recovering-the-lost.

10. She added this comment to a thread and then sent me the comment so I could quote it.

4. Does Character Still Count and Does Morality Still Matter?

1. David French, "Do the Southern Baptist Convention's Resolutions Contain a Partisan Caveat?," *National Review*, December 22, 2016, https://www.nationalreview.com/corner/do-southern-baptist-conventions-resolutions-contain-partisan-caveat/.

2. "Resolution On Moral Character Of Public Officials," Southern Baptist Convention, Salt Lake City, Utah, 1998. http://www.sbc.net/resolutions/773/resolution-on-moral-character-of-public-officials.

3. David French, "Do the Southern Baptist Convention's Resolutions Contain a Partisan Caveat?," *National Review*, December 22, 2016, https://www. nationalreview.com/corner/do-southern-baptist-conventions-resolutions-contain-partisan-caveat/.

4. David French, Twitter Post, December 27, 2019, https://twitter.com/ DavidAFrench/status/1210671328874942464.

5. Tucker Carlson, "Tucker Carlson: The real reason so many Christians are willing to support Trump," Fox News, December 24, 2019, https://www.foxnews.com/ opinion/tucker-carlson-christians-support-trump.

6. Although I do not have a link for this quote, which I read online and quoted from memory, a senior staff member with Franklin Graham confirmed its general accuracy to me. He explained, "Franklin would use that quote not to say he engages in politics more than his father, but the environment in America is much different than in the 50's even through the 90's and media coverage and treatment of people has played it much differently today."

7. For this editorial, by Mark Galli, see Chapter Eleven.

8. David Prager, "A Response to the Editor of Christianity Today," Townhall, December 24, 2019, https://townhall.com/columnists/dennisprager/2019/12/24/ a-response-to-the-editor-of-christianity-today-n2558477.

9. This is a paraphrase.

10. David Prager, "What Does Adultery Tell Us About Character?," Townhall.com, December 6, 2011, https://townhall.com/columnists/dennisprager/2011/12/06/ what-does-adultery-tell-us-about-character-n1025372.

11. I'm speaking of Heidi Cruz, the wife of Senator Ted Cruz, and then Carly Fiorina.

12. This time it was the father of Ted Cruz, Rafael Cruz.

13. Daniel White, "Watch Trump Talk About His Private Parts at the Debate," *Time*, March 3, 2016, https://time.com/4247366/republican-debate-donald-trump-small-hands-penis/.

14. Callum Borchers, "Meryl Streep was right. Donald Trump did mock a disabled reporter," *The Washington Post*, January 9, 2017, https://www.washingtonpost.com/ news/the-fix/wp/2017/01/09/meryl-streep-was-right-donald-trump-did-mock-a-disabled-reporter/.

15. Callum Borchers, "Ann Coulter says she can prove Donald Trump never mocked a reporter's disability. (She can't.)," *The Washington Post*, September 1, 2016, https:// www.washingtonpost.com/news/the-fix/wp/2016/09/01/ann-coulter-says-she-can-prove-donald-trump-never-mocked-a-reporters-disability-she-cant/.

16. Michael Brown, "Why Evangelical Christians Should Not Support Donald Trump," Townhall, November 29, 2015, https://townhall.com/columnists/ michaelbrown/2015/11/29/why-evangelical-christians-should-not-support-donald-trump-n2086230.

17. Chris Thurman, "You foolish evangelicals, Trump has bewitched you," *The Christian Post*, December 4, 2019, https://www.christianpost.com/voice/you-foolish-evangelicals-trump-has-bewitched-you.html.

18. For my response to Dr. Thurman, see here: Michael Brown, "Are Evangelicals Who Support Trump Fools?," *The Stream*, December 6, 2019, https://stream. org/are-evangelicals-who-support-trump-fools/; for his response to me, see here: Chris Thurman, "Yes, evangelicals, it is foolish to support Trump," *The Christian Post*, December 10, 2019, https://www.christianpost.com/voice/yes-evangelicals-it-is-foolish-to-support-trump.html; for my response to his response, see here: Michael Brown, "When a Christian Psychologist Makes Trump Into a Monster,"

The Stream, December 10, 2019, https://stream.org/christian-psychologist-makes-trump-monster/. For his apology, which I immediately and publicly accepted, see here: Chris Thurman, "To President Trump, evangelicals who support him, and Michael Brown: An apology and a challenge," *The Christian Post*, December 16, 2019, https://www.christianpost.com/voice/to-president-trump-evangelicals-who-support-him-and-michael-brown-an-apology-and-a-challenge.html.

19. *The Immoral Majority*, 82-83.

20. Ibid., 81.

21. Ibid., 81-82.

22. Leada Gore, "Dr. James Dobson responds to 'Christianity Today's' call for Trump removal," AL.com, December 23, 2019, https://www.al.com/news/2019/12/dr-james-dobson-responds-to-christianity-todays-call-for-trump-removal.html.

23. See Michael Brown "The Evangelical Elites vs. the Evangelical Deplorables: An Attempt at Mediation," The Stream, December 26, 2019, https://stream.org/the-evangelical-elites-vs-the-evangelical-deplorables-an-attempt-at-mediation/.

24. Dr. Michael L. Brown, Twitter Post, August 19, 2019 https://twitter.com/DrMichaelLBrown/status/1163530586939625479.

25. Donald J. Trump, Facebook Post, October 8, 2016, https://www.facebook.com/watch/?v=10157844642270725.

26. "Melania Trump Says Husband's Words Are 'Unacceptable' and Don't Represent Man She Knows," ABC News, October 8, 2016, https://abcnews.go.com/Politics/melania-trump-husbands-words-unacceptable-represent-man/story?id=42670225.

27. Wayne Grudem, "Trump Should Not Be Removed from Office: A Response to Mark Galli and Christianity Today," Townhall, December 30, 2019, https://townhall.com/columnists/waynegrudem/2019/12/30/trump-should-not-be-removed-from-office-a-response-to-mark-galli-and-christianity-today-n2558657.

28. Ibid.

29. Jonathan Pointer, Twitter Post, December 6, 2019, https://twitter.com/JonathanPointer/status/1203061679313113089.

30. https://www.facebook.com/ryan.cataldo.3

31. For a detailed article, but clearly *not* pro-Trump, see David A. Graham "Are Children Being Kept in 'Cages' at the Border?," *The Atlantic*, June 18, 2018, https://www.theatlantic.com/politics/archive/2018/06/ceci-nest-pas-une-cage/563072/.

32. For one key voice, see Laurie Goodstein, "'I Know I Will Be Criticized': The Latino Evangelical Who Advises Trump on Immigration," *The New York Times*, March 27, 2018, https://www.nytimes.com/2018/03/27/us/evangelical-dreamers-rodriguez.html.

33. For one important example, see Michael Brown, "Joe Biden and the Charlottesville Lie That Won't Die," The Stream, December 23, 2019, https://stream.org/joe-biden-charlottesville-lie-wont-die/.

34. "President Trump's Policies Continue to Benefit All Americans, Especially the Disadvantaged," Whitehouse.gov, September 10, 2019, https://www.whitehouse.gov/articles/president-trumps-policies-continue-benefit-americans-especially-disadvantaged/.

35. Robert P. George, Facebook Post, December 27, 2019, https://www.facebook.com/robert.p.george.39/posts/10219398644569471; I corrected a few spelling errors in the post.

36. Jim Daly "Jim Daly: Christianity Today is wrong to want Trump removed – Here's the evangelical argument in his favor," Fox News, December 23, 2019, https://

www.foxnews.com/opinion/jim-daly-christianity-today-is-wrong-to-want-trump-removed-heres-the-evangelical-argument-for-him.

37. Andrew T. Walker, "Understanding Why Religious Conservatives Would Vote for Trump," *National Review*, February 10, 2020, https://www.nationalreview.com/2020/02/2020-election-religious-conservatives-trump-voters/.

38. "White Evangelicals See Trump as Fighting for Their Beliefs, Though Many Have Mixed Feelings About His Personal Conduct," Pew Research Center, March 12, 2020, https://www.pewforum.org/2020/03/12/white-evangelicals-see-trump-as-fighting-for-their-beliefs-though-many-have-mixed-feelings-about-his-personal-conduct/.

5. The 'Cult of Trump' vs. 'Trump Derangement Syndrome'

1. "Trump: 'I Could Stand In the Middle Of Fifth Avenue And Shoot Somebody And I Wouldn't Lose Any Voters'," Real Clear Politics, January 23, 2016, https://www.realclearpolitics.com/video/2016/01/23/trump_i_could_stand_in_the_middle_of_fifth_avenue_and_shoot_somebody_and_i_wouldnt_lose_any_voters.html.

2. Harold Ritter, Twitter Post, February 5, 2020, https://twitter.com/HaroldRitter9/status/1225138811363110915. He was responding to my article, Michael Brown, "After the State of the Union: A Friendly Word to Never Trumpers," The Stream, February 6, 2020, https://stream.org/after-the-state-of-the-union-a-friendly-word-to-never-trumpers/.

3. Shane Claiborne, Twitter Post, January 28, 2020, https://twitter.com/ShaneClaiborne/status/1222037524354420736.

4. Shane Claiborne, Twitter Post, February 1, 2020, https://twitter.com/ShaneClaiborne/status/1223488570691915781.

5. Shane Claiborne, Twitter Post, January 31, 2020, https://twitter.com/ShaneClaiborne/status/1223114273108328449.

6. New York: Free Press, 2019.

7. *The Cult of Trump*, xi-xii.

8. Ibid., xii.

9. Ibid., xvii.

10. Jesef, Amazon.com Product Review, November 26, 2019, https://www.amazon.com/gp/customer-reviews/R2BNLH7JA912N2/ref=cm_cr_arp_d_rvw_ttl?ie=UTF8&ASIN=1982127333.

11. Joe Weisenthal, "Newsweek Likens Obama To Jesus—Calls Second Term 'The Second Coming'," *Business Insider*, January 18, 2013, https://www.businessinsider.com/newsweek-on-obamas-second-coming-2013-1.

12. Joseph Curl, "Obama, not Trump, the true menace to the media," *Washington Times*, April 30, 2019, https://www.washingtontimes.com/news/2019/apr/30/obama-not-trump-true-menace-media/?fbclid=IwAR1Sk3duEGoV2k_IxKtNIqGvzi7mvS9cmVol1LlxLzItE1XG-kQPK5stm_w.

13. The blurb on Amazon reads in part, "De La Torre argues that centuries of oppression and greed have effectively ruined evangelical Christianity in the United States. Believers and clerical leaders have killed it, choosing profits over prophets. The silence concerning—if not the doctrinal justification of—racism, classism, sexism, and homophobia has made white Christianity satanic. Prophetically calling Chris-

tian nationalists to repentance, De La Torre rescues the biblical Christ from the distorted Christ of white Christian imagination."

14. Miguel A. De La Torre, "Christianity and the Cult of Trump," UTNE Reader, August 2019, https://www.utne.com/politics/cult-of-trump-ze0z1908zhoe.

15. John Pavlovitz, "The Doomsday Cult of Trump," Johnpavlovitz.com, February 4, 2019, https://johnpavlovitz.com/2019/02/04/when-someone-you-love-joins-a-cult/.

16. Benjamin E. Zeller, "The Cult of Trump? What "Cult Rhetoric" Actually Reveals," Religion & Politics, October 29, 2019, https://religionandpolitics.org/2019/10/29/the-cult-of-trump-what-cult-rhetoric-actually-reveals/.

17. Ibid.

18. Sharday Mosurinjohn, "Why it's wrong to refer to the 'cult of Trump'," The Conversation, January 9, 2020, http://theconversation.com/why-its-wrong-to-refer-to-the-cult-of-trump-128103.

19. Ibid.

20. Andrew T. Walker, "Understanding Why Religious Conservatives Would Vote for Trump," *National Review*, February 10, 2020, https://www.nationalreview.com/2020/02/2020-election-religious-conservatives-trump-voters/.

21. Karlyn Borysenko, "After Attending a Trump Rally, I Realized Democrats Are Not Ready For 2020," Medium.com, February 11, 2020, https://gen.medium.com/ive-been-a-democrat-for-20-years-here-s-what-i-experienced-at-trump-s-rally-in-new-hampshire-c69ddaaf6d07.

22. Ibid.

23. Ibid.

24. Ibid.

25. "Trump derangement syndrome," Wikipedia, May 4, 2020, https://en.wikipedia.org/wiki/Trump_derangement_syndrome. Reflecting the exact opposite meaning is definition #2 offered on the Urban Dictionary: "Trump Derangement Syndrome (TDS) is a mental condition in which a person has been driven effectively insane due to their love of Donald Trump, to the point they will abandon all logic and reason." "Trump Derangement Syndrome," Urban Dictionary, https://www.urbandictionary.com/define.php?term=Trump%20Derangement%20Syndrome. For a spiritual explanation to this phenomenon, see John Fraser, *The Truth Behind Trump Derangement Syndrome: There Is More Than Meets the Eye* (n.p.: JF Publications, 2019).

26. Rob Whitley, "Is "Trump Derangement Syndrome" a Real Mental Condition?," Psychology Today Blog, January 4, 2019, https://www.psychologytoday.com/us/blog/talking-about-men/201901/is-trump-derangement-syndrome-real-mental-condition.

27. Michael Brown, "Am I Tuning In At the Wrong Times, or Does CNN Really Have Trump Derangement Syndrome?," The Stream, May 19, 2018, https://stream.org/cnn-trump-derangement-syndrome/.

28. Charles Hurt, "No Cure In Sight For Donald Trump Derangement Syndrome Sweeping Elite," Rasmussen Reports, January 27, 2016, https://www.rasmussenreports.com/public_content/political_commentary/commentary_by_charles_hurt/no_cure_in_sight_for_donald_trump_derangement_syndrome_sweeping_elite.

29. Ibid.

6. Did God Uniquely Raise Up Donald Trump?

1. Donald J. Trump, Twitter Post, April 30, 2020, https://twitter.com/realDonaldTrump/status/1255710938075889664

2. Donald J. Trump, Twitter Post, April 30, 2020, https://twitter.com/realDonaldTrump/status/1255714490554953736. Less extreme was this short tweet in all caps, sent out at 8:11 AM on April 30, 2020: "DIRTY COP JAMES COMEY GOT CAUGHT!" See Donald J. Trump, Twitter Post, April 30, 2020, https://twitter.com/realDonaldTrump/status/1255832117583495169.

3. Michael Brown, "Donald Trump, President of the United States by the Sovereign Intervention of God," Askdrbrown.org, November 9, 2016, https://askdrbrown.org/library/donald-trump-president-united-states-sovereign-intervention-god.

4. Ben Parker, Stephanie Steinbrecher, and Kelsey Ronan, "Lest We Forget the Horrors: A Catalog of Trump's Worst Cruelties, Collusions, Corruptions, and Crimes. the Complete Listing (So Far). Atrocities 1-546." McSweeneys.net November 5, 2018, https://www.mcsweeneys.net/articles/the-complete-listing-so-far-atrocities-1-546.

5. Glenn Kessler, Salvador Rizzo and Meg Kelly, "President Trump made 18,000 false or misleading claims in 1,170 days," *The Washington Post*, April 14, 2020, https://www.washingtonpost.com/politics/2020/04/14/president-trump-made-18000-false-or-misleading-claims-1170-days/.

6. Robert Dhondrup, *Liar-in-Chief: The Lies of President Trump* (n.p.: n.p., 2017).

7. Bishop Talbert Swan, Twitter Post, November 4, 2019, https://twitter.com/TalbertSwan/status/1191475697648320513; for my response, see Michael Brown, "The Religion of White Supremacy?," The Stream, November 10, 2019, https://stream.org/the-religion-of-white-supremacy/.

8. Tré Goins-Phillips, "Progressive Bishop: 'I'll Take My Chances on Hell' If Heaven Is 'Full of American Evangelicals'," faithwire.com, June 26, 2018, https://www.faithwire.com/2018/06/26/progressive-bishop-ill-take-my-chances-on-hell-if-heaven-is-full-of-american-evangelicals/. For my further interaction with Bishop Swan, see ASKDrBrown, "Dr Brown Blesses Bishop Swan," YouTube Video, November 18, 2019, https://youtu.be/UgIojsmM9wY.

9. The full title is *Was America Founded as a Christian Nation? A Historical Introduction* (rev. edition, Louisville, KY: Westminster John Knox Press, 2016.

10. Grand Rapids, MI: Eerdmans, 2018.

11. *Believe Me*, 12.

12. John Fea, "Hey Court Evangelicals, What's Wrong With Mike Pence?," Thewayofimprovement.com, December 19, 2019, https://thewayofimprovement.com/2019/12/19/hey-court-evangelicals-whats-wrong-with-mike-pence/.

13. Ibid.

14. Fea, *Believe Me*, 10.

15. Ibid., 16.

16. Ibid., 37. More fully, he wrote (151), "The evangelical road to Donald Trump has been marked by the politics of fear, power, and nostalgia." Note also the title of Bob Woodward's bestselling book *Fear: Trump in the White House*, cited below, Chapter Sixteen, note 1.

17. Fea, *Believe Me*, 37-38.

18. Ibid., 38, his emphasis.

19. John Fea, "David Barton: "Trump is God's Guy"," Thewayofimprovement.com,

June 30 ,2016, https://thewayofimprovement.com/2016/06/30/david-barton-trump-is-gods-guy/.

20. Neil Macdonald, "Donald Trump, anointed of God — seriously?: Neil Macdonald," CBC News, Nov 5, 2019, https://www.cbc.ca/news/opinion/opinion-neil-macdonald-trump-white-evangelicals-1.5346659.

21. "God And Trump: The Offensive Notion Of Divine Anointment," *Church & State Magazine*, June 2019, https://www.au.org/church-state/june-2019-church-state-magazine/editorial/god-and-trump-the-offensive-notion-of-divine.

22. Burlington, Ontario, Canada: Castle Quay Books, 2020.

23. *God's Man*, 17.

24. Ibid., 23.

25. Ibid., 24.

26. Ibid., 35-36. The original online link is no longer available.

27. Ibid., 46.

28. Ibid., 89.

29. The events are conflated together in Wallnau's account, but James Beverley has confirmed the actual sequence with me.

30. Ibid., 45-46, emphasis in the original.

31. Ibid., 98.

32. Keller, TX: Killer Sheep Media, 2016.

33. *God's Chaos Candidate*, 7.

34. Ibid., 8-9.

35. Ibid., 11.

36. Ibid.

37. See Chapter Fourteen.

38. *God's Chaos Candidate*, 7.

39. Ibid., 14-15.

40. Antoine Simonin, "The Cyrus Cylinder," *Ancient History Encyclopedia*, January 18, 2012, https://www.ancient.eu/article/166/the-cyrus-cylinder/.

41. "Cyrus Cylinder Translation," Livius.org, April 16, 2020, https://www.livius.org/sources/content/cyrus-cylinder/cyrus-cylinder-translation/.

42. Ibid., 29-30.

43. Ibid., 30.

44. Jerome R. Corsi, Ph.D., *Killing the Deep State: The Fight to Save President Trump* (West Palm Beach, FL: Humanix Books, 2018). Regarding the "one world order," see below, Chapter Fourteen.

45. Michael Brown, "The Election of Donald Trump Tells Us That Anything is Possible," February 5, 2017, https://stream.org/election-donald-trump-tells-us-anything-possible/.

46. During this interview: Line of Fire Radio, "One Book on Homosexuality and the Church," thelineoffire.org, December 15, 2015, http://thelineoffire.org/2015/12/15/two-new-books-on-homosexuality-and-the-church/.

47. Ibid.

48. Bruce G. Kauffmann, "Winston Churchill's Many Vices," HistoryLessons.net, https://historylessons.net/winston-churchills-many-vices.

49. Aris Folley, "Televangelist's show sells $45 Trump coin as 'point of contact' to God," *The Hill*, May 16, 2019, https://thehill.com/blogs/blog-briefing-room/news/443997-televangelist-sells-45-trump-coin-being-peddled-to-believers-as.

50. For the first American president likened to Cyrus, namely, Harry S. Truman, see

Craig von Busek, *I Am Cyrus: Harry S. Truman and the Rebirth of Israel* (Raleigh, NC: Straight Street Books, 2019).

7. Does a Vote for Trump Really Hurt Our Witness?

1. Dr. Michael L. Brown, Twitter Post, August 14, 2019, https://twitter.com/DrMichaelLBrown/status/1161809373766832129.
2. Brian Flood, "CNN contributor Joe Lockhart says all Trump supporters are racist: 'Don't hide it like a coward'," Fox News, July 29, 2019, https://www.foxnews.com/media/cnn-joe-lockhart-trump-supporters-racist.
3. Tim Hains, "MSNBC's Donny Deutsch: If You Vote For Trump, "You Own The Blood That Happens"," Real Clear Politics, August 9, 2019, https://www.realclearpolitics.com/video/2019/08/09/msnbcs_donny_deutsch_if_you_vote_for_trump_you_own_the_blood_that_happens.html.
4. Michael Brown, "The Issue is How God Feels, Not How We Feel," The Stream, August 25, 2019, https://stream.org/the-issue-is-how-god-feels-not-how-we-feel/ (typos corrected).
5. Danielle Kurtzleben, "Study: News Coverage Of Trump More Negative Than For Other Presidents," NPR, October 2, 2017, https://www.npr.org/2017/10/02/555092743/study-news-coverage-of-trump-more-negative-than-for-other-presidents.
6. "Media Trump Hatred Shows In 92% Negative Coverage Of His Presidency: Study," Investor's Business Daily, October 10, 2018, https://www.investors.com/politics/editorials/media-trump-hatred-coverage/.
7. Brent Bozell and Tim Graham, "Here's Undeniable Proof That the Media Despises Trump," The Daily Signal, June 26, 2019, https://www.dailysignal.com/2019/06/26/heres-undeniable-proof-that-the-media-despises-trump/.
8. Brian Flood, "Broadcast news slams Trump with 96 percent negative coverage since impeachment inquiry began, study says," Fox News, November 12, 2019, https://www.foxnews.com/media/broadcast-news-trump-impeachment-inquiry-negative-coverage.
9. Carla Bleiker, "Study: German media extremely negative about Trump," DW.com, May 25, 2017, https://www.dw.com/en/study-german-media-extremely-negative-about-trump/a-38974231.
10. I have heard this in various forms for three years now. For a larger question, see Daniel Cox, "Could Trump Drive Young White Evangelicals Away From The GOP?," FiveThirtyEight, August 20, 2019, https://fivethirtyeight.com/features/could-trump-drive-young-white-evangelicals-away-from-the-gop/.
11. Thom S. Rainer, " The Rise of the Religious "Nones"," Thomrainer.com, March 12, 2012, https://thomrainer.com/2012/03/the_rise_of_the_religious_nones/.
12. Michael Gryboski, "US decline in religious affiliation may be slowing: researchers," February 12, 2020, https://www.christianpost.com/news/us-decline-in-religious-affiliation-may-be-slowing-researchers.html.
13. See, e.g., Jeffrey M. Jones, "U.S. Church Membership Down Sharply in Past Two Decades," Gallup, April 18, 2019.
14. Christianna Silva, "America's Largest Churches Are All Anti-LGBT and Led By Mostly White Men," *Newsweek*, January 6, 2018, https://www.newsweek.com/americas-100-largest-churches-are-anti-lgbt-and-led-white-men-773017.

15. For an outsider's perspective on a strong, pro-Trump church (specifically, Pastor Jack Graham's First Baptist in Dallas), see Angela Denker, *Red State Christians: Understanding the Voters Who Elected Donald Trump* (Minneapolis: Fortress Press, 2019), Chapter One. Those watching Graham's sermons on TV over the years would think of him as a gospel preacher far more than as a supporter of Trump.

16. Caleb Parke, "65,000 college students ring in New Year worshipping Jesus," Fox News, December 31, 2019, https://www.foxnews.com/faith-values/new-years-eve-college-christian-passion-worship-atlanta.

17. Ryan P. Burge, "Evangelicals Show No Decline, Despite Trump and Nones," *Christianity Today*, March 21, 2019, https://www.christianitytoday.com/news/2019/march/evangelical-nones-mainline-us-general-social-survey-gss.html.

18. Douglas Todd, "B.C. breaks records when it comes to religion and the lack thereof," *Vancouver Sun*, May 9, 2013, https://vancouversun.com/news/staff-blogs/b-c-breaks-records-when-it-comes-to-religion-and-the-lack-thereof.

19. See, e.g., Derek Thompson, "Three Decades Ago, America Lost Its Religion. Why?," *The Atlantic*, September 26, 2019, https://www.theatlantic.com/ideas/archive/2019/09/atheism-fastest-growing-religion-us/598843/; Peter Wolfgang, "The Religious Right Drove People Away and Helped Create the 'Nones'," The Stream, February 24, 2020, https://stream.org/the-religious-right-drove-people-away-and-helped-create-the-nones/.

20. "Young adults around the world are less religious by several measures," Pew Research Center, June 13, 2018, https://www.pewforum.org/2018/06/13/young-adults-around-the-world-are-less-religious-by-several-measures/.

21. See the article cited in n. 19, above.

8. Did We Vote Our Pocketbook or Our Principles?

1. *Immoral Majority*, 159-163.

2. Wayne Grudem, "Why Voting for Donald Trump Is a Morally Good Choice," Townhall, July 28, 2016, https://townhall.com/columnists/waynegrudem/2016/07/28/why-voting-for-donald-trump-is-a-morally-good-choice-n2199564.

3. Samuel Smith, "Evangelicals more concerned about healthcare, economy than religious liberty, abortion: poll," *The Christian Post*, September 30, 2019, https://www.christianpost.com/news/evangelicals-more-concerned-about-healthcare-economy-than-religious-liberty-abortion-poll.html.

4. *The Immoral Majority*, 160-161.

5. Peter Wolfgang, "A Social Conservative Chooses Buttigieg," The Stream, February 14, 2020, https://stream.org/social-conservative-chooses-democratic-candidate-answer-shock/

6. https://www.facebook.com/AskDrBrown/posts/im-doing-some-of-my-own-polling-to-compare-it-with-other-scientific-national-pol/3591619677530275/.

7. See Dr. Michael L. Brown, Twitter Post, August 28, 2019, https://twitter.com/DrMichaelLBrown/status/1166851032669970432 and Dr. Michael L. Brown, Twitter Post, August 28, 2019, https://twitter.com/DrMichaelLBrown/status/1166851356151484422.

8. A Losen San Miguel, Twitter Post, September 30, 2019, https://twitter.com/alosensanmiguel/status/1178709198970015744.

9. Tim Hairston, Twitter Post, September 30, 2019, https://twitter.com/TimHairston7/status/1178699338614235136.

10. Originally found at https://twitter.com/BurkeCNN/status/1222884927827562496 and often retweeted, but the tweet has since been removed.

11. Oyindamola Bola, "Black Protestants: Unified for 2020," PRRI, January 8, 2020, https://www.prri.org/spotlight/black-protestants-unified-for-2020/.

12. Samuel Smith, "Evangelicals more concerned about healthcare, economy than religious liberty, abortion: poll," *The Christian Post*, September 30, 2020, https://www.christianpost.com/news/evangelicals-more-concerned-about-healthcare-economy-than-religious-liberty-abortion-poll.html.

13. Ibid.

14. "White Evangelicals See Trump as Fighting for Their Beliefs, Though Many Have Mixed Feelings About His Personal Conduct," Pew Research Center, March 12, 2020, https://www.pewforum.org/2020/03/12/white-evangelicals-see-trump-as-fighting-for-their-beliefs-though-many-have-mixed-feelings-about-his-personal-conduct/.

15. ASKDrBrown, "Dr. Brown Speaks with Prof. Jay Richards about the Virus, the Economy, and Science," YouTube video, March 24, 2020, https://www.youtube.com/watch?v=1_vma9Alo-U.

16. Richard Smith, "5 Myths About the Largest Natural Disaster Relief Effort in History," The Stream, April 7, 2020, https://stream.org/5-myths-about-the-largest-natural-disaster-relief-effort-in-history/.

9. Responding to a Passionate Plea from 'Progressive' Christians

1. "An Open Letter to Evangelicals of Moral Conscience," Global Center for Religious Research, January 18, 2020, https://www.gcrr.org/evangelicals-and-trump?fbclid=IwAR2jyQcPHOWya7yQwwFi6zwaleB18jVddaJHawQ9Es47GmxFqzJ0his5Mc8.

2. My emphasis.

3. Dr. Darren M. Slade, "Open Letter to Conscientious Evangelicals: Your Silence is Complicity! End the Trump Cult!," Global Center for Religious Research, January 26, 2020, https://www.gcrr.org/post/open-letter-to-conscientious-evangelicals-your-silence-is-complicity-end-the-trump-cult; for an irenic response, see Tom Gilson, "Anti-Trump 'Open Letter to Evangelicals' Comes With Inflammatory, Inaccurate Blog Post Behind It," The Stream, January 28, 2019, https://stream.org/open-letter-evangelicals-comes-with-inflammatory-inaccurate-blog-post/.

4. Russell Moore, "Have Evangelicals Who Support Trump Lost Their Values?," *The New York Times*, September 17, 2015, https://www.nytimes.com/2015/09/17/opinion/have-evangelicals-who-support-trump-lost-their-values.html.

5. Dr. Darren M. Slade "Mohler Discusses Evangelical Support for Trump," YouTube Video, December 30, 2018 https://www.youtube.com/watch?v=s6hsLy0dimA&feature=youtu.be. Mohler's comments were in response to the ten-year old audio tape containing inexcusable, repulsive comments made by Trump about women.

6. "Addendum B: A Short List of Mr. Trump's Immoral and Corrupt History," Global Center for Religious Research, https://www.gcrr.org/addendum-b.

7. For example, Trump is accused of, "Publicly endorsing Roy Moore, an accused child molester," but many would claim that the accusations were bogus. Or, to cite another example, Trump is accused of, "Being pathologically unrepentant and

unremorseful about any of his sinful behavior." But as we noted above, Chapter Four, Trump has expressed publicly remorse for at least some of his past actions, quite clearly. More importantly, since he began his presidential campaign, he has not been guilty of repeating some of his past, sinful actions, at least in terms of sexual sins (that is, as far as we know).

8. "An Open Letter to Evangelicals of Moral Conscience," Global Center for Religious Research, January 18, 2020, https://www.gcrr.org/evangelicals-and-trump?fbclid=IwAR2jyQcPHOWya7yQwwFi6zwaleB18jVddaJHawQ9Es47GmxFqzJ0his5Mc8.

9. Michael L. Brown, *Donald Trump Is Not My Savior: An Evangelical Leader Speaks His Mind About the Man He Supports as President* (Shippensburg, PA: Destiny Image, 2018).

10. Jim Wallis, "Who Will Call Out the President's Racism?," *Sojourners*, July 18, 2019, https://sojo.net/articles/who-will-call-out-presidents-racism.

11. Jim Wallis, "The Legacy of Barack Obama," *Sojourners*, March 2017, https://sojo.net/magazine/march-2017/legacy-barack-obama.

12. Rich Lowry, "Obama the abortion extremist," Politico, August 23, 2012, https://www.politico.com/story/2012/08/the-abortion-extremist-080013.

13. Michael Brown, "Equivocating or Evolving, President Obama is Wrong Either Way," Townhall, May 12, 2012, https://townhall.com/columnists/michaelbrown/2012/05/12/equivocating-or-evolving-president-obama-is-wrong-either-way-n823824.

14. Greg Mitchell, "Jim Wallis, Evangelical Leader, Defends Obama, Rips Dobson," *Huffington Post*, May 25, 2011, https://www.huffpost.com/entry/jim-wallis-evangelical-le_b_109138 (the article's original date was June 25, 2008; it was updated in 2011).

15. Alan Bean, "Homosexuality, Abortion, and Political Ideology," Friendsofjustice.blog, July 2013, https://friendsofjustice.blog/2013/07/04/homosexuality-abortion-and-political-ideology/. Beneath the title, the caption reads, "WRITTEN BY ALAN BEAM," but beneath that, it reads, "By Charles Kiker, July, 2013," and the end of the article is followed by "Charles Kiker."

16. Ibid.

17. Michael Paulson, "Pastor Led Son's Gay Wedding, Revealing Fault Line in Church," *The New York Times*, July 12, 2014, https://www.nytimes.com/2014/07/13/us/a-pastor-his-son-and-the-test-of-gay-marriage.html.

18. John Pavlovitz, Twitter Post, December 15, 2018, https://twitter.com/johnpavlovitz/status/1074102401358069760.

19. John Pavlovitz, Twitter Post, December 15, 2018, https://twitter.com/johnpavlovitz/status/1074102763657801728.

20. For the record, I have made repeated efforts to reach out to Pastor Pavlovitz, ranging from offering to sit with him in private to having him as a guest on my show. He has not responded to a single invitation to date. And, as with many of those in the "progressive" camp, I find points of solidarity with Rev. Pavlovitz, along with points of deep disagreement.

21. "Very Reverend Penny Bridges," San Diego LGBT Pride, https://sdpride.org/pennybridges/.

22. Mike Clawson, "Support (Finally!) for Gays at the "Harvard" of Christian Colleges," Patheos, April 29, 2011, https://friendlyatheist.patheos.com/2011/04/29/support-finally-for-gays-at-the-harvard-of-christian-colleges/ (Clawson had not yet earned his Ph.D. at the time he wrote this).

23. Ibid.
24. Scot McKnight, "Christianity Tomorrow," *Christianity Today*, January 21, 2020, https://www.christianitytoday.com/scot-mcknight/2020/january/christianity-tomorrow.html.
25. New York: Basic Books, 2006.
26. For my responses to Galli (and a related *Christianity Today* article, backing Galli), see Chapter Eleven.
27. For example, one of the signers if Rabbi Charles Isbell, a Semitic scholar known in particular for his work on ancient Aramaic incantations.

10. What Would Bonhoeffer Do?

1. Jim Wallis, "International Bonhoeffer Society Calls for 'Ending Donald Trump's Presidency' in 'Statement of Concern'," *Sojourners*, January 16, 2020, https://sojo.net/articles/international-bonhoeffer-society-calls-ending-donald-trumps-presidency-statement-concern. For the full statement, see "The Board of Directors of the International Bonhoeffer Society – English Language Section, Issues Statement of Concern," The Bonhoeffer Center, January 15, 2020, https://thebonhoeffercenter.org/index.php?option=com_content&view=article&id=208:statement-issued-by-the-board-of-directors-of-the-international-bonhoeffer-society-english-language-section-january-15-2020&catid=12&Itemid=208.
2. See Lori Brandt Hale and Reggie L. Williams, "Is This a Bonhoeffer Moment?," *Sojourners*, February, 2018, https://sojo.net/magazine/february-2018/bonhoeffer-moment.
3. Eric Metaxas, *Bonhoeffer: Pastor, Martyr, Prophet, Spy* (Nashville, TN: Thomas Nelson, 2010).
4. "The Board of Directors of the International Bonhoeffer Society – English Language Section, Issues Statement of Concern," The Bonhoeffer Center, January 15, 2020, https://thebonhoeffercenter.org/index.php?option=com_content&view=article&id=208:statement-issued-by-the-board-of-directors-of-the-international-bonhoeffer-society-english-language-section-january-15-2020&catid=12&Itemid=208.
5. John Avion, "Wingnuts Excerpt-Bush Derangement Syndrome," The Daily Beast, August 1, 2010, https://www.thedailybeast.com/wingnuts-excerpt-bush-derangement-syndrome.
6. Ibid.
7. Ibid.
8. Rory Cooper, "Gore Vidal Wishes He Had "Murdered" President Bush," October 30, 2009, https://www.dailysignal.com/2009/10/30/gore-vidal-wishes-he-had-murdered-president-bush/.
9. Ibid.
10. David Emery, "Did Joe Biden Tell a Racially Mixed Audience that Republicans Would 'Put Y'All Back in Chains'?," Snopes, May 15, 2019, https://www.snopes.com/fact-check/joe-biden-put-yall-back-in-chains/
11. Carlos Lozada, "A literary guide to hating Barack Obama," *The Washington Post*, August 25, 2016, https://www.washingtonpost.com/news/book-party/wp/2016/08/25/a-literary-guide-to-hating-barack-obama/
12. Eugene Scott, "Obama's evolution from downplaying identity politics to acknowledging the prevalence of tribalism," *The Washington Post*, November 30, 2018,

https://www.washingtonpost.com/politics/2018/11/30/obamas-evolution-downplaying-identity-politics-acknowledging-prevalence-tribalism/.

13. "President Trump's Policies Continue to Benefit All Americans, Especially the Disadvantaged," Whitehouse.gov, September 10, 2019, https://www.whitehouse.gov/articles/president-trumps-policies-continue-benefit-americans-especially-disadvantaged/.

14. Jerome Hudson, "Hudson: A Deplorable Moment for Every Black American in the Country," Breitbart News, May 22, 2020, https://www.breitbart.com/entertainment/2020/05/22/deplorable-moment-every-black-american-this-country/.

15. Rajan Menon, "Trump's War on the Poor Includes Our Children," The Nation, February 4, 2020, https://www.thenation.com/article/economy/child-poverty-trump/.

16. Jessica Taylor, "State Of The Union: 'Tonight, I Ask You To Choose Greatness,' Trump Says," WXXI News, February 5, 2019, https://www.wxxinews.org/post/tonight-i-ask-you-choose-greatness-trump-says.

17. German Lopez, "The First Step Act, explained," Vox, February 5, 2019, https://www.vox.com/future-perfect/2018/12/18/18140973/state-of-the-union-trump-first-step-act-criminal-justice-reform.

18. Daniel Trotta, "Trump revokes Obama guidelines on transgender bathrooms," Reuters, February 22, 2017, https://www.reuters.com/article/us-usa-trump-lgbt/trump-revokes-obama-guidelines-on-transgender-bathrooms-idUSKBN161243.

19. Matthew Colangelo, "Racial Equality Under Trump," *Democracy Journal*, March 22, 2017, https://democracyjournal.org/briefing-book/racial-equality-under-trump/.

20. Karina Piser, "Trump Is Cutting Food Stamps During a Pandemic," *The New Republic*, March 13, 2020, https://newrepublic.com/article/156912/trump-cutting-food-stamps-pandemic.

21. Katherine Rodriguez, "6.1 Million Individuals Off Food Stamps Under Donald Trump," Breitbart, February 15, 2020, https://www.breitbart.com/economy/2020/02/15/6-1-million-individuals-off-food-stamps-under-donald-trump/.

22. Annie Karnie, "Trump Focuses on Black Economic Gains and Support for Historically Black Colleges," *The New York Times*, September 10, 2019, https://www.nytimes.com/2019/09/10/us/politics/trump-black-colleges.html.

23. Thomas B. Edsall, "Trump Has His Sights Set on Black Voters," March 4, 2020 https://www.nytimes.com/2020/03/04/opinion/trump-black-voters.html.

24. Joseph Guzman, "Ex-NFL player declares Trump America's 'first black president'," *The Hill*, February 28, 2020, https://thehill.com/changing-america/respect/diversity-inclusion/485162-ex-nfl-player-declares-trump-first-black.

25. Amaya Verde and Patricia Vélez Santiago, "Trump's cabinet is far from reflecting the racial diversity of the United States," Univision, January 23, 2017, https://www.univision.com/noticias/politica/trumps-cabinet-is-far-from-reflecting-the-racial-diversity-of-the-united-states.

26. In keeping with the concerns of the IBS, I should note that Trump critics, quite commonly if not almost universally, believe that he is a racist. According to *New York Times* columnist Nicholas Kristof, Trump is "racist to the bone." See Nicholas Kristof, "Trump Is Racist to the Bone," *The New York Times*, July 17, 2019, https://www.nytimes.com/2019/07/17/opinion/donald-trump-racist.html.

27. See, e.g., Joseph Guzman, "Ex-NFL player declares Trump America's 'first black

president',"" The Hill, February 28, 2020, https://thehill.com/changing-america/
respect/diversity-inclusion/485162-ex-nfl-player-declares-trump-first-black.

28. AskDrBrown, "Ethiopian Immigrant's Prayer Goes Viral: 'Thank you for waking up our nation!',"" YouTube Video, October 10, 2019, https://youtu.be/ncxja3dpYX8.

29. Fox 10 Phoenix, "FULL EVENT: President Trump remarks at Young Black Leadership Summit 2019," YouTube Video, October 4, 2019, https://www.youtube.com/watch?v=gTDoC9VqIWs.

30. Elizabeth Dias, "'Shame on Him': Evangelicals Call Out Trump on Syria," The New York Times, October 10, 2019, https://www.nytimes.com/2019/10/10/us/evangelicals-syria-trump-criticism.html.

31. Hank Berrien, "Barack Obama's ICE Chief: Don't Blame Trump, 'Cages' For Illegals Were Built By Obama Administration," The Daily Wire, June 27, 2019, https://www.dailywire.com/news/barack-obamas-ice-chief-dont-blame-trump-cages-hank-berrien.

32. Ashe Schow, "REPORT: Trump Administration Has Reunited 95% Of Migrant Children With Their Families Or Sponsors," The Daily Wire, July 18, 2019, https://www.dailywire.com/news/report-trump-administration-has-reunited-95-ashe-schow.

33. Robert Kraychik, "Dr. Nicole Saphier: Trump's 'Strict Border Control' Helped Reduce Opiod Overdose Deaths," Breitbart News, January 31, 2020, https://www.breitbart.com/radio/2020/01/31/dr-nicole-saphier-trumps-strict-border-control-helped-reduce-opioid-overdose-deaths/.

34. "The German Churches and the Nazi State," The United States Holocaust Memorial Museum, https://encyclopedia.ushmm.org/content/en/article/the-german-churches-and-the-nazi-state.

35. Ibid. See also Michael L. Brown, Our Hands Are Stained with Blood: The Tragic Story of the Church and the Jewish People (second edition; Shippensburg, PA: Destiny Image, 2019); Colin Barnes, They Conspire Against Your People: The European Churches and the Holocaust (Broadstairs, Kent, UK: King's Divinity Press, 2014).

36. "The German Churches and the Nazi State," The United States Holocaust Memorial Museum, https://encyclopedia.ushmm.org/content/en/article/the-german-churches-and-the-nazi-state.

37. Metaxas, Bonhoeffer, 180.

38. Ibid., 181.

39. Ibid., 185.

40. "The German Churches and the Nazi State," The United States Holocaust Memorial Museum, https://encyclopedia.ushmm.org/content/en/article/the-german-churches-and-the-nazi-state.

41. Ed Kilgore, "Why Trump's Evangelical Allies Are Enraged Over His Betrayal of the Kurds," New York Intelligencer, October 8, 2019, https://nymag.com/intelligencer/2019/10/trumps-evangelical-allies-are-upset-about-his-syria-policy.html.

42. Elizabeth Dias, "'Shame on Him': Evangelicals Call Out Trump on Syria," The New York Times, October 10, 2019, https://www.nytimes.com/2019/10/10/us/evangelicals-syria-trump-criticism.html.

43. Lulu Garcia-Navarro, "Trump Could Lose Evangelical Support Over Turkey-Kurds Issue," NPR, October 13, 2019, https://www.npr.org/2019/10/13/769848640/trump-could-lose-evangelical-support-over-turkey-kurds-issue.

44. Ed Kilgore, "Why Trump's Evangelical Allies Are Enraged Over His Betrayal of the

Kurds," *New York Intelligencer,* October 8, 2019, https://nymag.com/intelligencer/ 2019/10/trumps-evangelical-allies-are-upset-about-his-syria-policy.html.

45. Metaxas, *Bonhoeffer*, 193.
46. Ibid., 194.
47. Ibid., 307-308.
48. Ibid., 308.
49. There is no question that pro-Trump, alt-right antisemites, who profess to be Christians, have rallied around Trump in Hitler-like ways, as documented by the Holocaust historian Debora E. Lipstadt, in *Antisemitism: Here and Now* (New York: Knopf Doubleday, 2019), 29-41.

11. The Shot Heard Around the Evangelical World

1. "Our History," *Christianity Today,* https://www.christianitytoday.org/who-we-are/our-history/.
2. Mark Galli, "Trump Should Be Removed from Office," *Christianity Today,* December 19, 2019, https://www.christianitytoday.com/ct/2019/december-web-only/trump-should-be-removed-from-office.html.
3. James A. Beverley and Annette Johnson, eds., *Evangelical Civil War: Mark Galli, Christianity Today and Donald Trump* (forthcoming, Concord, NC: EqualTime Books, 2020). Had the full text of all the articles been published, it would have amounted to roughly 125,000 words, or more than 400 pages long.
4. Private communication, related to me by Beverley.
5. I cannot quantify this minority in precise terms, but if 19 percent of white evangelicals did not vote for Trump in 2016, joined by a larger percentage of black and Hispanic evangelicals, that would suggest the minority is not insubstantial.
6. See John Zmirak, "Want to Understand the Impeachment? Watch Richard Jewell," The Stream, December 19, 2019, https://stream.org/want-to-understand-the-impeachment-dont-watch-the-hearings-watch-richard-jewell/, for a clear philosophical perspective.
7. See throughout this book, and note Michael Brown, "A Reality Check for Christian Supporters of President Trump," The Stream, December 19, 2019, https://stream.org/reality-check-christian-supporters-president-trump/.
8. Michael Brown, "Let the Politicians Focus on Politics While Pastors Focus on the Gospel," The Stream, December 18, 2019, https://stream.org/let-politicians-focus-politics-pastors-focus-gospel/.
9. Timothy Dalrymple, "The Flag in the Whirlwind: An Update from CT's President," *Christianity Today,* December 22, 2019, https://www.christianitytoday.com/ct/2019/december-web-only/trump-evangelicals-editorial-christianity-today-president.html.
10. See Chapter Seven.
11. Here are two representative articles, one from America and one from the UK, respectively: Joe Marusak, "Franklin Graham banned from Liverpool, England, because of LGBTQ 'hatred,' mayor says," *Charlotte Observer,* January 28, 2020, https://www.charlotteobserver.com/news/local/article239715428.html and Harriet Sherwood, "US preacher Franklin Graham tries to reverse UK tour cancellations," *The Guardian,* February 7, 2020, https://www.theguardian.com/world/2020/feb/07/us-preacher-franklin-graham-will-try-to-reverse-uk-tour-cancellations.
12. https://fire-international.org/.

13. AskDrBrown, Facebook Post, December 22, 2019, https://www.facebook.com/AskDrBrown/posts/3972687246090181

14. Dr. Michael L. Brown, Twitter Post, December 22, 2019, https://twitter.com/DrMichaelLBrown/status/1208893128821878787.

15. Heather Timmons "Christianity Today again slams Trump, raises issue of 'unconditional loyalty'," Thomson Reuters Foundation News, December 24, 2019, http://news.trust.org/item/20191224023342-ynppd

16. Tom Sykes, "Editor Quits Amid Evangelical Newspaper Civil War Over Trump," The Daily Beast, December 24, 2019, https://www.thedailybeast.com/napp-nazworth-christian-post-editor-quits-amid-evangelical-newspaper-civil-war-over-trump

17. Allan Hugh, "God did not elect Trump, people did," The Hill, December 24, 2019, https://thehill.com/opinion/white-house/475685-god-did-not-elect-trump-people-did

18. Gary Abernathy, "In the age of Trump, it's OK to be (deeply) conflicted," The Washington Post, December 23, 2019, https://www.washingtonpost.com/opinions/2019/12/23/age-trump-its-okay-be-deeply-conflicted/.

19. See again Beverley, Evangelical Civil War, and note especially Melissa Barnhart, "Nearly 200 evangelical leaders slam Christianity Today for questioning their Christian witness," The Christian Post, December 22, 2019 https://www.christianpost.com/news/nearly-200-evangelical-leaders-slam-christianity-today-for-questioning-their-christian-witness.html.

20. Cited in John Grano and Richard Land, "Christianity Today and the problem with 'Christian elitism'," The Christian Post, December 23, 2019, https://www.christianpost.com/news/christianity-today-and-the-problem-with-christian-elitism.html.

21. Ibid. A colleague of Mark Galli's informed me that Galli did not intend his comments to sound so elitist, nonetheless, the statement was made publicly, leaving some damage and misunderstanding in its wake.

22. Anthony L. Fisher, "Trump attacked the evangelical magazine Christianity Today by calling it 'radical left,' and it shows just how meaningless the phrase has become for him," Business Insider, December 20, 2019, https://www.businessinsider.com/trump-attack-christianity-today-evangelical-all-critics-radical-far-left-2019-12.

23. Isaac Chotiner, "Why the Editor of Christianity Today Decided to Rebuke Trump," The New Yorker, December 21, 2019, https://www.newyorker.com/news/q-and-a/why-the-editor-of-christianity-today-decided-to-rebuke-trump.

24. Allison Gordon, "Evangelical editor who criticized Trump doesn't believe he'll change minds," CNN, December 20, 2019, https://www.cnn.com/2019/12/20/politics/mark-galli-christianity-today-evangelicals-cnntv/index.html.

25. See again Chapter Six.

12. When the Left Demonizes the Right

1. New York: Bloomsbury Publishing, 2020.

2. Tom Gilson, "Freedom From Religion Foundation & New Book Reveal Distortions Driving Anti-Christian Policy," The Stream, May 7, 2019, https://stream.org/distortion-driving-anti-christian-policy/.

3. "The Power Worshippers: Inside the Dangerous Rise of Religious Nationalism," Amazon.com Product Listing, https://smile.amazon.com/Power-Worshippers-

Dangerous-Religious-Nationalism-ebook/dp/B07YKWVJ2H/ref=sr_1_1?
dchild=1&keywords=katherine+stewart&qid=1588989722&sr=8-1.

4. ASKDrBrown, "Progressive Christian Leader: White Evangelicals Uphold 'Slave Holder Religion'," YouTube Video, July 30, 2019, www.youtube.com/watch?v=Xk2gXRhQUes.

5. Ibid.

6. Tom Gilson, "Freedom From Religion Foundation & New Book Reveal Distortions Driving Anti-Christian Policy," The Stream, May 7, 2019, https://stream.org/distortion-driving-anti-christian-policy/.

7. Ibid.

8. "The Power Worshippers: Inside the Dangerous Rise of Religious Nationalism," Amazon.com Product Listing, https://smile.amazon.com/Power-Worshippers-Dangerous-Religious-Nationalism-ebook/dp/B07YKWVJ2H/ref=sr_1_1?dchild=1&keywords=katherine+stewart&qid=1588989722&sr=8-1.

9. Michael Brown, "Is It 'Theological Malpractice' for Ministers to Pray for Trump?," The Stream, July 18, 2017, https://stream.org/is-it-theological-malpractice-for-ministers-to-pray-for-trump/.

10. Katherine Stewart, "Why Trump Reigns as King Cyrus," The New York Times, December 31, 2018, https://www.nytimes.com/2018/12/31/opinion/trump-evangelicals-cyrus-king.html.

11. Chapter Six.

12. See Michael L. Brown, Saving a Sick America: A Prescription for Moral and Cultural Transformation (Nashville, TN: Thomas Nelson, 2017), 29-41.

13. Mary Eberstadt, "Regular Christians Are No Longer Welcome in American Culture," Time Magazine, July 29, 2016, http://time.com/4385755/faith-in-america/.

14. David Limbaugh, Persecution: How Liberals Are Waging War Against Christians (Washington, DC: Regnery Publishing, 2003).

15. Michael Brown, "Speak Up and Speak Out in 2019," Askdrbrown.org, December 31, 2018, https://askdrbrown.org/library/speak-and-speak-out-2019.

16. George Yancey and David A. Williamson, So Many Christians, So Few Lions (Lanham, MD: Rowman & Littlefield, 2015).

17. Jay Richards, "On Communism and Socialism, Many Americans are Still Clueless," The Stream, August 7, 2017, https://stream.org/on-communism-and-socialism-many-americans-are-still-clueless/.

18. Tom Gilson, "Leftist Totalitarianism: Your 'Freedom of Conscience' Under State Control," The Stream, January 2, 2019, https://stream.org/leftist-totalitarianism-freedom-conscience-state-control/.

19. Dennis Prager, "The Left Will Make 2019 a Dark Year," Townhall.com, January 1, 2019, https://townhall.com/columnists/dennisprager/2019/01/01/the-left-will-make-2019-a-dark-year-n2538310.

20. Michael L. Brown, "The Rotten Fruit of Radical Feminism and Identity Politics," Askdrbrown.org, November 27, 2017, https://askdrbrown.org/library/rotten-fruit-radical-feminism-and-identity-politics.

21. Jennifer Hartline, "It's Not Kavanaugh. It's Roe.," The Stream, September 20, 2018, https://stream.org/not-kavanaugh-roe/.

22. Lowell "Max" Johnson, Twitter Post, March 13, 2020, https://twitter.com/MaxTheWretched/status/1238640864173359105.

23. Brown, Donald Trump Is Not My Savior.

24. Michael L. Brown, "The Left's Hatred of Mike Pence Undermines Its Hatred of

Donald Trump," Askdrbrown.org, September 12, 2018, https://askdrbrown.org/library/left%E2%80%99s-hatred-mike-pence-undermines-its-hatred-donald-trump.

25. Katherine Stewart, "The Religious Right's Hostility to Science Is Crippling Our Coronavirus Response," *The New York Times*, March 27, 2020, https://www.nytimes.com/2020/03/27/opinion/coronavirus-trump-evangelicals.html

26. See Michael L. Brown, *When the World Stops: Words of Hope, Faith, and Wisdom in the Midst of Crisis* (Lake Mary, FL: Charisma House, 2020), 55-69. See also Michael Brown, "When Churches Say No to the Government," The Stream, April 5, 2020, https://stream.org/when-churches-say-no-to-the-government/; and Joseph Mattera, "9 Reasons Why Churches Should Respect the Coronavirus Ban on Gatherings," Josephmattera.org, April 2, 2020, https://josephmattera.org/9-reasons-why-churches-should-respect-the-coronavirus-ban-on-gatherings/.

27. See, e.g., Shant Shahrigian, "De Blasio, Cuomo go on defensive over initial responses to coronavirus outbreak," *New York Daily News*, March 29, 2020, https://www.nydailynews.com/coronavirus/ny-coronavirus-bill-de-blasio-20200329-ebyymp5jknel7dy63ymjeb4mdu-story.html; see also Natalie Colarossi, "8 times world leaders downplayed the coronavirus and put their countries at greater risk for infection," *Business Insider*, April 11, 2020, https://www.businessinsider.com/times-world-leaders-downplayed-the-coronavirus-threat-2020-4.

28. Tom Pappert, "FLASHBACK: Biden Called Trump's COVID_19 China Travel Ban 'Xenophobia'," National File, May 26, 2020, https://nationalfile.com/flashback-biden-opposed-trumps-chinese-coronavirus-travel-ban-as-xenophobia/.

29. Ian Schwartz, "Dr. Anthony Fauci: Travel Ban To China Absolutely Made A Difference," Real Clear Politics, March 12, 2020, https://www.realclearpolitics.com/video/2020/03/12/dr_anthony_fauci_travel_ban_to_china_absolutely_made_a_difference.html.

30. Leah MarieAnn Klett, "Pew: Most white evangelicals don't think COVID-19 poses a major threat to Americans' health," *The Christian Post*, March 27, 2020, https://www.christianpost.com/news/pew-most-white-evangelicals-dont-think-covid-19-poses-a-major-threat-to-americans-health.html?uid=07ed4df3d9&utm_source=The+Christian+Post+List&utm_campaign=f6791ba7d7-EMAIL_CAMPAIGN_2020_03_27_04_13&utm_medium=email&utm_term=0_dce2601630-f6791ba7d7-4263913.

31. Dan Zak, "One of America's top climate scientists is an evangelical Christian. She's on a mission to persuade skeptics." *The Washington Post*, July 15, 2019, https://www.washingtonpost.com/lifestyle/style/one-of-americas-top-climate-scientists-is-an-evangelical-christian-shes-on-a-mission-to-convert-skeptics/2019/07/12/9018094c-8d2a-11e9-adf3-f70f78c156e8_story.html.

13. What If Hillary Had Been Elected?

1. Dr. Michael L. Brown, Twitter Post, December 22, 2019, https://twitter.com/DrMichaelLBrown/status/1208919964620640257.

2. New York: HarperOne, 2016.

3. Ibid., 5-6.

4. Ibid., 29, emphasis in the original.

5. For a balanced assessment of Jefferson's actual beliefs, see Mark A. Beliles and Jerry Newcombe, *Doubting Thomas?: The Religious Life and Legacy of Thomas Jefferson* (New York: Morgan James Publishing, 2014).

6. Prothero, *Why Liberals Win*, 34.

7. Ibid.

8. Cited in ibid., 276, n. 56.

9. Ibid., 41.

10. Ibid., 43, emphasis in the original.

11. "What was the Second Great Awakening?," Christianity.com, https://www.christianity.com/church/the-2nd-great-awakening-11630336.html.

12. Prothero, *Why Liberals Win*, 16.

13. Ibid., 4.

14. Ibid., 242.

15. "1800 United States Census," Wikipedia, May 24, 2020, https://en.wikipedia.org/wiki/1800_United_States_Census.

16. Emma Newburger, "Obama warns Democrats against going too far left: 'We have to be rooted in reality'," CNBC, November 16, 2019, https://www.cnbc.com/2019/11/16/obama-warns-democrats-against-going-too-far-left.html.

17. "US election 2020: Obama issues warning to 'revolutionary' Democrats," BBC News, November 16, 2019, https://www.bbc.com/news/world-us-canada-50445743.

18. Michael L. Brown, *It's Time to Rock the Boat: A Call to God's People to Rise Up and Preach a Confrontational Gospel* (Shippensburg, PA: Destiny Image, 1993), 145.

19. Ibid., 146.

20. Ibid., 146-147.

21. Prothero, *Why Liberals Win*, 19.

22. Tim Stafford, "The Abolitionists," *Christianity Today*, https://www.christianitytoday.com/history/issues/issue-33/abolitionists.html.

23. Elizabeth Nash and Joerg Dreweke, "The U.S. Abortion Rate Continues to Drop: Once Again, State Abortion Restrictions Are Not the Main Driver," Guttmacher Institute, September 18, 2019, https://www.guttmacher.org/gpr/2019/09/us-abortion-rate-continues-drop-once-again-state-abortion-restrictions-are-not-main.

24. Michael J. New, "The Best Metrics of Pro-Life Progress," *National Review*, January 18, 2019, https://www.nationalreview.com/2019/01/pro-life-cause-measurable-progress-stay-the-course/.

25. For encouraging details, see https://www.lovelife.org/proofofimpact and https://charlotte.cities4life.org/.

26. Madison Feller, "What You Need To Know About 'Fetal Heartbeat' Bills," *ELLE*, May 7, 2019, https://www.elle.com/culture/career-politics/a26836112/fetal-heartbeat-abortion-bills/.

27. Tim Hains, "CNN's Jeffrey Toobin: Alabama Abortion Law Will Overturn Roe v. Wade; "They've Won"," Real Clear Politics, May 16, 2019, https://www.realclearpolitics.com/video/2019/05/16/cnns_jeffrey_toobin_alabama_abortion_law_will_end_roe_v_wade_theyve_won.html.

28. Susan Miller, "The young are regarded as the most tolerant generation. That's why results of this LGBTQ survey are 'alarming'," *USA Today*, June 24, 2019, https://www.usatoday.com/story/news/nation/2019/06/24/lgbtq-acceptance-millennials-decline-glaad-survey/1503758001/.

29. Ibid.

30. For related thoughts, see Michael L. Brown, *Outlasting the Gay Revolution: Where Homosexual Activism Is Really Going and How to Turn the Tide* (Washington, DC: WND Books, 2015); idem, *Saving a Sick America*, especially 178-189. To be sure, Christians should be kind and compassionate to all people. But from a conservative, biblical perspective, rejecting LGBTQ activist goals is a positive thing.

31. "MassResistance "Drag Queen" victories continue as parents make a difference!," Massresistance.org, November 7, 2019, https://www.massresistance.org/docs/gen3/19d/MR-Drag-Queen-victories_110719/index.html,

32. https://www.nytimes.com/2020/04/01/sports/transgender-idaho-ban-sports.html.
    Talya Minsberg, "'Boys Are Boys and Girls Are Girls': Idaho Is First State to Bar Some Transgender Athletes," *The New York Times*, April 1, 2020,
        https://www.nytimes.com/2020/04/01/sports/transgender-idaho-ban-sports.html.

33. Scottie Andrew, "This year, at least six states are trying to restrict transgender kids from getting gender reassignment treatments," CNN, January 22, 2020, https://www.cnn.com/2020/01/22/politics/transgender-healthcare-laws-minors-trnd/index.html.

34. For a critical assessment, see Miriam Valverde, "Trump claims he got rid of the Johnson Amendment. Is that true?," Politifact, July 18, 2017, https://www.politifact.com/factchecks/2017/jul/18/donald-trump/trump-claims-he-got-rid-johnson-amendment-true/.

35. News 19 WLTX, "Right to Pray in Public Schools President Trump announcement: full video," YouTube Video, January 16, 2020, https://youtu.be/FvS1ShJrs6o.

36. Betsy DeVos, "Betsy DeVos: Religious liberty in our schools must be protected," *USA Today*, January 17, 2020, https://www.usatoday.com/story/opinion/2020/01/17/betsy-devos-religious-liberty-schools-protected-first-amendment-column/4488287002/.

37. Ibid.

14. Trump, the 'New World Order,' and Israel

1. "New World Order (professional wrestling)," Wikipedia, May 30, 2020, https://en.wikipedia.org/wiki/New_World_Order_(professional_wrestling).

2. Hua Hsu, "A Global Government Is Waiting in the Wings," *New York Intelligencer*, November 15, 2013, https://nymag.com/news/features/conspiracy-theories/new-world-order/.

3. See here for a recent, related "Rothschild" claim: David Emery, "Did Facebook Executive Jeff Rothschild Say 'We Need a Third World War'?," Snopes, May 18, 2018, https://www.snopes.com/fact-check/jeff-rothschild-third-world-war/.

4. "New World Order (politics)," Wikipedia, May 11, 2020, https://en.wikipedia.org/wiki/New_world_order_(politics).

5. George H.W. Bush, "The other 9/11: George H.W. Bush's 1990 New World Order speech," *The Dallas Morning News*, September 8, 2017, https://www.dallasnews.com/opinion/commentary/2017/09/08/the-other-9-11-george-h-w-bush-s-1990-new-world-order-speech/.

6. Rodney & Adonica Howard-Browne, Facebook Post, March 14, 2016, https://www.facebook.com/rodneyadonicahowardbrowne/photos/a.83442597437/10154002928097438/?type=1&theater.

7. The Jim Bakker Show, "We Are In A Last Minute Reprieve - Rodney Howard Browne on The Jim Bakker Show," YouTube Video, July 4, 2019, https://youtu.be/hMA0J3jVFbo.

8. "We Are In A Last Minute Reprieve - Rodney Howard Browne on The Jim Bakker Show," *Charisma Magazine*, https://www.charismamag.com/video/42115-rodney-howard-browne-trump-has-all-but-destroyed-the-new-world-order.

9. For insights on how other conservative leaders failed to see the appeal of Trump's candidacy before 2016, see Chris Buskirk and Seth Leibsohn, *American Greatness: How Conservatism Inc. Missed the 2016 Election and What the D.C. Establishment Needs to Learn* (Washington, DC: WND Books, 2017). The foreword by William J. Bennett is also insightful.

10. Ibid.

11. "Former British Prime Minister Gordon Brown Voices Support of One World Government," Behold Israel, March 28, 2020, https://beholdisrael.org/former-british-prime-minister-gordon-brown-voices-support-of-one-world-government/. This article, posted on March 28, 2020 on a Messianic Jewish, Israeli website that focuses on end-time prophecy, notes that, "Earlier this week, amid the ever-spreading pandemic of the coronavirus, former British Prime Minister Gordon Brown voiced his support of a 'temporary' world government. He argued that no one country would be able to come up with a solution on their own and that international leaders will need to work together to form a solution."

12. "Angela Merkel complains that Trump is Destroying The New World Order," PCMD News, May 19, 2019, https://pcmdnews.com/angela-merkel-complains-that-trump-is-destroying-the-new-world-order/. The article also traces the history of the "new world order" concept, both in terms of conspiratorial theories and contemporary manifestations.

13. Colum Lynch, "Trump's War on the World Order," *Foreign Policy*, December 27, 2018, https://foreignpolicy.com/2018/12/27/trumps-war-on-the-world-order/.

14. Patrick Buchanan, "Will the Coronavirus Kill the New World Order?," Real Clear Politics, March 13, 2020, https://www.realclearpolitics.com/articles/2020/03/13/will_the_coronavirus_kill_the_new_world_order_142650.html.

15. This is not to imply that all globalism is bad but rather that a particular type of globalism can be very dangerous.

16. *God, Trump, and the 2020 Elections*, 27.

17. See Gen 12:1-3, and note Michael L. Brown, "Will God Really Bless Those Who Bless Israel?", in Mae Elise Cannon, ed., *A Land Full of God: Christian Perspectives on the Holy Land* (Eugene, OR: Wipf & Stock, 2017), 67-74.

18. Alex Leff and Emily Feng, "Trump Angers China By Signing Law Backing Hong Kong Protesters," NPR, November 28, 2019, https://www.npr.org/2019/11/28/783529916/trump-angers-china-by-signing-law-backing-hong-kong-protesters.

19. Bert M. Farias, *The Tumultuous 2020s and Beyond: A New Era for America, the Church, and the Nations* (n.p.: Holy Fire Ministry, 2019), 11, emphasis in the original.

20. Ibid., 12.

21. Ibid., 13.

15. Trump Is Trump

1. John Haltiwanger, "Trump tweets about ratings for his coronavirus press briefings for the 3rd day in a row as US death toll surpasses 18,000 and unemployment nears 17 million," *Business Insider*, April 20, 2020, https://www.businessinsider.com/trump-boasts-about-ratings-coronavirus-press-briefings-death-toll-rises-2020-4.
2. Cited in ibid. See also KJ Edelman, "'You Should Be Saying Congratulations': Here Are 116 Times Trump Has Praised His Own Coronavirus Response," Mediaite, April 9, 2020, https://www.mediaite.com/trump/you-should-be-saying-congratulations-here-are-116-times-trump-has-praised-his-own-coronavirus-response/.
3. Patrick Knox, "WITH FRIENDS LIKE THESE Piers Morgan rips Trump for 'failing on almost every level' with coronavirus briefings and 'will make him lose election'," *The Sun*, April 19, 2020, https://www.the-sun.com/news/706519/piers-morgan-rips-trump-coronavirus-briefings-lose-election/. For a highly contentious briefing where the president needed to say, "It's not about me," see Nikki Schwab, "Donald Trump furiously defends his handling of coronavirus and plays video of Andrew Cuomo praising him that annoys him by stopping early - and then compares himself to Abraham Lincoln," *Daily Mail*, April 19, 2020, https://www.dailymail.co.uk/news/article-8235063/Trump-shows-clips-Cuomo-praising-defends-coronavirus-response.html.
4. Email from Pastor Garlow, sent 5-7-20.
5. Ibid.
6. Brian Stelter and Hadas Gold, "Piers Morgan says his friend President Trump is 'failing the American people'," CNN, April 19, 2020, https://www.cnn.com/2020/04/19/media/reliable-sources-piers-morgan/index.html.
7. Tamara Keith, "A Look At A Solemn Dignified Transfer Ritual For Fallen Soldiers," NPR, February 11, 2020, https://www.npr.org/2020/02/11/804955928/anguish-raw-emotions-at-ceremony-for-fallen-soldiers-as-trump-looks-on.

16. The Bottom Line Is Simple

1. New York: Simon & Schuster, 2018.
2. New York: Penguin Press, 2020.
3. New York: Henry Holt & Co., 2018.
4. New York: Penguin Press, 2017.
5. New York: Harper Collins, 2018.
6. Updated edition, New York: Thomas Dunne Press, 2019.
7. Pat Ralph and Ellen Cranley "22 new books that reveal the inner workings of the Trump administration," *Business Insider*, March 12, 2019, https://www.businessinsider.com/books-about-trump-white-house-2018-9.
8. Lee, ed., *Dangerous Case*, x.
9. "Anti-Obama Books," Good Reads Listopia, https://www.goodreads.com/list/show/38977.Anti_Obama_Books.
10. For spirited responses to Never Trump Christians, see John Zmirak, "The Last Gasp of NeverTrump Christians," The Stream, May 12, 2020, https://stream.org/the-last-gasp-of-nevertrump-christians/ and John Zmirak, "David 'Vichy' French

Wants Christians to Surrender," The Stream, July 1, 2019, https://stream.org/david-vichy-french-wants-christians-to-surrender/.

11. Regarding LGBT issues, Trump has consistently pushed back against various aspects of LGBT activism, earning him the derision of the left. See, e.g., Tess Bonn, "Human Rights Campaign head: Trump the 'worst president on LGBTQ issues ever'," The Hill, November 7, 2019, https://thehill.com/hilltv/rising/469512-human-rights-campaign-president-trump-is-worst-president-on-lgbtq-issues-ever. At the same time, he has done things like appoint openly gay Richard Grenell as an acting member of his Cabinet, which was a first for a gay man.

12. John Zmirak, "The Last Gasp of NeverTrump Christians," The Stream, May 12, 2020, https://stream.org/the-last-gasp-of-nevertrump-christians/.

13. Ibid. Of course, some would claim he did act lawlessly.

14. Used with permission.

15. Washington, DC: Regnery, 2005.

16. Hugh Hewitt, "It's the Supreme Court, stupid," Washington Examiner, July 31, 2016, https://www.washingtonexaminer.com/its-the-supreme-court-stupid.

17. Rebecca R. Ruiz, Robert Gebeloff, Steve Eder and Ben Protess, "A Conservative Agenda Unleashed on the Federal Courts, New York Times, March 16, 2020, https://www.nytimes.com/2020/03/14/us/trump-appeals-court-judges.html.

18. Daniel Bush, "Trump's conservative picks will impact courts for decades," PBS, October 25, 2019, https://www.pbs.org/newshour/politics/trumps-conservative-picks-will-impact-courts-for-decades.

19. Cori Petersen and CJ Szafir, "Trump Is Remaking the Federal Judiciary at a Historic Rate," Real Clear Politics, January 4, 2020, https://www.realclearpolitics.com/articles/2020/01/04/trump_is_remaking_the_federal_judiciary_at_a_historic_rate__142073.html.

20. Richard A. Arenberg, "The Trumpification of the federal courts," The Hill, January 6, 2020, https://thehill.com/opinion/judiciary/476796-the-trumpification-of-the-federal-courts.

21. Ian Millhiser, "What Trump has done to the courts, explained," Vox, February 4, 2020, https://www.vox.com/policy-and-politics/2019/12/9/20962980/trump-supreme-court-federal-judges.

22. To Change the World: The Irony, Tragedy, and Possibility of Christianity in the Late Modern World (Oxford and New York: Oxford University Press, 2010), 12.

23. Believe Me, 7, citing Hunter, To Change the World, 234, 280.

24. I reviewed the listing of shows on the major Christian and radio networks nationally in support of this statement. For a larger analysis of online sermons, see "The Digital Pulpit: A Nationwide Analysis of Online Sermons," Pew Research Center, December 16, 2019, https://www.pewforum.org/2019/12/16/the-digital-pulpit-a-nationwide-analysis-of-online-sermons/.

25. I reviewed different lists of bestselling evangelical books in 2019 and 2020 in support of this statement.

26. Michael L. Brown, "The Left's Hatred of Mike Pence Undermines Its Hatred of Donald Trump," Askdrbrown.org, September 12, 2018, https://askdrbrown.org/library/left%E2%80%99s-hatred-mike-pence-undermines-its-hatred-donald-trump.

27. Chris Pandolfo, "Maxine Waters openly admits she's going for 'impeachment' of Trump — AND Pence," Conservative Review, September 10, 2018, https://www.conservativereview.com/news/maxine-waters-openly-admits-shes-going-for-impeachment-of-trump-and-pence/.

28. Philip Schuyler, Twitter Post, September 11, 2018, https://twitter.com/FiveRights/status/1039452268658139136.

29. Andrew Buncombe, "Mike Pence is worse than Donald Trump, says Omarosa," Yahoo News, September 11, 2018, https://www.yahoo.com/news/mike-pence-worse-donald-trump-140900151.html.

30. Frank Bruni, "Mike Pence, Holy Terror," *The New York Times*, July 28, 2018, https://www.nytimes.com/2018/07/28/opinion/sunday/mike-pence-holy-terror.html.

31. Ibid.

32. Ibid.

33. Savannah Barker, "Who should liberals fear more: President Trump or a potential President Pence?," Tylt, December 10, 2017, https://thetylt.com/politics/trump-pence-dangerous.

34. Jane Mayer, "The Danger of President Pence," *The New Yorker*, October 16, 2017, https://www.newyorker.com/magazine/2017/10/23/the-danger-of-president-pence.

35. Frank Jacobs, "How Dubya Used the Book of Ezekiel as a Blueprint for the Iraq War," Bigthink.com, January 15, 2016, https://bigthink.com/strange-maps/gog-and-magog-or-dubyas-biblical-mind-map.

36. WCNC, "Franklin Graham banned from UK conference center over gay rights," YouTube Video, January 29, 2020, https://www.youtube.com/watch?v=KATmypoQskE.

37. Michael Brown, "The Left's Message to Samaritan's Purse: You Cannot Be Christian," The Stream, April 22, 2020, https://stream.org/the-lefts-message-to-samaritans-purse-you-cannot-be-christian/.

38. While not exact instances in every case, none of them are hypothetical; see, e.g., Michael L. Brown, *A Queer Thing Happened to America: And What a Long Strange Trip It's Been* (Concord, NC: EqualTime Books, 2011); idem, *Outlasting the Gay Revolution*.

39. See immediately above, n. 37.

17. Ten Essential Keys for Passing the Trump Test

1. "ICYMI: Sen. Cruz: It's Time to Break the Washington Cartel," U.S. Senator Ted Cruz, June 24, 2015, https://www.cruz.senate.gov/?p=press_release&id=2363; see also Gregory Kreig, "Cruz campaign: Donald Trump has been Washington 'cartel paymaster'," CNN, January 19, 2016, https://www.cnn.com/2016/01/19/politics/donald-trump-ted-cruz-cartel-paymaster/index.html.

2. This does not mean that I necessarily agree with Jerome Corsi's, *Killing the Deep State*.

3. I addressed similar themes in the last chapter of *Donald Trump Is Not My Savior*, laying out these seven points: 1) We must rise above the political fray. 2) Regardless of party affiliation, we must remain independent. 3) We must stay involved. 4) God uses unlikely vessels, but character still matters. 5) We must stand for the issues near and dear to the Lord's heart. 6) Sometimes, we must function as the president's loyal opposition. 7) Our calling goes beyond patriotism. There is some overlap, then, with the content of this chapter, but everything that is written here is new and does not borrow directly from that chapter, which should be read independently.

4. *Commentary on Daniel*, 2.44–45.

5. *Homilies on 1 John 1.12* (with reference to Daniel 2:34)

6. See Justin Taylor, "An FAQ on America as a "City on a Hill"," The Gospel Coalition, July 21, 2016, https://www.thegospelcoalition.org/blogs/evangelical-history/an-faq-on-america-as-a-city-on-a-hill/ and "Ronald Regan and "The Shining City Upon a Hill"," Our Lost Founding, January 11, 2020, https://ourlostfounding.com/ronald-reagan-and-the-shining-city-upon-a-hill/.

7. "Porn Stats: Which Country Produces And Hosts The Most Porn?," Fight the New Drug, November 22, 2017, https://fightthenewdrug.org/porn-stats-which-country-hosts-most-porn/.

8. Charlotte Pence Bond, "'A National Tragedy': America Leads World in Single-Parent Homes," Light Workers, https://www.lightworkers.com/america-leads-world-in-single-parent-homes/.

9. https://www.usdebtclock.org/

10. James Pasley, "20 staggering facts about human trafficking in the US," *Business Insider*, July 25, 2019, https://www.businessinsider.com/human-trafficking-in-the-us-facts-statistics-2019-7.

11. "World Prison Populations," BBC News, http://news.bbc.co.uk/2/shared/spl/hi/uk/06/prisons/html/nn2page1.stm.

12. See Michael L. Brown, "Digging Deeper into the Question of Racism in America," The Stream, May 10, 2020, https://stream.org/digging-deeper-into-the-question-of-racism-in-america/.

13. Michael Snyder, "NUMBER ONE? 20 Shameful Categories In Which America Leads The World," *Business Insider*, July 8, 2011, https://www.businessinsider.com/20-shameful-categories-america-leads-world-2011-7.

14. "When Faith Becomes a Means," C.S. Lewis Institute, October 2017, https://www.cslewisinstitute.org/Reflections_When_Faith_Becomes_a_Means. I'm not sure if this was done with specific intent, but when Fea cites this passage (see *Believe Me*, 91), he begins with, "Let him begin by treating the Patriotism . . . as part of his religion." While this buttressed Fea's argument, by including the words "the Pacifism," the reader would have realized that Lewis's point was broader than Fea's.

15. Brown, *Donald Trump Is Not My Savior*.

16. Dr. Michael L. Brown, Twitter Post, May 12, 2020, https://twitter.com/DrMichaelLBrown/status/1260256951058956289. My team subsequently turned this into a meme, also posting in on Instagram and Facebook. See drmichael-brown, Instagram Post, May 13, 2020, https://www.instagram.com/p/CAIDm_9Abz2/ and

17. Christopher Ingraham, "Somebody just put a price tag on the 2016 election. It's a doozy." *The Washington Post*, April 14, 2017, https://www.washingtonpost.com/news/wonk/wp/2017/04/14/somebody-just-put-a-price-tag-on-the-2016-election-its-a-doozy/.

18. Alexander Burns, Maggie Haberman, Jonathan Martin, and Nick Corasaniti, "A Sitting President, Riling the Nation During a Crisis," *The New York Times*, May 15, 2020, https://www.nytimes.com/2020/05/15/us/politics/president-trump-coronavirus-pandemic-response.html.

19. Martin Luther King, Jr. "A Knock at Midnight," The Martin Luther King, Jr. Research and Education Institute, https://kinginstitute.stanford.edu/king-papers/documents/knock-midnight.

20. T. Austin-Sparks, "Prophetic Ministry: Chapter 1 – What Prophetic Ministry Is,"

The Online Library of T. Austin Sparks, https://www.austin-sparks.net/english/books/001003.html; for details of original publication, see https://www.austin-sparks.net/english/books/prophetic_ministry.html.

21. Radley Balko, "There's overwhelming evidence that the criminal-justice system is racist. Here's the proof." *The Washington Post*, September 18, 2018, https://www.washingtonpost.com/news/opinions/wp/2018/09/18/theres-overwhelming-evidence-that-the-criminal-justice-system-is-racist-heres-the-proof/.

22. Michael Brown, "Digging Deeper Into the Question of Racism in America," The Stream, May 10, 2020, https://stream.org/digging-deeper-into-the-question-of-racism-in-america/.

23. Talia Ralph, "Reverend Billy Graham urges North Carolina to vote against gay marriage," The World, May 3, 2012, https://www.pri.org/stories/2012-05-03/reverend-billy-graham-urges-north-carolina-vote-against-gay-marriage. He said, "Watching the moral decline of our country causes me great concern. I believe the home and marriage is the foundation of our society and must be protected."

24. Jon Meacham, *American Gospel: God, the Founding Fathers, and the Making of a Nation* (New York: Random House, 2006), 215. See also Jana Riess, "Billy Graham, Franklin Graham, and the Dangers of Mixing Religion and Politics," Word & Way, October 15, 2019, https://wordandway.org/2019/10/15/billy-graham-franklin-graham-and-the-dangers-of-mixing-religion-and-politics/.

25. Note the responses to my Twitter poll conducted on May 21-22, 2020, asking the question: "Broadly speaking, which do you feel is more important in 2020 (and beyond)? Who wins the presidential election or the church preserving a solid testimony before the Lord?" Dr. Michael L. Brown, Twitter Post, May 21, 2020, https://twitter.com/DrMichaelLBrown/status/1263630254675046402. While a mildly surprising 23.3 percent answered with, "Both equally important," only 2.5 percent answered with, "Who wins," while a whopping 74.2 percent said, "Preserving our testimony."

26. See, e.g., Kristin MacLaughlin, "The Detrimental Effects of Pornography on Small Children," Net Nanny, December 19, 2017, https://www.netnanny.com/blog/the-detrimental-effects-of-pornography-on-small-children/ and Kimberly Perry, "What's the average age kids see Internet pornography?(quite young)," We Stand Guard, October 17, 2019, https://www.westandguard.com/what-s-the-average-age-kids-see-internet-pornography-quite-young. See further Brown, *Saving a Sick America*.

27. Charles Finney, "What is Revival?," Angelfire.com, http://www.angelfire.com/ca5/revolutionchurch/JEonRevival.html.

28. Ibid.

29. Ibid.

About the Author

MICHAEL L. BROWN *(Ph.D., New York University), is the host of the daily, nationally syndicated talk radio show, The Line of Fire, and is the author of more than 40 books and over 1,500 op-ed pieces. He is the founder and president of FIRE School of Ministry, has served as a visiting or adjunct professor at seven leading seminaries, and has contributed to major scholarly compendiums and journals. He has preached around the world, conducted debates on university campuses in America and abroad, and is committed to seeing a gospel-based, moral and cultural revolution.*

Visit AskDrBrown.org or follow us on social media.

 facebook.com/AskDrBrown

twitter.com/DrMichaelLBrown

instagram.com/drmichaelbrown